FIGHTING ADMIRALS OF THE SECOND WORLD WAR

FIGHTING ADMIRALS OF THE SECOND WORLD WAR

by

David Wragg

Pen & Sword
MARITIME

First published in Great Britain in 2009 by
Pen & Sword Maritime
an imprint of
Pen & Sword Books Ltd
47 Church Street
Barnsley
South Yorkshire
S70 2AS

ISBN: 978-1-84415-860-7

A CIP catalogue record for this book is
available from the British Library.

Typeset in 11/13pt Sabon by
Concept, Huddersfield, West Yorkshire

Printed and bound in England by
CPI UK

Pen & Sword Books Ltd incorporates the Imprints of Pen & Sword
Aviation, Pen & Sword Maritime, Pen & Sword Military, Wharncliffe
Local History, Pen & Sword Select, Pen & Sword Military Classics,
Leo Cooper, Remember When, Seaforth Publishing and
Frontline Publishing.

For a complete list of Pen & Sword titles please contact
PEN & SWORD BOOKS LIMITED
47 Church Street, Barnsley, South Yorkshire, S70 2AS, England
E-mail: enquiries@pen-and-sword.co.uk
Website: www.pen-and-sword.co.uk

Contents

Introduction

> *Command of the sea is the indispensable basis of security, but whether the instrument that commands swims, floats, or flies is a mere matter of detail.*
>
> Admiral Sir Herbert Richmond, RN, 1946

Sea power was an essential element in the Second World War. Without it, the Japanese would not have been able to attack the US Pacific Fleet at Pearl Harbor, and then undertake their conquest of South-East Asia and the East Indies; also without it, the Allies would not have been able to fight back and eventually carry the war to Japan. The German U-boats and surface raiders were countered by the convoy system, with first MAC-ships (merchant aircraft carriers) and then escort carriers, and the methodical hunting down of the battleship *Bismarck* and the *Panzerschiff*, or 'pocket battleship', *Graf Spee*. Sea power enabled the British to hang on to the island fortress of Malta and the Italian failure to use sea power effectively allowed the Maltese islanders to remain free. It was British sea power that meant that the Germans had little chance of invading England, and enabled the BEF to be rescued from Dunkirk and Cherbourg. It was sea power that enabled the Allies to land in North Africa, Sicily, then Italy and finally in France.

The application of sea power nevertheless demanded astute handling of huge fleets and the ability to plan effectively yet flexibly, while at the most senior levels the admirals had to be able to fight on two fronts, confronting the wishes of politicians when necessary.

Fighting Admirals of the Second World War looks at twenty-three of the leading admirals on both sides, at their careers, their personalities, their achievements and failures, all set against the backdrop of the global conflict which they were fighting, and the political climate of the times. The admirals are grouped under their navies, for which there is an introduction that sets the scene and explains the constraints under which these senior officers had to plan and operate. There are seven British (Cunningham, Fraser, Horton, Pound, Ramsay, Somerville, Tovey) and five US admirals (Fletcher, Halsey, King, Nimitz, Spruance), two German (Dönitz and Raeder), six Japanese (Koga, Kondo, Nagumo, Ozawa, Toyoda, Yamamato), one French (Darlan), justified by the problems faced by Vichy, including the courageous decision to scuttle the fleet rather than let it fall into German hands in late 1942, as well as one Dutch Admiral, Doorman, and one Italian, Riccardi. In selecting the list, their decisive role in the war is taken as the only criterion. They had to be strategists. British admirals in the Pacific, such as Vian, are excluded as they operated under overall US direction.

The Washington Naval Treaty of 1922 was very specific, allocating maximum tonnages to each navy of the signatory powers and in addition stipulating restrictions on the total tonnage for each type of warship; it also imposed maximum tonnages for individual vessels as well, with cruisers limited to 10,000 tons, for example, and capital ships to 35,000 tons, while aircraft carriers were limited to 27,000 tons, although both the British and Americans were allowed two carriers of up to 33,000 tons each.

Both the Royal Navy and the United States Navy were limited to a total warship tonnage of 525,000 tons, while Japan, a First World War ally, was limited to 315,000 tons; France and Italy were limited to 175,000 tons each. These limitations had some unexpected results, with all three of the largest 'treaty navies' having battlecruisers in excess of their permitted tonnage, and all three took the option of converting two of these ships into aircraft carriers, although the Japanese lost one of their battlecruisers while under conversion due to an earthquake and converted a battleship instead.

The statistics tell one story, but there were practical differences that meant that the state of the Royal Navy was worse than it might have been. The first of these was the determination of successive British inter-war governments to tighten the Washington restrictions, and drive down the tonnage of cruisers to much less than that allowed, aiming at a figure of around 8,500 tons for a heavy cruiser and 23,000 tons for an aircraft carrier. Not surprisingly, the future Axis powers took an opposing view, and consistently understated their tonnages. At the London Naval Conference of 1930, the

Japanese attempted to obtain parity with both the UK and the USA. Four years later, the Japanese formally notified the other Washington Naval Treaty signatories that she no longer considered herself bound by its restrictions. German desire for rearmament became increasingly clear after Hitler assumed absolute power in 1933, although the Paris Air Agreement of 1926 had already removed the restrictions on German commercial aviation and aircraft manufacture. The London Naval Treaty of 1935 paved the way for the reconstruction of the German Navy, restricted by the Washington Naval Treaty to a coastal defence force, granting Germany a total tonnage equivalent to 35 per cent of that of the Royal Navy, although within this figure, what can only be regarded as an oversight or collective memory loss allowed Germany parity with the Royal Navy in terms of submarines! The Germans even managed to build extra ships once new tonnage was permitted, ordering the battle-cruiser *Gneisenau* secretly.

Note: In this book, the admirals are dealt with by nationality, allowing an overview of the situation of each country and its navy, and then alphabetically, to avoid problems of changing ranks as they were promoted during the war years.

Chapter 1

The War at Sea – Europe

When asked, most people will view the Second World War as an air war, while the First World War, by contrast, evokes folk memories of the trenches on the Western Front. While there can be no doubt that the Second World War could have been lost in the air, nevertheless, it was also very much a war at sea, albeit one in which the aeroplane played a leading role from the Battle of the Coral Sea onwards, the first naval engagement when opposing fleets did not see each other, and ships were sunk by air-dropped munitions rather than by shellfire or torpedoes from surface vessels or submarines.

This image of a war that was predominantly naval applies most of all in the Pacific and Indian Oceans, and in the Netherlands East Indies. Certainly, there were actions on land, but it was sea power that enabled Japan to attack the United States Pacific Fleet at Pearl Harbor, and then to land on territory after territory as the Japanese sought to expand their empire south and west; but then finally it was sea power that enabled the United States in turn to take the war to the Japanese, with amphibious landings as the US Marine Corps island-hopped towards Japan. It was sea power in the form of the USN's submarines that cut Japan off from fuel, raw materials and food from the conquered territories, and it was sea power that enabled the Allies to strike at the oil refineries in the Netherlands East Indies.

Even in the European theatre, it was sea power that enabled the British and French to intervene in Norway; control of the sea enabled the two allies to extricate themselves from Norway and then allowed the British, with French help, to rescue the British Expeditionary Force from Dunkirk and the Cherbourg peninsula. It was the battle for conquest of the seas that made Malta so important and sea power that enabled the island to be resupplied, albeit whilst on the verge of starvation and on the brink of surrender. Less happily, sea power allowed an evacuation from Greece, and then from Crete.

No Phoney War at Sea

On looking back at the Second World War, at least in Europe, one often hears mention of the 'Phoney War', that period between the outbreak of war in September 1939 and the German invasion of Denmark and Norway the following April, when nothing seemed to happen. The Germans called this period the *Sitzkrieg*, the 'Sitting War', which was far more accurate as the opposing armies sat on opposite sides of the French Maginot Line. For the mass of the population, but especially for the civilian population, little seemed to happen after war broke out on 3 September 1939.

But there was no such thing as a phoney war at sea. On 3 September 1939, the very day that war broke out, the liner *Athenia*, 13,500 tons, was torpedoed off the Hebrides, without the warning required by the Hague Convention. Out of the 128 people who lost their lives, twenty-eight were Americans, giving Hitler the opportunity to argue that the ship had been the victim of a British attack intended to sour relations between Germany and the United States. The U-boat commander was to claim later that he had mistaken the ship for either a Q-ship or an armed merchant cruiser.

Whatever view one might take of these arguments, the Germans were determined to bring the war home to the Royal Navy at the outset. During the first months of the war, losses at sea became all too commonplace. Just two weeks after war broke out, on 17 September 1939, after flying had ended for the day, the aircraft carrier *Courageous* was torpedoed by *U-29* and sunk while on an anti-submarine sweep. The carrier sank in just twenty minutes, taking 500 men with her, many of whom would have been trapped below decks in the dark. Submarine sweeps were wasteful and hazardous, akin to looking for a needle in a haystack given the available intelligence at the time. Worse was to follow. It was to be small consolation that the first German aircraft to be shot down, on 26 September, was accounted for by fighters from *Ark Royal*, for on 14 October, *U-47* penetrated the sheltered anchorage at Scapa Flow in Orkney and torpedoed the battleship *Royal Oak*, which sank with the loss of 833 lives. The submarine had fired two salvoes, each of three torpedoes, with two torpedoes of the first salvo missing and the one that made contact failing to explode properly, but forty-five minutes later, a second salvo exploded under the battleship, detonating her magazine.

November was no better, for on the 23rd, while on convoy escort duty, the armed merchant cruiser *Rawalpindi*, a former P&O liner, was sunk by the German battlecruisers *Gneisenau* and *Scharnhorst* off Iceland. This was an unequal contest, between the finest ships in the *Kriegsmarine* at the time and a ship that not only lacked the fire-power, armour and speed of her adversaries, but also lacked the capability of being able to match their rate of fire and gunnery direction.

This succession of losses was reversed before the year ended with the first British victory of the war. The brighter news came from the South Atlantic, where on 13 December, the cruisers *Ajax*, *Achilles* and *Exeter* encountered the German 'pocket' battleship, or *Panzerschiff*, *Admiral Graf Spee*, that had been commerce raiding, near the mouth of the River Plate. Despite being outgunned, using superior tactics which caused the *Graf Spee* to divide her fire, the three cruisers managed to so damage her that she had to seek refuge in Montevideo, in neutral Uruguay, where she was allowed three days for temporary repairs; instead, she put all but a skeleton crew ashore and put to sea on 17 December simply to be scuttled. Had she not been scuttled, her opponents were ready to resume the Battle of the River Plate. Many theories have been advanced for this success, including the inability of the German ship to direct her fire in two directions simultaneously, or that she might have mistaken the two light cruisers, *Ajax* and *Achilles*, for destroyers.

Hunting for commerce raiders was slightly easier than chasing submarines, especially with the growing number of British ships with radar, while battleships and cruisers at the time still carried seaplanes for aerial reconnaissance, although obviously the support of an aircraft carrier was far better. The danger was that the heavier armed units of the *Kriegsmarine* could usually outgun the cruisers sent to catch them – 11-inch guns were far superior in range and in the damage that they could inflict than the 8-inch guns of a heavy cruiser, let alone a light cruiser's 6-inch main armament. British cruisers on foreign stations were exercised in dealing with a German surface raider, and by a curious twist of fate, during one such exercise in 1938, the heavy cruiser *Exeter* had played the part of a German *Panzerschiff*, or pocket battleship. The Germans believed that their *Panzerschiffs* could only be countered by a British capital ship, but this was far from true. Perhaps it showed some foresight that before the outbreak of war, one of the *Graf Spee*'s sisters, *Deutschland*, was renamed *Lutzow* because someone thought of the impact on the nation's morale if *Deutschland* was sunk! In 1940, the *Panzerschiffs* were redesignated as heavy cruisers.

As early as 16 October 1939, the Luftwaffe had mounted a raid on British warships moored in the Firth of Forth. On this occasion the need to avoid civilian casualties was very much in mind. The nine Junkers Ju88 bombers of *Kampfgeschwader 30* had as their target the battlecruiser *Hood*, but finding her in Rosyth Dockyard, turned their attention to the two cruisers *Edinburgh* and *Southampton*, and both ships were bombed, although the damage to *Edinburgh* was slight. *Southampton* received a direct hit from a 1,100-lb armour-piercing bomb that went through the port side before travelling down through three decks and out through the starboard side, after which it exploded causing further damage to the ship. Had the bomb exploded before it emerged, the ship could have been lost.

The concern for civilian life was not to last long and at the height of the 'blitz', the Royal Navy's three main home bases at Chatham, Portsmouth and Plymouth were to be heavily bombed.

While the Royal Navy had been quick to introduce a convoy escort system on the outbreak of war, having learnt the harsh lessons of the First World War, German naval operations were seriously inhibited at first, both by the blockade and the need for submarines and surface raiders to sail around the north of Scotland and through the Denmark Strait to reach their operational waters. The fall of France gave the Germans established naval ports with open access to the Bay of Biscay and beyond. The more direct route from Germany down the North Sea and through the Straits of Dover was judged to be too risky – a factor that was to be made good use of later when planning the audacious 'Channel Dash'.

Meanwhile, the Royal Navy had also spent the first few months of the war engaged in other activities. The widespread belief in 1939 was that the fighting, once it started, would see a repeat of the trench warfare of the First World War, but in any case, the territorial integrity of France had to be defended from the almost inevitable German assault. Between September 1939 and June 1940, half a million men and 89,000 vehicles were moved to France across the English Channel without loss. Despite fears that German U-boats would intervene, only one passed safely through the Straits of Dover. So successful were the defensive minefields laid by the Royal Navy that during October 1939, by which time the last of 3,600 mines had been laid to create a barrier, three U-boats were lost.

Nevertheless, the Second World War saw the Royal Navy at a disadvantage on the other side of the British Isles, where it felt the loss of its bases in the Irish Republic, even though these were supposed to be available under treaty. The lost treaty bases were Berehaven in the south and Lough Swilly in the north. The latter was relatively easy to replace, with nearby Londonderry across the border in Northern Ireland becoming a handy substitute with the advantage that it also had airfield facilities to the east at Eglinton, now known as Derry City Airport. The Western Approaches would have benefited from the base at Berehaven, as would the Atlantic convoys, but Devonport, near Plymouth, remained operational despite heavy German aerial attack, while new bases more conveniently sited grew at Milford Haven near the western extremity of South Wales, further north at Liverpool, and on the Clyde in Scotland.

Other steps were also taken to improve the security of merchant vessels, so that by March 1941, the Admiralty Defensively Equipped Merchant Ship (DEMS) organization had equipped 3,434 ships with anti-submarine guns, and had also provided one or more close-range anti-aircraft guns for 4,431 British and Allied ships. Initially, naval ratings and army gunners were seconded, but later merchant seamen were trained to take their place.

Opening Rounds

The Royal Navy had intervened after the German invasion of Denmark and Norway. Denmark was overwhelmed quickly as German forces swept over the border as well as sending an invasion fleet directly into the harbour at Copenhagen. Intervention by Britain and France was simply not possible, but Norway was a different case. Here defence was aided by the terrain and by the loss of key German commanders in the invasion, which also gave the Norwegian government time to move out of Oslo and organize resistance by the country's small armed forces. Alerted to the impending invasion, the Royal Navy had already started to mine Norwegian waters on 8 April, the day before the invasion started. An Anglo-French expeditionary force with an initial 13,000 men was quickly assembled and by mid-April British and French troops landed in Norway, with the landings covered by the aircraft carrier *Furious*, which then moved to the role of aircraft transport, while the newest carrier, *Ark Royal*, took over protection of the landing fleet and forces ashore. The Mediterranean Fleet aircraft carrier *Glorious* was immediately recalled to home waters, while *Eagle*, in the Indian Ocean, was ordered to the Mediterranean.

The Norwegian campaign with few good airfields available ashore, was ideally suited to carrier operations, had sufficient ships been available with aircraft of adequate performance. As it was, the Luftwaffe gained the upper hand as early as 10 April, when it mounted an attack against ships of the Home Fleet south-west of Bergen, sinking a destroyer and causing minor damage to the battleship *Rodney* and three cruisers, *Devonshire*, *Glasgow* and *Southampton*, only recently repaired after her earlier encounter with German airmen.

The battle was far from one-sided, however, and an even greater success was scored against the German fleet that same day when Blackburn Skuas of Nos 800 and 803 Naval Air Squadrons, flying from HMS *Sparrowhawk*, and RNAS Hatston on Orkney, attacked and sank the German light cruiser *Konigsberg* at Bergen, the first major warship to be sunk by naval aircraft.

The Royal Navy proved that it could give a good account of itself, also on 10 April, with the first destroyer action in Narvik Fjord, when British destroyers sank two German destroyers and several merchantmen, but with two British destroyers being sunk. Far more successful was the second destroyer action at Narvik, often referred to as the 'Second Battle of Narvik', with the battleship *Warspite* and nine destroyers sinking the remaining eight German destroyers on 13 April.

Nevertheless, the Norwegian Campaign failed, due in part to the shortage of airfields ashore and the lack of high-performance aircraft for the British aircraft carriers offshore. The withdrawal was marred by the loss of the British aircraft carrier HMS *Glorious* to the German battlecruisers *Scharnhorst* and *Gneisenau*. One reason for withdrawal, apart from the poor progress being made ashore, was the need to reinforce British and French units in France, but it was too late.

The Royal Navy organized the evacuation of the British Expeditionary Force, mainly from Dunkirk, in Operation Dynamo, coordinated by Admiral Bertram Ramsay at Dover. The operation moved 338,226 British and French troops to the south of England. Inevitably, most of the ships used were civilian owned and manned, including not just merchant vessels and fishing boats, but private craft as well, many of which did sterling work moving troops from the beaches and the shallows out to ships moored in deeper water, although two-thirds of those evacuated were taken off the harbour's east mole straight onto ships. Meanwhile, other warships were used to keep German naval units, and especially E-boats, from the evacuation fleet, and to provide anti-aircraft cover during the period of the evacuation. Nothing larger than a destroyer could get close enough to help, but the Fleet Air Arm also assisted by lending several of its Swordfish squadrons to RAF Coastal Command to provide short-range reconnaissance and anti-shipping measures.

The Dunkirk evacuation was costly, with nine British and French destroyers and eight troopships lost, and out of the officially recorded 848 civilian vessels and small naval craft that took part, no less than seventy-two were lost to enemy action and another 163 lost in collisions, with forty-five damaged.

Next, the French surrender saw the creation of what was effectively a puppet state by the Vichy French, which meant that the allegiance of the surviving French Navy units could not be taken for granted. Bad enough to lose an ally with its ships and seamen – even worse would be to have them transferred to German control. Those French ships that had escaped to Portsmouth were quickly seized on 3 July under cover of darkness, while measures were put in hand to neutralize the ships sharing Alexandria in Egypt with the Royal Navy, repatriating most of their crews and ensuring that the guns could not be used. The big problem was the fate of the substantial number of major fleet units at ports in France's African territories, divided between Oran, and nearby Mers-el-Kebir, in Algeria and Dakar in West Africa.

After the fall of France, there was the danger that the French fleet could be used by the Germans, or that Vichy France might join the Axis powers. The need to obtain the surrender of the French fleet, or at least neutralize it, was an unwelcome task, dealing with men who had been allies so recently. Tackling the French fleet was an unwelcome task for the Royal Navy, whose personnel were all too aware that until recently this had been an ally. Vice Admiral Sir James Somerville, in command of Force H based on Gibraltar, was anxious to avoid a battle with the French, but in the end found his ships engaging those of his former ally at Mers-el-Kebir and Oran.

The Convoys

The statistics for Second World War convoys on the North Atlantic alone were impressive. During the war years there were 2,889 escorted trade convoys to and from the UK, with a total of 85,775 ships. There were in addition another 7,944 coastal convoys, comprising 175,608 ships. This latter figure has to be put into perspective, for after the fall of France coastal convoys did not operate through the English Channel because of the danger of enemy attack, and instead their cargo became yet another burden for the railways. It should also be remembered that since the same ship would, while it survived, take part in many convoys, the chances of a ship surviving the war were much less than these figures might suggest.

Although it would be foolhardy to ignore the protection offered by a convoy and its escorts, the convoy system was not compulsory and not universally accepted. Fast troopships, such as the former liners *Queen Mary* and *Queen Elizabeth*, sailed alone, relying on speed to keep them safe. Many of the ships lost from convoys were stragglers, ships that for one reason or another could not keep up with the rest of the convoy and so became vulnerable to attack.

The convoy war was the reason for many innovations. Destroyers were seen at one and the same time as too important to risk on convoys, and their design intended for high speed made them uncomfortable at convoy speeds in the open ocean, so the small but cheap and cheerful corvettes of the Flower-class soon appeared. The need for dedicated anti-submarine or anti-aircraft vessels also saw the re-invention of the frigate, a type of ship that had gradually disappeared in the late nineteenth century. Armed merchant cruisers were converted passenger liners, but soon proved vulnerable to enemy cruisers and although they did sterling service, their role was sacrificial until later when the surviving ships became auxiliary anti-aircraft cruisers. More useful were the catapult-armed merchant ships, the CAM-ships, with a solitary fighter to provide air cover, but as this couldn't return to the ship and either had to fly ashore or, more usually, ditch, this was very much a single-shot solution. Better still were the merchant aircraft carriers, MAC-ships, with converted tankers carrying three Fairey Swordfish and grain ships carrying four, which were used in the anti-submarine and reconnaissance role. Most effective of all were the escort carriers, initially merchant ships converted to carry aircraft, but later versions used merchant hull designs and were laid down to be escort carriers, capable of conversion for merchant duties at the end of hostilities. Escort carriers could carry a mix of aircraft – fighters as well as anti-submarine aircraft.

In the North Atlantic, the main threat to the convoys occurred in what was variously known as the 'Atlantic Gap', or the 'Black Gap', that part of the North Atlantic during which convoys were outside the protection of shore-based maritime reconnaissance aircraft. The gap reduced steadily as longer-range aircraft became available, but land-based aircraft always suffered from the disadvantage that for every aircraft flying over and around a convoy, another had to be on its way back to base, with yet another one on its way out. At the base for these aircraft, there would be several more aircraft undergoing maintenance, refuelling and rearming while their crews took a well-earned rest. The presence of the venerable Swordfish with a convoy forced many U-boat commanders to remain submerged, so that they couldn't catch up with the convoy, and while the Swordfish often did attack and destroy a U-boat, in many cases the best results came from Swordfish and escort vessels working together. It was the convoy war and the need to protect trade that saw the birth of Canadian and Dutch naval aviation, brought into being as part of the Fleet Air Arm, and at first fully integrated with it. Even before the United States entered the war, American warships started to escort convoys as far as mid-ocean, ostensibly to protect neutral shipping but in fact showing the country's support for the UK and the occupied nations of Europe.

The convoys through the Bay of Biscay suffered similar problems to those in the North Atlantic once France had fallen and both the *Kriegsmarine* and the Luftwaffe had access to French bases. These convoys often divided at Gibraltar, with part of the convoy proceeding to Malta and, in the early days, Alexandria, while the rest would steam to destinations in Africa and beyond. Once the Axis made the passage across the Mediterranean all but impassable, convoys for Egypt also sailed via the Cape and the Suez Canal. This was taking the long way round and the much lengthened route made heavy demands on shipping, and on the supply of escorts.

A weakness of the German U-boat campaigns was that submarine commanders made and received a significant volume of radio transmissions, sending reports back to HQ and being given instructions. The Germans believed these communications to be secure, using their Enigma codes, but these codes had been broken by the British after a German submarine, *U-570*, had been captured by a British escort vessel south of Iceland in August 1941. The capture of the submarine was kept secret, although she was commissioned into British service as HMS *Graph*. The possession of the codes and British Ultra intelligence was a crucial factor in winning the Battle of the Atlantic, but it also provided significant advance warning elsewhere as well.

The U-boats were not the only threat to Allied merchant shipping, especially during the early days of the war. German surface raiders were a major threat and in addition to auxiliary or armed cruisers – converted merchantmen – the Germans also used their major surface units, including the battleship *Bismarck*. The reason for this was simple. As we will see in the chapters on Erich Raeder and Karl Dönitz, the German Navy was not ready for war because in surface vessels it was vastly inferior to the Royal Navy, and remained so throughout the war. *Bismarck* was sunk by the Royal Navy's Home Fleet and Force H. Eventually, Germany's major surface units in the North Atlantic, the battlecruisers *Scharnhorst* and *Gneisenau*, and the heavy cruiser *Prinz Eugen*, which is believed to have fired the shell that blew up the British battlecruiser *Hood*, were stuck in port in France until the famous Channel Dash that saw them escape to Germany. With the last German battleship, *Tirpitz*, and the *Scharnhorst*, lurking in Norwegian fjords, these ships were a constant source of anxiety for the Allies once the convoys to Murmansk and Archangel were introduced after the Soviet Union entered the war. They did at least serve a useful purpose for Germany, as the Royal Navy and the Royal Air Force mounted attacks on the *Tirpitz* until at last she was sunk by the RAF, and the Royal Navy sunk the *Scharnhorst* at sea in the Battle of the North Cape.

The Arctic convoys saw those aboard the merchantmen and the warships fighting both the weather and the Germans, but after the disaster that was Convoy PQ17, from PQ18 onwards, escort carriers were normally provided and did much to ensure better chances of survival for the ships.

Nevertheless, from the purely naval point of view, the most dangerous convoys were those across the Mediterranean in the struggle to sustain the defence of Malta. This situation was so bad that fast minelayers and large mine-laying submarines were pressed into service to keep the Maltese islands going in between convoys, which often failed to get through. The operations of the fast minelayers were known as the 'club runs', while those of the submarines were known as the 'magic carpet'. Even escort carriers were of little use in the intense fighting that these convoys suffered, and so the large fleet carriers and battleships had to be pressed into service.

Bringing the Enemy to Battle

At first, only in the Mediterranean was a major sea battle possible, but after Cunningham's victory at the Battle of Punta Stilo, or Calabria, the Italian Navy, the *Regia Marina*, kept out of the way. Nevertheless, the Italian Navy had six large battleships and it was important that these be neutralized, so the idea of an air attack on the Italian fleet in its main forward harbour of Taranto, first considered during the Italian invasion of Abyssinia, present-day Ethiopia, was revived. Twenty-one Fairey Swordfish biplanes were sent against Taranto from the new fast armoured carrier *Illustrious*, and for the cost of just two shot down, and the loss of the crew of one of these, three Italian battleships were put out of action, while other ships and harbour installations were damaged.

One of the great mysteries of the Second World War was that the Italians made relatively little use of their battle fleet, bearing in mind that they had three times as many battleships as the Germans. Raeder, the Commander-in-Chief of the German *Kriegsmarine*, saw the occupation of Malta as crucial to success in the Mediterranean. The islands were poorly defended with a small garrison and at first no official fighter cover – what there was consisted of just three Gloster Sea Gladiator biplanes 'borrowed' from the Royal Navy and flown by flying-boat pilots. On the first day of Italy being involved in the Second World War, it would have been easy to send these ships to bombard Malta, and especially the capital Valletta, and the famous three cities on the other side of the Grand Harbour. A long bombardment, with bombing raids in any breaks, would have brought the islands (Malta consists of three inhabited islands: Malta itself, Gozo and Comino) to their knees and made invasion feasible. The failure to take Malta meant that, until the famous British victory at El Alamein, the Axis powers had great difficulty in keeping their forces in North Africa supplied. Before the war, the Royal Air

Force and the British Army had agreed that Malta could not be defended, and it was only the Admiralty's persistence that Malta could be a base for submarines and light forces that ensured that it was not demilitarized and abandoned, as the Channel Islands had been. Just as the Pacific was to be the theatre in which the USN's submarines mounted a highly successful campaign, the Mediterranean was where British submarines triumphed, thanks to their base in Malta. Maintaining Malta as a base was far from easy, as already noted, and submarines in port often had to remain submerged during daylight hours to avoid being bombed. The famous convoy, Operation Pedestal, of August 1942, which saved the island from starvation and running out of fuel, as well as surrender, took an escort that included four large fleet aircraft carriers, of which one, *Eagle*, was sunk.

Punta Stilo was the only battle in the Second World War when two full battle fleets actually engaged. The United States Navy was later to come close to such an engagement during the final stages of the Battle for Guadalcanal, but one of the two US battleships suffered an electrical failure and could not fire her guns. The Imperial Japanese Navy attempted to force such an engagement at Leyte Gulf, but again failed as carrier-borne aircraft took over. All other engagements either involved a single capital ship on one side or the other, or were between carrier-borne aircraft, while the opposing fleets were out of sight and beyond gun range.

Nevertheless, one theme that occurs in this book time and time again is the desire of so many of the admirals involved on both sides to bring about a decisive naval battle. This is not surprising since every one of them was not only born into the nineteenth century, but all of them spent their early days at sea in the era of the big ship, when the battleship was the ultimate deterrent and air power was just an impractical dream. One of the Japanese admirals even saw service at the Battle of Tsushima in 1905, while British and Germans were at Jutland.

It was the rise of naval air power that meant that big ship to big ship gunnery duels were almost a thing of the past, but not quite, and even the sinking of the *Bismarck*, aided by naval air power, was left to more traditional methods for the *coup de grâs*.

The real turning point in the war in Europe was in fact the invasion of North Africa, Operation Torch, on 8 November 1942, the first assault on Axis-held territory and the first big amphibious assault mounted by the Allies. This quickly brought about the surrender of the Vichy French forces in the area when Admiral Darlan ordered resistance to cease after just two days of fighting, but the campaign continued until May 1943 as German forces in Tunisia mounted a strong defence. Well over 200 British naval vessels were involved, as well as Free Dutch ships, and sixteen Fleet Air Arm squadrons. The operation was a success for Cunningham and for Ramsay.

The problem was, of course, that neither the Germans nor the Italians were able to use sea power effectively, other than by their submarines. At the Battle of the Barents Sea in December 1942, Hitler finally lost patience with thc surfacc fleet as the Royal Navy mounted a gallant defence of Russian Convoy JW51B on 31 December 1942, when the convoy was threatened by the German heavy cruiser *Hipper*. Ten Royal Navy warships were involved.

Almost a year later, in December 1943, the Battle of the North Cape was the result of an attack on Arctic convoys by the German battlecruiser *Scharnhorst*, which was sunk with heavy loss of life. In addition to gunfire from the cruisers *Belfast* and *Jamaica*, then joined by the battleship *Duke of York*, a feature of the operation was a daring torpedo attack under heavy fire by four destroyers, *Savage*, *Saumarez* and *Scorpion*, plus the Norwegian *Stord*, at 3,000 yards in the early evening, while later four more destroyers, *Musketeer*, *Opportune*, *Virago* and *Matchless* attacked at even closer range. In all, twelve British ships were involved.

Both these engagements were without the use of naval air power, as indeed were the landings at Anzio, Operation Shingle, on 22 January 1944, which were intended to by-pass German resistance to the Allied advance on Rome. Almost sixty warships were involved, including fourteen minelayers, although there was no Fleet Air Arm involvement. Good natural defensive positions and appalling weather helped the German resistance, and even supplying forces ashore proved difficult, solved by using amphibious DUKWs and lorries, which were loaded in Naples and then driven ashore at Anzio. Many warships were lost, including the cruisers *Penelope* and *Spartan*, and the destroyers *Inglefield* and *Janus*, as well as a dozen or so minor warships.

Coming after the successes in North Africa and the landings on Sicily – albeit these were costly because of bad weather – and then at Salerno, Anzio was a nasty shock to Allied confidence. Fortunately, despite being postponed for twenty-four hours due to bad weather, the landings at Normandy still went ahead. This required a massive effort by the Royal Navy and the United States Navy, but out of 1,212 warships deployed on 6 June 1944, 78 per cent were British, ranging from drifters to battleships, whose role was to provide a heavy bombardment of the German defences. Not all of the troops were put ashore from ships, with a substantial force either air-landed by glider or parachuted to seize important bridges before the Germans could destroy them.

Chapter 2

The War at Sea – The Pacific

The Japanese attack on the United States Pacific Fleet in its forward base at Pearl Harbor in Hawaii on 7 December 1941 brought the United States into the Second World War. Recklessly, when the USA declared war on Japan in response to this act of aggression, which was made without a prior declaration of war, Hitler took the opportunity to declare war on the United States. It is interesting to speculate just what might have happened had he not done so, but it was inevitable that once hostilities began, the US would probably have decided, within months if not weeks, to extend the war to Germany and Italy.

The USA was then placed in the situation that it had to fight a war on two fronts: in Europe and the Atlantic, and in the Pacific. In both theatres sea power was essential, but the difference was that the availability of British bases, mainly in England, allowed the United States Army Air Force to join the Royal Air Force in the bombing campaign against Germany, while in the Pacific it was the greatest naval war of all time, and even included the biggest naval battle in history at Leyte Gulf. So it happened that the Japanese could not have attacked the United States without its carrier force, and without its carrier force in turn, the United States could not have fought its way across the Pacific to the Japanese home islands. Before that, of course, the daring Doolittle raid jolted Japanese preconceptions about their invincibility.

Faced with action on two fronts, and responding to an unprovoked attack on its territory, the temptation for many Americans was first to settle the score with Japan. Nevertheless, the US President, Franklin Roosevelt, opted for a 'Germany first' policy. Contrary to the perceptions of many Britons, this was accepted willingly by the

Commander-in-Chief and Chief of Naval Operations for the USN, Admiral Ernest King. The reason for doubting his commitment to this policy was King's pronounced and abrasive Anglophobia, which left him as one of the most unpopular wartime service leaders. 'Germany first' was not so much a reflection of US support for the UK so much as a hard-headed assessment that Germany could be finished first, and that then the US forces deployed in Europe, along with those of the UK, could be transferred to the Far East.

The use of the Royal Navy in the Pacific was not welcomed by all USN commanders. Neither King nor Nimitz favoured this, but it was a political decision taken by Roosevelt. Nimitz did insist that the Royal Navy must provide its own bases and fleet support rather than use those of the hard-pressed USN, and this happened, with the Royal Navy using Australia for its main bases, while it also had Addu Atoll, now Gan, as a secret refuelling base in the Indian Ocean. Cape Town was another base.

There were also those Americans who did not see why they should help a colonial power recover its possessions. In fact, while this was another reason for the British wanting to be present in the Far East, there was also the not unimportant point that they wished to be seen to be supporting the two dominions, Australia and New Zealand, which had already done so much to help in the war in Europe. Between the wars, the British Government had promised to send a large fleet to protect these two countries should they be threatened by Japan, but by the time Japan entered the war, the Royal Navy was already fully stretched in European waters and the mid-Atlantic.

Despite these initial objections, the USN did help the Royal Navy in gearing up for massed air attack, with the USS *Saratoga* operating alongside HMS *Illustrious* in the early attacks on the oilfields and refinery at Sabang, a small island off the coast of Sumatra, with the first attack on 19 April 1944. Earlier, when the USN had found itself short of aircraft carriers, HMS *Victorious* had been transferred to the USN, operating briefly as the USS *Robin*.

During the attack on Okinawa, despite their earlier objections, the USN found the newly formed British Pacific Fleet to be invaluable in attacking Japanese air bases on the islands of the Sakishima Gunto, easing the pressure on the US Pacific Fleet and also preventing the Japanese from sending reinforcements.

Even before the Royal Navy returned to the Pacific, there was an important invasion to be conducted in the Indian Ocean, off the coast of East Africa. Operation Ironclad, the invasion of Madagascar, may seem like a sideshow during a global war, but it was occupied by the Vichy French and available to Axis forces, while well positioned to block British convoys to Egypt, which by this stage of the war had to steam past the Cape of Good Hope north towards the Suez Canal. On 5 May 1942, British forces invaded, taking the Vichy French by surprise. An advance party of just fifty Royal Marines were embarrassed by the number of prisoners taken. Just over thirty ships were involved, including two aircraft carriers, *Indomitable* and *Illustrious*, and the elderly battleship *Ramillies*, as well as eight naval air squadrons. Initially it was intended that only part of the island should be occupied, and the operation is referred to simply as 'Diego Suarez' in the Royal Navy's honours list, but in the end the entire island had to be occupied. It was the only invasion during the Second World War that was an 'all-British' affair.

Turning the Tide

While there were carrier aircraft attacks on ports in New Guinea occupied by the Japanese, the first strike at Japan itself came from a USAAF officer, the then Colonel James 'Jimmy' Doolittle who planned and led Operation Shangri-La, the raid by North American B-25 Mitchell bombers against Tokyo on 18 April 1942. The aircraft took off from the aircraft carrier USS *Hornet*, which required great skill on the part of the pilots as the leading aircraft had little flight deck left in which to make their take-off run, but it caught the Japanese by surprise as they believed that they were safely out of reach of American bombers. While the attack caused little real damage, in part because the aircraft were tasked to bomb too many targets, it caused the Japanese to reassess their strategy, which became more defensive. Had the attack concentrated on the Emperor's palace, it might have shortened the war, but the targets were too widely dispersed for real impact, although the operation was as a significant a boost to US morale as it undermined that of the Japanese.

The first significant naval battle of the Pacific War and the first to be completely between aircraft carriers, and with the ships of the opposing fleets not coming into sight of one another, was the Battle of the Coral Sea between the United States and Japanese navies on 8 May 1942.

On 3 May, the Japanese had landed unopposed on Tulagi and Guadalcanal in the eastern Solomon Islands, but on 4 May, they were surprised by aircraft from the USS *Yorktown*, with Task Force 17, which sank a destroyer and three minesweepers. The two largest Japanese carriers, *Shokaku* and *Zuikaku* entered the Coral Sea on 5 May. The following day, both sides refuelled at sea, unaware that they were separated by just 70 miles, despite aerial reconnaissance.

During the night of 7/8 May, the two American carriers *Yorktown* and *Lexington* were so close to the two Japanese carriers that six Japanese aircraft attempted to land on the *Yorktown.* On the morning of 8 May, reconnaissance aircraft from both sides discovered each other, with the fleets some 200 miles apart. Both sides launched air strikes at more or less the same time, with the Japanese sending ninety aircraft and the Americans seventy-eight. While *Zuikaku* escaped into a rainstorm, *Shokaku* was hit by three bombs, forcing her to withdraw, but she survived due to the poor performance of the American air-launched torpedoes. Meanwhile, Japanese aircraft attacked the two American carriers in three waves, with two attacking *Lexington* from both sides and the third attacking *Yorktown.* Eleven torpedoes were launched at the *Lexington*, but her commanding officer managed to avoid them before two more struck the ship, causing a massive explosion to run through the ship as her aviation fuel tanks ruptured, followed by a second blast twenty minutes later. Further explosions followed, wrecking the machinery and at 2000, the ship having been abandoned, a destroyer torpedoed the burning wreck.

On paper, the battle was a major Japanese victory, with the loss of one small carrier against a major US fleet unit, but *Shokaku* had been damaged and would not be available for the forthcoming Battle of Midway, when she would be sorely needed, while a Japanese advance on Port Moresby had been abandoned. The Japanese had also lost many experienced naval airmen, without having the training programme to replace them quickly or easily.

On 3–7 June 1942 just six months after the attack on Pearl Harbor, the Battle of Midway came as no surprise to the Americans, as Ultra intelligence had already given warning of both the objective and the likely date. This enabled Admiral Nimitz, to concentrate his forces to defend Midway atoll. In anticipation of a strong defence at Midway, the Japanese sent a diversionary raiding force north to the Aleutians, but the USN disregarded this realizing that it was unimportant.

During the afternoon of 3 June, USAAF Boeing B-17 Fortress bombers were sent to attack the Midway invasion force, but enjoyed little success against ships under way at sea. Despite this, the Japanese failed to fly effective reconnaissance missions, leaving large areas of sea uncovered.

At dawn, the Japanese sent more than a hundred aircraft to Midway to destroy the defences, but at the same time, shore-based aircraft of both the USAAF and USN from Midway found the Japanese carriers and attacked, disrupting the formation of the fleet and killing a number of crewmen working on the open decks in strafing attacks. The Japanese mounted an intense AA barrage and scrambled Zero fighters, which accounted for seventeen American aircraft.

The Japanese attack on Midway's shore installations caused considerable damage, but failed to put the airfield or the defences out of action. The Japanese commander, Vice Admiral Nagumo, decided to send a second wave to complete the operation and keep the US forces under pressure, but, as will be seen later, confusion reigned as the aircraft were armed, and then the munitions were changed, while the strike was also delayed waiting for returning aircraft to land on the carriers.

As first-wave aircraft landed and were moved down into the hangars, and with second-wave aircraft brought up and ranged ready for take-off, the first American aircraft arrived. Flying low over the sea, the first wave of torpedo-bombers suffered heavy losses, but the second wave of dive-bombers hit the *Kaga* with four 1,000-lb bombs. That day, the Japanese lost the *Akagi*, *Hiryu* and *Soryu* as well as the *Kaga*, while the USN lost the *Yorktown*. The Japanese admiral, Nagumo, had to be dissuaded from going down with his ship. Midway marked the end of Japanese ambitions, although the war still had to be won.

Advancing towards Japan

Despite the victory at Midway, Japan could not be regarded as being defeated as she still possessed strong forces. King appropriately enough called this the period of the 'offensive-defensive', with the period up to Midway being the defensive, while the USN would later move to the offensive. His order of priorities was the capture of the Santa Cruz Islands and Tulagi, followed by army General MacArthur taking Lae, Salamaua and the north-east coast of New Guinea, with the island fortress of Rabaul later, and then other positions in New Guinea. Nevertheless, it took from the landings on Guadalcanal and Tulagi on 7 August 1942 until 29 January 1943 for success to be achieved. In the interim there were almost continual naval actions as the Japanese sought to regain the initiative, including the Battle of the Solomon Islands and then the Battle of the Santa Cruz Islands, followed by the First Night Battle off Guadalcanal on 12/13 November 1942 and the Second Night Battle on 14/15 November, with the night battles seeing surface vessel engagements without the carrier-borne air power that was typical of so many naval engagements in the Pacific. On 13 November, the cruiser USS *Juneau*, damaged during the first night battle, was sunk by the Japanese submarine *I26*.

Wrangling between the Navy and the Army over who should take the lead in the Pacific, which General Douglas MacArthur saw as the most important theatre of war and for which he pressed for priority against Roosevelt's 'Germany first' strategy, led to the theatre being divided. MacArthur was given the South-West Pacific Area, while Nimitz became Commander-in-Chief Pacific Ocean Areas, or CINCPOA, with overall command of all land and air forces in his area as well as naval forces.

Compared to the slick organization of amphibious assaults later in the Pacific War, the landings on Guadalcanal, Operation Watchtower, were a makeshift affair, and many of those involved nicknamed it 'Operation Shoestring', but the naval leaders had no option. Not landing was out of the question as the Japanese were close to finishing an air base, Henderson Field, and once this was operational, an invasion would be more costly as any force would be subjected to strong Japanese air attack. The island had to be invaded and taken as soon as possible by whatever means were available. As it was, the Japanese fought doggedly and even ran reinforcements and supplies through to the island at night under a system nicknamed the 'Tokyo Express' by the Americans. As mentioned later, the performance of the US carrier commander, Vice Admiral Fletcher, was criticized during this campaign.

Many of the aircraft used at Guadalcanal were those of the United States Marine Corps. The use of USMC aircraft at Guadacanal was at this stage by no means unusual, with a third of the ground-attack aircraft being flown by Marine pilots. It was all the more surprising that the following year Admiral Chester Nimitz, the commander of US forces in the Pacific, should decide to omit carrier training from the syllabus, especially as the new escort carriers were starting to become available, many of which were used to cover amphibious assaults and could have been designated 'Marine carriers'. In making this decision, which seems so strange with the benefit of hindsight, Nimitz was probably considering the extra time taken to train pilots in the difficult art of carrier-deck landings. The restriction was later removed.

At the same time, the USMC's flying had evolved from the original intent of providing an aerial observation-post role for forces once ashore. The same process had happened to some extent in the United States Army some years earlier. During the Solomons campaign the USMC had revived the AOP role, borrowing twenty-four Piper O-1 Cub high-wing monoplanes from the United States Army. The aircrew and maintenance personnel for this important task came not from the existing ranks of Marine Corps pilots but from those Marines who had peacetime experience of private flying! Not only did it not denude the combat squadrons of experienced personnel, it also meant that the pilots of the AOP aircraft were often those who had the necessary experience of gunnery and so were well placed to help with artillery direction.

After this, the USN and USMC started the push towards Rabaul, first securing the Solomons and then the Gilbert Islands. There were landings on New Guinea, cutting off a sizeable Japanese army.

It was far away from these battles that the last traditional naval battle was fought, in the Battle of the Komandorski Islands on 26 March 1943. The Imperial Japanese Navy was escorting a convoy to the Aleutians with Vice Admiral Hosagaya commanding four cruisers and four destroyers. The USN attacked with a force of two cruisers and four destroyers under Rear Admiral McMorris. The two fleets fought, line against line, until their ammunition ran out. The cruiser USS *Salt Lake City* and a destroyer were both damaged, as was the Japanese cruiser *Nachi*. In what was otherwise an inconclusive engagement, the Japanese convoy turned back expecting an American air attack.

Further south, the main offensive continued with the recapture of Attu by a US task force commanded by Rear Admiral Kinkaid, which landed the US 7th Division, covered by three battleships, an escort carrier, seven cruisers and twenty-one destroyers, as well as troop transports, on 11 May 1943. It took until the end of the month to crush Japanese resistance.

There was a pause for some weeks, probably while the US forces trained for the next amphibious assault, on 30 June 1943, at Rendova Island. The landings on Rendova were the first to use modern landing craft, not only enabling troops to get ashore more quickly, but also to be accompanied by tanks and other vehicles. Under Rear Admiral Turner, the force included the first Landing Craft Tank (LCT), able to carry three heavy tanks, and the first landing Craft Infantry (LCI), with up to 400 men. Rendova was close to a major Japanese airfield on New Georgia, so a strong covering force consisting of several combat groups covered the landings, with two aircraft carriers, three escort carriers, five battleships and a cruiser and destroyer screen. As the Japanese attempted to resupply their forces ashore, several night actions followed. In one of these, in the Kula Gulf on the night of 5/6 July, Rear Admiral Ainsworth led a group of three cruisers and four destroyers against Rear Admiral Akiyama's force of ten destroyers, sinking two Japanese destroyers, but the cruiser USS *Helena* was torpedoed by a Japanese destroyer and sunk. On the night of 12/13 July, another night action started, off the neighbouring island of Kolombangara, when Rear Admiral Izaki approached with a cruiser and nine destroyers, of which four had troop reinforcements aboard. They were intercepted once again by Ainsworth, this time with three cruisers and ten destroyers. In a night gunnery action, the Japanese cruiser *Jintsu* blew up, but the Japanese destroyers made a torpedo attack and damaged all three Allied cruisers, the USS *Honolulu* and *St Louis*, and HMNZS *Leander*.

Back on the Aleutians, the USN landed 34,000 men on the island of Kiska on 15 August 1943 after a two-week heavy bombardment, only to find that the Japanese had evacuated the island before the bombardment had started. This was unusual, as the Japanese frequently fought to the death, even to the extent that they would shoot anyone who attempted to surrender, and would also kill women and children rather than let them be captured by the Allies.

The Americans would often by-pass a Japanese strongpoint, preferring to isolate it rather than engage in a costly and time-consuming assault. They by-passed Kolombangara in favour of landings on Vella Lavella in the Solomons on 15 August.

September 1943 saw landings on Lae and Salamaua by General MacArthur's forces which were allocated responsibility for New Guinea.

After a further interval, the US 3rd Marine Division landed on Bougainville in the Solomons, on 1 November 1943, and despite heavy fighting, many Japanese troops managed to hold out in the dense jungle in the island interior until the war ended. The next day, the Japanese sent two heavy and two light cruisers with six destroyers, under Rear Admiral Omori, for an attack that night on the invasion force, which was protected by Rear Admiral Merrill with four cruisers and eight destroyers. American naval gunfire, radar controlled, sank the cruiser *Sendai* and a destroyer, while another cruiser, the *Haguro* was damaged. The cruiser *Denver* was hit, but the shells failed to explode, and the destroyer *Foote* was hit by fire from another American destroyer. The fact that the US Marines would already have landed from their ships was not unusual. Time and time again, the Imperial Japanese Navy failed to stop the transports before they reached their destination and so stop another Allied landing, and then would take great risks to attack the largely empty transports.

Keeping the pressure on the Japanese with heavy bombardments and air attacks before landings was an American speciality in the Pacific, softening up Japanese positions in advance. Kiska was one of the few instances where the Japanese left rather than face the landings, largely because the Aleutians were of little value to them other than posing the constant threat to the Americans of them being used for a possible invasion of Alaska.

On 5 November, the USN mounted the first of a number of heavy air raids on Rabaul, with ninety-seven aircraft from the carriers *Saratoga* and *Princeton*, commanded by Rear Admiral Sherman. They hit and damaged six Japanese cruisers for the loss of ten aircraft. The operation was repeated on 11 November, but with 185 aircraft from Rear Admiral's Montgomery's force of three carriers, *Essex*, *Bunker Hill* and *Independence*. They damaged the cruiser *Agano* and sank a submarine. A Japanese aerial attack from Rabaul was beaten off before they could score any hits on the American ships. As the US landing fleet was off Bourgainville, for once the Japanese attempted to attack before it reached its destination, but again they were beaten off with heavy losses, although they scored torpedo hits on two US cruisers.

Essex and *Independence* were both examples of new classes of American carriers. The Essex-class ships were large fleet carriers while the Independence-class were light carriers converted from Cleveland-class light cruisers in a bid to accelerate carrier construction. In fact, the Essex-class ships were built so quickly that it is doubtful whether the Independence-class were really needed, especially as they suffered from narrow flight and hangar decks. Perhaps the efficiency of US industry surprised even the USN! As the war progressed, the so-called escort carriers were so numerous that many were pressed into service as aircraft transports or to carry aircraft used to provide support for the Marines and troops once ashore.

Before the end of the month, Vice Admiral Raymond Spruance, in command of the newly formed US Fifth Fleet, with Rear Admiral Pownall in command of his carriers, was ready to support the landings on the Gilbert Islands. This was the largest naval force assembled so far, with six aircraft carriers and five Independence-class light carriers, carrying 700 aircraft, as well as five battleships, six cruisers and twenty-one destroyers. Starting on 19 November, the Fifth Fleet attacked Japanese airfields on the islands of Tarawa and Makin, so that the Japanese had simply no air power left in the eastern Marshall Islands and the Gilbert Islands when the US 2nd Marine Division landed on 20 November, backed up by the US 27th Infantry Division, which had the support of eight escort carriers with a total of 216 aircraft, as well as seven battleships and six heavy cruisers. This was the first landing to use the new dock-landing ships, which could launch landing craft from a dock at the stern once it was flooded. Makin was captured on the first day following heavy fighting, but it took until 23 November to secure Tarawa. The operation was not without some cost, as the light carrier *Independence* was hit by an air-dropped torpedo, and on 24 November, the escort carrier *Lipscombe Bay* was sunk by the Japanese submarine *I175*. As the year drew to a close, carrier-borne aircraft struck at Kwajalein Atoll, but the new Essex-class carrier *Lexington* was struck by an air-dropped torpedo, while MacArthur's troops landed on the south coast of New Britain on 15 December, to be followed by the US 1st Marine Division landing on the western end of the island on 26 December.

The Fifth Fleet was the name of the formation commanded by Vice Admiral Raymond Spruance, but when he was ashore planning his next operation, command switched to Vice Admiral William 'Bull' Halsey, and the title became the Third Fleet, switching back again when Halsey went ashore for his planning. The task forces comprising the fleet also switched identities, so that TF58, the carrier force, would alternate as TF38 when Halsey was in overall command.

While Japanese naval might was on the wane, that of the United States continued to grow. After further landings on New Guinea and New Britain at the beginning of January, a US carrier fleet, Task Force 58, under Vice Admiral Marc Mitscher, struck at Japanese airfields in the Marshall Islands between 29 January and 6 February 1944, covering landings. This had no less than 6 fleet carriers and 6 command light carriers, with a total of 730 aircraft, 8 battleships, 3 heavy and 3 light cruisers, and 36 destroyers. Once again, when the US landed the 4th Marine Division and the 7th Infantry Division on Kwajalein in the Marshall Islands on 31 Janury, the support provided by the Fifth Fleet included 8 escort carriers with 190 aircraft, as well as 7 battleships, 9 cruisers and 45 destroyers. The heavy bombardment provided by the battleships no doubt helped the Americans to take Kwajalein in a week.

Mid-February saw III Amphibious Force under Rear Admiral Wilkinson land the 3rd (New Zealand) Division on Green Island, to the east of New Britain.

The Fifth Fleet sent part of its carrier force and six battleships, with a strong cruiser and destroyer escort, to attack Truk, in the Caroline Islands, on 17 and 18 February. Although Truk was a large Japanese base, there were few worthwhile targets in the harbour for aircraft from the five large carriers and four light carriers, or for the guns of the six battleships. Carrier-borne aircraft attacked and sank the cruiser *Naka*, while the battleships sank the auxiliary cruiser *Katori* as well as two destroyers. Between them, the aircraft and the battleships also sank twenty-six Japanese merchantmen, and no less than 300 out of 365 Japanese combat aircraft were lost compared with just twenty-five US aircraft. Seven Japanese torpedo-bombers managed to get through to score a single hit on the aircraft carrier *Intrepid*. On 17 February, the so-far unused reserves of the landing on Kwajalein, the 27th Infantry Division, were landed on a westerly atoll in the Marshall Islands, and after four days of fighting, the Japanese were defeated.

Carrier-borne aircraft attacked Japanese-held islands in the Marianas on 23 February. By this time, the USN was getting further from its bases and suffering the problem of a good forward base, but this was resolved on 29 February by MacArthur's troops, the 1st Cavalry Division, taking Manus in the Admiralty Islands, north of New Guinea, after fierce fighting. The island had a deep harbour and was ideal for the construction of a naval base. By late March, the major Japanese fortress of Rabaul was encircled.

The return of the Royal Navy to the Pacific was by way of the Indian Ocean, with the fast armoured aircraft carrier HMS *Illustrious* initially operating alongside the USS *Saratoga* for operations against Sabang on Sumatra, starting on 19 April 1944. The news was not all good for the Allies, even at this late stage, as the build-up of strong Royal Navy forces in the East was marred by an ammunition ship exploding in the harbour at Bombay, now Mumbai, on 14 April. The explosion completely destroyed eleven ships, and badly damaged another nine, while the fire in the port continued for fourteen days.

Although the amphibious assaults and major naval battles made the headlines, the usual wartime role of warships continued. Between 19 and 31 May 1944, the destroyer USS *England* sank six Japanese submarines in just fourteen days, setting a Second World War record for a single ship.

Battle of the Philippine Sea

Attacks by Mitscher's carrier-borne aircraft on the Palau Islands at the end of March preceded the US landings on Hollandia on 22 April, while the landings were given air cover in addition to that provided by the US Seventh Fleet, which was the landing fleet, with its eight escort carriers. By the end of the month, further attacks were being made on Truk as the USN prepared for its assault on the Marianas. As the next step towards the invasion of the Marianas, between 11 and 17 June, Task Force 58's carriers was divided into four groups to destroy Japanese air power on the islands, and while the Japanese Navy Air Force and Japanese Army Air Force attempted to strike back, they did so without success. On 15 and 16 June, two carrier combat groups attacked the Bonin Islands, part way to Japan, to prevent the Japanese from flying in reinforcements to the Marianas, destroying 300 Japanese aircraft for the loss of just twenty-two USN.

The first landings in the Marianas were on the island of Saipan, on 15 June 1944. This was one of the most heavily defended islands encountered by the Americans thus far, with 22,700 Japanese troops and 6,700 sailors, determined to fight as they expected only to have to hold the island until the Imperial Japanese Navy intervened. Vice Admiral Turner's Task Force 52 landed V Amphibious Corps as well as the US 2nd and 4th Marine Divisions, keeping the 27th Infantry Division in reserve. TF52 comprised 550 ships including 8 escort carriers with 170 aircraft, 7 battleships, 11 cruisers and 50 destroyers, while another 4 escort carriers carried replacement aircraft for the battle.

Eventually, Vice Admiral Ozawa did arrive, with no less than five large aircraft carriers and four light carriers, with a total of 430 aircraft, while the USN Fifth Fleet had seven large aircraft carriers and eight light carriers with 890 aircraft. The opposing battle fleets were more evenly balanced, with Spruance having 7 battleships against Ozawa's 5, of which 2, *Yamato* and *Musashi*, had 18-inch guns which outranged those of the USN; there were also 8 US heavy cruisers against 11 Japanese, but 13 US light cruisers compared with just 2 for the Japanese, and 67 US destroyers against just 28 Japanese.

One indication of the increasingly desperate state of the Imperial Japanese Navy was that in April 1944, the Japanese Navy Air Force had fewer than a hundred pilots available for duty in the central Pacific, not simply because of the predations of American fighters, but also due to sickness, especially malaria. When 500 new pilots and 500 radio operators graduated from the training school at Kasumigaura, their training was still incomplete and, of course, they lacked combat experience. The new airmen were sent to Admiral Ozawa to continue their training, but he was running short of airfields and his carriers, based at Tawi Tawi in the Sulu Islands, seldom went to sea for fear of attack by US submarines. While there were still nine Japanese carriers left following the completion of the new *Taiho* on 7 March, both *Shokaku* and *Zuikaku* were badly battered and in need of a refit. Most of those that remained were best described as light carriers, although some approximated more to escort carriers.

Nevertheless, those ashore defending the Marianas were right in believing that the IJN would be coming to their aid, as the Japanese planned a strong counter-attack using both carrier and shore-based aircraft. This was the basis of the Battle of the Philippine Sea, but known informally to the USN as the 'Marianas Turkey Shoot', so high were the casualties amongst Japan's declining air forces.

Ozawa's plan was to get the US Fifth Fleet between his carriers and the Japanese Army Air Force bases in the Marianas, so that the Americans could be attacked from both sides. He anticipated his aircraft striking at the Americans and then continuing to land at Guam and Rota to refuel and rearm, so that they could then mount a second strike on the Fifth Fleet on their return to the carriers – in effect what became known in the later stages of the air campaign in Europe as 'shuttle bombing'. Ozawa divided his carrier force into two, while Kurita had a van force with three carriers.

Both navies sent submarines into the Philippine Sea, although only the American submarines saw action, engaging Japanese warships and also providing additional reconnaissance.

Japanese reconnaissance aircraft first sighted the American carriers during the afternoon of 18 June, but at this stage Mitscher was still unaware of the exact position of the Japanese carriers.

The following morning, realizing that he was vulnerable to Japanese attack, Mitscher had most of his fighters prepared and either in the air on combat air patrols or ranged on deck ready for take-off at an early hour. It was not until 1000 hrs that the first Japanese attacks came, but these were shore-based aircraft from Guam. Additional aircraft were launched from the carriers to reinforce the CAP and in the fierce dogfights that ensued, just twenty-four out of the sixty-nine Japanese aircraft sent against the Fifth Fleet survived. The next wave consisted of 130 aircraft, of which ninety-eight were shot down. These attacks were followed by the first of four waves of carrier-borne aircraft but, anticipating an attack, Mitscher had positioned his fighters 50 miles ahead of the fleet, and once again the Japanese suffered heavy losses, with those aircraft that managed to evade the fighters being caught by the intense anti-aircraft fire put up by the ships. Just twenty or so of them managed to press home their attack, and hits were scored on the battleship *South Dakota* and the carriers *Wasp* and *Bunker Hill*, but all three continued in action. Even those aircraft that managed to reach the shore bases in Guam were attacked and destroyed by American fighters as they landed. Ozawa had viewed Guam as an unsinkable aircraft carrier – unsinkable perhaps, but it lacked manoeuvrability!

While USN aircraft were attacking the airfields in Guam, the Japanese carriers were themselves under attack from below the waves. At 0911 hrs, just after the Japanese aircraft had taken off, the submarine *Albacore* torpedoed the *Taiho*, Ozawa's flagship, and a gigantic aviation fuel explosion destroyed the ship and killed half her crew. Later, at 1220, another submarine, the *Cavalla*, put three torpedoes into *Shokaku* and three hours later she also blew up as aviation fumes ignited, and sank. During the afternoon just a hundred aircraft returned to the Japanese carriers. Ozawa meanwhile had moved his flag to the cruiser *Naguro*.

Japanese tactics when attacking ships at sea differed little from those of the Americans, which was not surprising since the nature of the aircraft dictated how the mission should be flown. Torpedo aircraft attacked low, at no more than 200 feet, while the dive-bombers remained at medium altitude ready to start their dive onto the selected target.

Having lost three-quarters of his aircraft and two of his largest carriers, Ozawa had little option but to withdraw, and after darkness fell started to steam slowly to the north-west. Mitscher realized that this could be a major opportunity. By this time, some of his carriers were low on fuel, but he made the most of this problem by leaving them behind to neutralize enemy air power on Guam. Mitscher sent three carriers under Rear Admiral Clark in pursuit of Ozawa's fleet. Reconnaissance aircraft from TF58 were launched starting at 0530 on 20 June. Despite reports from American submarines that had spotted the Japanese fleet, looking for even ships as large as aircraft carriers in the vast reaches of the Pacific was akin to searching for a needle in a haystack, and it was not until 1500 hrs that an American aircraft located the retreating Japanese. At this stage, Ozawa's ships were at extreme range from the pursuing American carriers.

The American pilots struggled to use as little fuel as possible, flying their aircraft on as lean a mixture as possible, thereby taking a full two hours to reach the Japanese fleet. They had plenty of time to think about the difficulty of operating at full pressure over the combat zone and then returning to their ships, knowing that if they didn't manage to conserve enough fuel, they would in all probability have to ditch in the sea at night, and hope to be rescued by the advancing fleet.

The Japanese were heavily dependent on AA fire for their survival as Ozawa had just thirty-five fighters left to protect his fleet. One problem with dive-bombing was that pilots could not see whether their bombs had hit the target as they had to pull back the control column as they released their bombs, allowing themselves enough height above the target for the aircraft to bring its nose up – the steeper the dive, the more room needed to pull up and climb away, another danger for the inexperienced, especially in the fading light.

The carrier *Hiyo* was so badly damaged that she sank within two hours in yet another fuel-vapour explosion. Two of the fleet's precious tankers were also sunk. Of the other carriers, *Zuikaku*, *Junyo*, *Ryuho* and *Chiyoda* were all badly damaged, as was the battleship *Haruna* and a cruiser. Just twenty American aircraft were shot down in the attack.

Heavy US losses occurred on the return flight, but not from enemy action. Eighty USN aircraft were lost during this time after running out of fuel. Mitscher wanted the pursuit to continue, but on hearing of the losses, Spruance forbade it. In any case, even though the fighters could carry small bombs, it was the torpedo-bombers and dive-bombers that would be needed to inflict real damage on the Japanese, and almost all of these had been lost. In all, the attack and the homeward run saw forty-nine American aviators killed, despite most of those ditching being rescued. Nagumo, whose career seems to have been marked with missed opportunities and failures, later committed hari-kari ashore on Saipan after learning of the defeat. Many other senior Japanese officers on the island also seem to have committed suicide, although there is some doubt about this as it may have been an accident.

Japanese aircraft losses were so high that the Americans promptly described the Battle of the Philippine Sea as the 'Marianas Turkey Shoot'. Ozawa had lost three aircraft carriers and 400 carrier-borne aircraft, as well as another fifty aircraft based ashore. American losses overall were 130 aircraft and seventy-six aircrew.

On 24 June, Mitscher took three of his four carrier groups to Eniwetok for refuelling and replenishment, while Clark took the fourth group to attack Iwo Jima and the Pagan Islands. It was not until 9 July that Japanese resistance on Saipan ended, and on 21 July, the Americans landed on Guam. Task Force 53 under Rear Admiral Connolly put III Amphibious Corps ashore with the support of many of the battleships and escort carriers involved in the landings on Saipan, while Mitscher's carriers sent their aircraft to attack Japanese bases within range of the Marianas to prevent them from harassing the invading troops. It took several weeks for Japanese resistance on Guam to be broken, but the island then became the major US base in the western Pacific.

Landings on Tinian followed next, on 24 July, when Task Force 52 put V Amphibious Corps ashore, with US Army heavy artillery ashore on Saipan joining the battleships in providing heavy fire support.

Command of the fast naval force, the Third Fleet, passed from Vice Admiral Ghormley to Admiral William 'Bull' Halsey, who had acquired his nickname because of his short temper, impatience and physique. Halsey had been in overall command of the carriers involved in the Doolittle raid in 1942. The Third Fleet was given the task of further weakening Japanese air power to help the next set of landings. Halsey started his campaign with attacks by carrier aircraft on the Bonin Islands between 31 August and 2 September, followed on 7 September by four days of air raids on Japanese forces in the southern Philippines, when Mitscher's redesignated Task Force 38 sent all of its aircraft to attack airfields and naval installations, finding resistance to be light. This was followed by attacks on the central Philippines on 12/13 September, before the fleet withdrew to prepare to support the next round of landings.

Meanwhile, on 15 September, the capture of Morotai finally brought the US Army Air Force into the war in the Pacific after a period when their main effort had been attacking Japanese forces in Burma, using Consolidated B-24 Liberators, an aircraft known for its long range. The eastern islands in the Sundra Group were now within USAAF range.

Between 15 and 23 September, Rear Admiral Wilkinson took Task Force 31 to land III Amphibious Corps on the Palau Islands, an important stepping stone between Guam, Saipan and the Philippines. No less than twelve escort carriers were used on this operation, as well as the battleships *Pennsylvania*, *Tennessee*, *Maryland*, *West Virginia* and *Mississippi*, with eight cruisers and twenty-seven destroyers. The undefended Ulithi Atoll was also seized and a forward naval base constructed.

Meanwhile, on 24 August, the Royal Navy in the Indian Ocean sent aircraft from the carriers *Victorious* and *Indomitable* to attack Padang on Sumatra, and there were also air attacks on the airfield at Sabang, which was later bombarded by the British Eastern Fleet. Between 17 and 19 October, these two carriers plus *Illustrious* attacked the Nicobar Islands, Indian territories close to the coast of Burma and occupied by the Japanese.

The Philippines

On 21 and 22 September, TF38 attacked Manila Harbour, sinking three destroyers and twenty merchantmen, as well as causing extensive damage to harbour installations and to airfields ashore. Attacks on Japanese shipping and airfields in the central Philippines by aircraft from Mitscher's redesignated TF38 continued on 24 September, destroying 1,200 Japanese aircraft, many of them on the ground, and a further thirteen ships, all for the loss of seventy-two USN aircraft. The attacks showed that the defence of the Philippines was far weaker than the Americans had expected, and led them to advance the date for the first landings from December to October. General MacArthur, who had been in command of the defence of the Philippines when the Japanese invaded in 1942, had pressed to be given command of the liberation force, and the ships and landing craft of the newly formed Central Pacific Command under Admiral Nimitz were placed under MacArthur's overall command, leaving Halsey's Third Fleet to operate independently.

But first the Americans wanted to take the vital island of Formosa, close to the coast of China, and also within easy range for heavy bombers heading for the Philippines and for the Japanese island of Okinawa, as well as Japan itself. Formosa also sat comfortably close to the shipping lanes between Japan and its empire, or, more importantly, the resources that the empire could send home to Japan.

Operations against Okinawa and Formosa by TF38's seventeen aircraft carriers started on 10 October and lasted for six days. Halsey used 340 aircraft to attack Okinawa on 10 October, before attacking targets on northern Luzon in the Philippines and then attacking Formosa, home to the Imperial Japanese Navy's 2nd Air Fleet under Vice Admiral Fukudoma. The first day of action against Formosa, 12 October, saw a major air battle develop in which the Japanese lost 160 aircraft to the USN's forty-three. Over the next couple of days, the IJN attempted to send its aircraft against the Allied fleet, but only succeeded in making one torpedo strike on the cruiser USS *Canberra* (the only American warship to have been named after a foreign city as a tribute to HMAS *Canberra*, lost in the Guadalcanal campaign) and then the *Houston*. The *Houston* was later hit a second time. Over the seven days, the Japanese lost 600 aircraft against ninety by the USN.

Finally, on 20 October, MacArthur's troops landed on Leyte, with Vice Admiral Kinkaid's US Seventh Fleet putting the US Sixth

Army ashore at Tacloban. Halsey's Third Fleet continued its attacks on Luzon and other parts of the Philippines to keep the Japanese from attacking the landing force, but they still managed to put a torpedo into the cruiser *Honolulu* and a bomb into the cruiser HMAS *Australia*.

What then transpired was the Battle of Leyte Gulf, which ran from 23 to 26 October, and which is covered in greater detail in the chapter on Halsey. The Philippines were invaluable to the Japanese as their loss would cut the sea lanes between the Japanese Home Islands and their sources of fuel and raw materials in the Netherlands East Indies and Malaya. The greatest naval battle in history, it consisted of four parts, with an air-sea battle in the Sibuyan Sea on 24 October, a night battle in the Surigao Straits on 25 October, followed by a further battle off Samar, and finally an air-sea battle off Cape Engano. Japanese strategy was for Ozawa to send his carrier fleet, by this time down to just 116 aircraft, to lure Halsey to the north, and allow Vice Admiral Kurita with the Japanese battle fleet to attack from the west. Two other battle fleets were also deployed. This was not just a desperate attempt to seek a decisive naval battle, but also an opportunity to use the Japanese battleships, which had been largely by-passed in a war that favoured the submarine and the aircraft carrier.

What happened was the loss of much that remained of the Imperial Japanese Navy, while US losses were heavier than they might have been because of the intervention of massed kamikaze suicide attacks. The USN lost a light carrier and 2 escort carriers, as well as 3 destroyers, while the IJN lost a large aircraft carrier, 3 light carriers, 3 battleships, 6 heavy cruisers, 4 light cruisers and 11 destroyers, with 10,000 men killed compared to the USN's 1,500.

The Battle of Leyte Gulf meant that the USN no longer had to face serious Japanese opposition at sea. In operations after the battle to the east of the Philippines, during November 1944, no less than 800 Japanese aircraft were shot down, and an entire reinforcement troop convoy bound for Leyte was destroyed, with the loss of three more cruisers and thirteen destroyers. Kamikaze pilots sank one US destroyer and hit five large aircraft carriers and two light carriers.

Beneath the surface, the USN's submarines continued to exact their steady toll of Japanese shipping. Yet it was an exceptional success on 21 November, when the *Sealion* sank the battleship *Kongo*, and an even better day on 27 November when the *Archerfish* sank the new aircraft carrier *Shinano* in the Japanese Inland Sea before she could enter service (the loss was such that the USN would not believe the report until it could be verified after the war had ended). Another new carrier, the *Unryu*, was later sunk by the *Redfish*.

Nevertheless, Halsey's refusal to take proper action on receiving adverse meteorological reports resulted in the episode known as 'Halsey's Typhoon', which saw three destroyers sunk and three light carriers damaged, with 146 aircraft either swept overboard or wrecked by the waves. This was a blemish on his record that many of his peers would neither forgive nor forget.

As the New Year broke, the British Eastern Fleet was operational, and on 4 January 1945, aircraft from the aircraft carriers *Illustrious*, *Indefatigable*, *Indomitable* and *Victorious* attacked the oil refineries in north-eastern Sumatra; they were at sea again on 24 and 29 January for further strikes on the refinery at Palembang.

By spring, the Philippines had been largely recaptured except for isolated pockets of resistance. Before this, on 16–17 February, Mitscher's TF58,with no less than 16 aircraft carriers, 9 battleships, 14 cruisers and 77 destroyers, mounted the first large-scale US air attack on the Japanese home islands, destroying some 500 Japanese aircraft at a cost of 88 for the USN. While the USAAF's heavy bombers had been mounting raids over Japan from the previous autumn, to ensure that these aircraft had fighter protection, the Americans decided to take Iwo Jima to provide an air base for fighters. Once again the Fifth Fleet provided air cover, including Mitscher's TF58, while TF51 comprised a landing force of some 500 ships, including eleven escort carriers, seven battleships and five cruisers, for the amphibious assault on 19 February. The island was strongly garrisoned and, starting on 21 February, there were numerous kamikaze attacks, sinking the escort carrier *Bismarck Sea*; although the *Saratoga* was hit six times, she was saved. It took a month to suppress Japanese opposition.

On 18–19 March, further heavy attacks were mounted on Japan, including the Inland Sea, with 10 fleet carriers and 6 light carriers sending no less than 1,200 aircraft, supported by 8 battleships and 2 battlecruisers, 16 cruisers and 64 destroyers. A furious response from Vice Admiral Ugaki's 5th Air Fleet resulted in five aircraft carriers being hit, with the *Franklin* suffering a thousand casualties.

On 1 April, the USN and RN were together for the landings on Okinawa, defended by 77,000 Japanese troops and 10,000 IJN personnel. Spruance led the US Fifth Fleet, with Mitscher's TF58 reinforced by the British Pacific Fleet with four aircraft carriers and 220 aircraft, two battleships and five cruisers. The landing fleet, TF51, had 430 ships, including ten battleships, thirteen cruisers and eighteen escort carriers with 540 aircraft. On 6 April, kamikaze attacks began against TF51's ships, while the battleship *Yamato* put to sea heading for Okinawa with a cruiser and eight destroyers on a 'one-way' suicide mission as she only had sufficient fuel to reach the battle zone. The following day, *Yamato* was sunk by 280 US aircraft which also sank the cruiser and four of the destroyers. Nevertheless, the kamikaze attacks continued for another six weeks, with 2,000 aircraft sinking twenty-six US ships, although none were larger than a destroyer, and damaging another 164, including three US and three British carriers, as well as three US battleships.

By this time, with France liberated, the Marine Nationale was back in the war, and on 11 April, the British Eastern Fleet, with the battleships *Queen Elizabeth* and the French *Richelieu*, as well as two escort carriers, two cruisers and five destroyers, bombarded Sabang again. Later, on the night of 15/16 May, British destroyers sank the Japanese heavy cruiser *Haguro* in the Straits of Malacca.

Japanese resistance on Okinawa was finally broken by the end of June, but at the cost of 48,000 US casualties. Towards the end of July, the US Third Fleet attacked Japan in preparation for the eventual landings, and sank almost every remaining major Japanese warship, including the aircraft carrier *Amagi* and three battleships. The last attacks by the Third Fleet were between 9 and 14 August, but by that time the atomic bombs had been dropped on Hiroshima on 6 August and Nagasaki on 9 August, which eventually led to Japan's surrender. There was still an anti-surrender faction that included many senior naval officers and surrender could not be taken for granted until the surrender document was signed.

Chapter 3
The United States Navy

The United States Navy started to grow rapidly even before the First World War, and afterwards its development was entwined with the Washington Naval Treaty of 1922 that allowed it to become one of the two strongest navies in the world. No longer would it leave the Royal Navy in the position that it could equal the two strongest navies in the world. Moreover, unlike the Royal Navy, it retained control of its own aviation between the two world wars, but also continued the system under which it operated as a purely 'blue water' navy, leaving operations in home waters to the United States Coast Guard, part of the US Department of Transportation (sic) in peacetime, but coming under USN control in wartime. Like the Royal Navy and Imperial Japanese Navy, the USN believed firmly in the aircraft carrier. With war threatening in Europe and then breaking out in September 1939, the USN expanded rapidly in the last days of peace, which for it lasted until 7 December 1941 when the Japanese attacked its forward Pacific base at Pearl Harbor in Hawaii. Japanese failure to knock out Pearl Harbor and destroy the Pacific Fleet, and the inability of the Japanese to appreciate the value of the Panama Canal, meant that within six months of the attack, the United States Navy was on the offensive and the Imperial Japanese Navy on the defensive.

Even before the United States was drawn into the conflict, the country started to assist the United Kingdom: convoys were escorted to a mid-Atlantic handover point on the pretext of protecting neutral shipping, while First World War destroyers were transferred to the Royal Navy in return for the use of British bases in the Caribbean, and on two occasions aircraft were delivered to Malta by the US carrier *Wasp*.

Alone amongst the major belligerent powers, the United States had the fuel, the raw materials and the industrial capacity, including the labour force, to fight and win a major war that for it meant fighting on two main fronts, in the Pacific and the North Atlantic, as well as playing a part in the war in North Africa and the Mediterranean, and helping to supply the Soviet Union. As the war progressed, US-built escort carriers enabled the Allies to win the convoy battles and then proved themselves invaluable in providing aircraft to cover invasions in Italy and the South of France, and island-hopping towards Japan across the Pacific.

Between the two world wars, the United States Navy developed a strong naval air arm, which included shore-based maritime-reconnaissance aircraft, and a strong submarine service, but lagged behind in anti-submarine warfare. Increasingly, Japan was seen as the most likely enemy as that country did not disguise its territorial ambitions in China. Germany was seen as less of a threat, but after the outbreak of war in Europe in 1939, the following year Congress passed the 'Two-Ocean Navy' measure that permitted the building of no less than 1,350,000 tons of new warships. It was just in time, and a country with fewer resources could not have completed this programme before the war ended. The 'Lend-Lease Act', which allowed the United States to lend war material, including warships and aircraft, to the United Kingdom in return for being able to use British bases around the world, but especially in the Caribbean, was also matched by 'reverse lend-lease', with British anti-submarine technology made available to the USN.

The US carrier fleet enabled the United States to strike back at Japan and take the war across the Pacific, with carrier-borne aircraft matching Japanese shore-based aircraft in combat, something which many considered impossible. Less well known was the role of the American submariners who fought the war's most successful anti-submarine campaign, and even though the actual tonnage sunk was less than that of the German U-boats in the Atlantic, they effectively cut Japan off from food, fuel and raw materials, so that as the war ended, many Japanese were starving and there was little fuel left. Japan's poor anti-submarine technology and the reluctance amongst IJN commanders to become involved in convoy protection meant that US submarine losses were very much less than those of the Germans. On the other hand, the submarine campaign was hampered at the start by unreliable torpedoes which often failed to explode, even when they hit the target, which could not always be taken for granted as they were as likely to run in circles as run straight.

On 7 December 1941, the day of the attack on Pearl Harbor, the United States Navy had 16 battleships, 7 aircraft carriers, 18 heavy cruisers, 19 light cruisers, 6 anti-aircraft cruisers, 171 destroyers and 114 submarines.

Chapter 4

Overcautious, or Simply Unlucky?

Admiral Jack 'Frank' Fletcher, USN (1885–1973)

Fletcher was the US admiral in command of several of the early campaigns in the Pacific, but he was blamed on more than one occasion for being overcautious, and maybe he was also just unlucky. Despite his reputation for caution and the loss of the carrier USS *Lexington*, he nevertheless stopped the Japanese from taking Port Moresby at the Battle of the Coral Sea, which could be said to have been a tactical victory for the Japanese, but a strategic victory for the United States.

Known throughout the United States Navy as 'Black Jack', Fletcher was born in Marshalltown, Iowa. He came from a naval family with an uncle who was an admiral. He attended the US Naval Academy at Annapolis from 1902 until 1906. On graduating, he served aboard the battleships USS *Rhode Island*, *Ohio* and *Maine*. In November 1909, he was posted to the destroyer *Chauncey*, part of the Asiatic Torpedo Flotilla and his first command was the *Dale* in April 1910. In March 1912, Fletcher returned to the *Chauncey* as her commanding officer. Posted to the battleship *Florida* in December 1912, he was at the occupation of Vera Cruz, Mexico, in April 1914, for which he was awarded the Medal of Honor for distinguished conduct.

During the First World War, he was a gunnery officer until September 1917, when he took command of the *Margaret* and later was posted to the *Allen* in February 1918 before taking command of the *Benham* in May, escorting convoys across the Atlantic, for which he was awarded the Navy Cross. From October 1918 to February 1919 he stood by the *Crane* at San Francisco as she fitted out, afterwards becoming commanding officer of the *Gridley* on her commissioning. Returning to Washington, he was head of the Detail Section, Enlisted Personnel Division in the Bureau of Navigation from April 1919 until September 1922.

After serving in the Philippines, he returned to the USA for a posting at the Washington Navy Yards in 1925. He completed the Senior Course at the Naval War College, Newport in June 1930, and afterwards became Chief of Staff to the Commander-in-Chief, US Atlantic Fleet in August 1931. In 1933 he was transferred to the Office of the Chief of Naval Operations, before becoming an aide to the Secretary of the Navy from November 1933 to May 1936. He took command of the *New Mexico*, flagship of Battleship Division Three in June 1936. In December 1937 he became a member of the Naval Examining Board and was appointed Assistant Chief of the Bureau of Navigation in June 1938. Promoted to rear admiral and returning to the Pacific on the outbreak of war in Europe, until December 1941 he commanded a succession of cruiser divisions. When Japan entered the war, he was commanding Task Force 11 with the carrier *Saratoga* and was sent to Wake Island, which was under bombardment by Japanese warships. On 22 December, Fletcher was recalled by a nervous Admiral Pye, who was acting as a replacement for the disgraced commander of the US Pacific Fleet, Rear Admiral Husband Kimmel, until Nimitz arrived.

For his part, Fletcher's arrival at Wake Island was delayed by his frequent sending away of his destroyers to refuel so that they would be ready for high-speed action. It thus happened that in the early stages of the Pacific War Fletcher acquired an unwanted reputation for being overcautious, as TF11 was late in arriving at Wake Island, and allowed the Japanese to take the island unopposed. In some ways his caution can be understood with hindsight, as this was a war that was fought at sea in a way that few senior officers of his generation could have envisaged, and given the vast distances of the Pacific and the unknown demands of steaming at high speed in combat, the worry about running low on fuel in mid-battle can be understood.

Nevertheless, in May 1942, it was Fletcher who turned back the Japanese in the Battle of the Coral Sea, and while they inflicted heavier losses on the USN than he managed against the Imperial

Japanese Navy, the strategic victory overall was his. One of the largest Japanese aircraft carriers, the *Shokaku*, was so badly damaged that she was not available for the next major move by the Japanese, against Midway. It also showed that the Japanese were no longer invincible, being fought to a standstill. The head of the USN, Admiral Ernest King, wrote to the British First Sea Lord, Admiral Sir Dudley Pound, that 'On the whole we had rather the better of it and we seem to have stopped the advance on Port Moresby for the time being.'

Fletcher was still in command at the Battle of Midway on 4 June 1942, but when his flagship, the aircraft carrier USS *Yorktown*, was unfortunately lost, Spruance took over tactical command and in the end also took the credit for the victory, which saw four Japanese aircraft carriers lost in a single day. This was sheer bad luck for Fletcher as the battle marked the turning point in the war at sea in the Pacific. From this time onwards, the Japanese had lost all hope of victory, or even fighting to a negotiated settlement, and Japanese strategy became defensive.

All of this could be defended or attributed to misfortune, the sad fortunes of war, but in August, with the Americans on what they called the 'offensive-defensive' and starting the long island-hopping advance to victory, what happened at Guadalcanal could not be explained away.

Promoted to vice admiral, Fletcher was put in command of a carrier force to protect the Guadalcanal landings. Code-named Operation Watchtower, the landings on Guadalcanal and Tulagi on 7 August 1942 followed an inter-service spat between the USN and the United States Army over which service should take the lead in the Pacific War. In the end, the USN and USMC were given the lead in the Pacific War, a wise move given that amphibious landing succeeded amphibious landing, while in North Africa and Europe, the Army would have enough to occupy its planners. 'Operation Watchtower' was prepared in considerable haste, causing some to describe it as 'Operation Shoestring', but it was necessary to act quickly before the Japanese could complete the air base, Henderson Field, and deploy aircraft there.

At Guadalcanal, Vice Admiral Ghormley took overall command of the operation, while Fletcher was in command of Task Force 61 with three aircraft carriers, the USS *Enterprise*, *Saratoga* and *Wasp*, as well as the battleship *North Carolina*, six cruisers and sixteen destroyers. At stake were the landings by 19,000 men from Major General Vandegrift's 1st Marine Division. A British officer, Rear Admiral Victor Critchley, commanded a force of cruisers to defend the transports.

The makeshift nature of the arrangements had been essential if the Americans were to act quickly and the Japanese were to be prevented from developing the defences of Guadalcanal and Tulagi. Had the enemy sufficient time to complete airfields, the invasion of the islands would have been much more difficult and costly. Initially, most of the fighting was on Tulagi, and at first the operation on Guadalcanal went well, but a steady war of attrition developed, especially around the key objective of Henderson Field, an airfield under construction. After losing twenty-one aircraft in a single day, Fletcher sought permission to withdraw, which Ghormley allowed, but the gap left in the US defences led to the Battle of Savo Island, which started during the early hours of 9 August. Allied warships under the British Rear Admiral Critchley, screening the transports, were surprised at midnight and defeated in little more than half an hour by a Japanese force of seven cruisers and one destroyer, commanded by Vice Admiral Gunichi Mikawa. After inflicting initial heavy losses on the US and Australian force offshore, sinking four cruisers, HMAS *Canberra*, USS *Astoria*, *Vincennes* and *Quincy*, and circling Savo Island, Vice Admiral Mikawa did not continue to attack the US transports for fear of being attacked by USN carrier-borne aircraft, not realizing that Fletcher had withdrawn. Fletcher is sometimes criticized because his carriers were at the far end of their nightly withdrawal, and although steaming back ready for the morning, were still too far to away to provide protection. Had the Japanese realized the disposition of the Allied ships, an attack on the transports and on troops ashore could have resulted.

When the Japanese attempted to reinforce their garrison ashore on Guadalcanal, the Battle of the Eastern Solomon Islands developed. After the Japanese managed to land reinforcements on Guadalcanal on 18 August, Henderson Field became the scene of intense fighting. The first batch of Japanese reinforcements – just 915 men – showed that the Japanese had seriously underestimated the strength of the US forces, and was wiped out in a battle on 21 August. A steady war of attrition was then started by the Japanese, with reinforcements being landed under cover of darkness in an operation dubbed the 'Tokyo Express' by the Americans. A more determined effort to reinforce their troops on Guadalcanal came in late August when the Japanese sent four transports to reinforce their troops on the island, but the four 'transports' were really just elderly destroyers and again the total number of troops to be landed totalled just 1,500 men, as the Japanese were still underestimating the size of the US forces.

The Japanese move found Vice Admiral Fletcher with TF61, still including the carriers *Enterprise* and *Saratoga*, but with the *Wasp* away refuelling, and a total of 176 aircraft available. His opponent was Vice Admiral Nagumo, who had survived the Battle of Midway and had retained his command. Nagumo, who was now responsible for ensuring the safe arrival of the transports, had three aircraft carriers, *Zuikaku* and *Shokaku*, with 131 aircraft between them, and the smaller *Ryujo*, with thirty-one aircraft which, with a cruiser and two destroyers, was to act as a diversionary force. Given the small size and number of the transports, Nagumo had a considerable number of surface vessels to protect these and his carriers, with three battleships, ten cruisers and twenty-one destroyers in addition to those with *Ryujo*, compared with Fletcher's single battleship, four cruisers and eleven destroyers.

The Americans were expecting increased Japanese activity and spotted *Ryujo* early on, but lost track of the Japanese ships by 21 August. On 23 August, American reconnaissance aircraft once again located the Japanese transports, but a strike launched from the US carriers failed to find them. The next day, *Saratoga*'s aircraft found the *Ryujo* at 1000 hrs some 300 miles north of TF61; this time the strike aircraft found her and promptly sunk her using bombs and torpedoes. Meanwhile, Japanese aircraft from *Shokaku* and *Zuikaku* found and attacked the USS *Enterprise*. The absence of the *Wasp* meant that, for the last time in the Pacific War, the Japanese had overall air superiority. Fighters from the *Enterprise* and the carrier's AA defences fought off the first wave of Japanese torpedo-bombers, but a second wave of dive-bombers managed to hit the *Enterprise* three times, starting fires, although these were soon extinguished and the ship remained capable of limited operations. Nevertheless, Fletcher took the blame for the absence of one of his carriers and the lack of local air superiority.

On 25 August, United States Marine Corps aircraft based ashore on Guadalcanal and Esperitu Sanctu attacked the Japanese troop transports, sinking the largest one and a destroyer escort, while a cruiser was also badly damaged. By this time, in addition to the ships lost, the Japanese had lost a total of ninety aircraft against just twenty US aircraft, and Nagumo decided to withdraw.

The United States had won yet another battle in the Pacific War, the Battle of the Eastern Solomon Islands. It is hard to see why the Japanese, having put so much effort into escorting such a pitiful reinforcement convoy, had not assumed a more aggressive role, and the only justification can be that the strategy was one of tying down US forces. Nor did the Japanese cut their losses and abandon the islands as, despite losing the battle, they continued to maintain the 'Tokyo Express', while the destroyers engaged on these runs also took the opportunity to shell Henderson Field. On 31 August, a more substantial force of 3,500 Japanese troops were landed on Guadalcanal, building up their forces to a total of 6,000 men by early September, by which time the Americans had 19,000 men on the island. These Japanese troops were defeated in a night battle on 13/14 September.

Later, in a rare offensive by Japanese submarines, the *I-19* attacked the *Wasp* with three torpedoes on 15 September, with the ship catching fire and eventually sinking. In the end, the US forces prevailed, but could not prevent the Japanese from successfully evacuating some 13,000 troops. A more determined bid by the Japanese to retake Guadalcanal saw the Combined Fleet escorting Japanese reinforcements from Rabaul on 11 October, with the Battle of Cape Esperance following that night, although this was inconclusive. The USMC forces ashore were subjected to heavy bombing by Japanese carrier aircraft after the battle, and Vice Admiral Gormley took the blame for failing to stop the Japanese landing reinforcements and bombing the American forces ashore; he was replaced by Vice Admiral 'Bull' Halsey.

Nevertheless, Fletcher was criticized for the premature withdrawal of his carriers, leaving the USMC units ashore without adequate air cover at a time when the Japanese Vice Admiral Nagumo had arrived with his aircraft carriers, the repaired *Shokaku*, her sister *Zuikaku* and the smaller *Ryujo*.

Fletcher was moved out of the way. In November 1942, he became Commander, Thirteenth Naval District and Commander, North Western Sea Frontier to calm fears amongst US and Canadian citizens of invasion from the north. A year later, he was placed in charge of the whole Northern Pacific area, remaining there until after Japan's surrender, when his forces occupied northern Japan.

Post-war, Fletcher was appointed chairman of the General Board of the Navy, but he was not promoted until he retired in May 1947, when he was given the four-star rank of Admiral. He had lost much of his naval records in combat and in retirement he refused to reconstruct them or collaborate with the official US naval historian for the war. Many believe that in return he received an inadequate appraisal and that this attitude was picked up by later authors.

Chapter 5

A 'Bull' in a China Shop

Fleet Admiral William 'Bull' Halsey, USN (1882–1959)

Despite a far from sparkling time as a student at the US Naval Academy, Halsey graduated in 1900. On 7 December 1941, by now a vice admiral with the Pacific Fleet, his carriers were at sea with heavy cruisers from Pearl Harbor, and so the most important targets for the attacking Japanese aircraft were safely out of the way. This was Halsey's good fortune: he had no inkling that the attack was imminent and US planners believed that a surprise attack by the Japanese would take the Philippines as the target of choice. Nevertheless, the absence of the US carriers was sufficient to so unnerve the commander of the Japanese task force that had launched the assault on Pearl Harbor that he refused to send a further strike later in the day, as had been originally planned, and concentrated on avoiding the American carriers.

Halsey was born into a naval family in Elizabeth, New Jersey, on 30 October 1882, the son of Captain William F. Halsey, Sr. USN. He waited two years for admittance to the US Naval Academy at Annapolis, and in frustration decided to study medicine and join the Navy as a doctor. Years later, Halsey admitted that he hadn't learnt much during his one and only year studying medicine, but had enjoyed himself!

He was eventually admitted to Annapolis from which he graduated in 1904 with several athletic honours, but a less than sparkling academic record. His early service was in battleships and torpedo craft at a time when the USN was expanding rapidly and was short of good officer material – Halsey was thus one of the few who were promoted directly from ensign to full lieutenant, skipping the rank of lieutenant (junior grade). Torpedoes and torpedo craft became a speciality for him, and he commanded the First Group of the Atlantic Fleet's Torpedo Flotilla throughout 1912 and 1913, being promoted to lieutenant commander. His First World War service, which included command of the destroyer USS *Shaw* in 1918, was sufficiently distinguished to earn a Navy Cross.

From 1922 unil 1925, Halsey was the US naval attaché in Berlin, Germany, after which he commanded the *Dale* during a European cruise. Promoted to captain, between 1930 and 1932 he led two destroyer squadrons, before being sent to the Naval War College in the mid-1930s. Afterwards, he learnt to fly, insisting on taking the full twelve-week pilot's course rather than the easier observer's, but must not have proved to be a natural pilot as he took longer than anyone else on his course to gain his wings. He took command of the carrier *Saratoga*, which was followed by command of the Naval Air Station at Pensacola, Florida, the USN's main air-training establishment. Halsey was promoted to rear admiral in 1938 and commanded various carrier divisions (equating to British carrier squadrons) for the next three years, before serving, as a vice-admiral, as Commander Aircraft Battle Force. On 7 December 1941, he was commanding the carrier division of the US Pacific Fleet.

If Halsey had been lucky on the first day of the war in the Pacific, thereafter he made his own luck. Many considered him to be reckless on occasion, but his enthusiasm for taking the offensive and his drive earned him the unswerving support of his Commander-in-Chief, Chester Nimitz, and gave the American public, shattered by the suddenness and audacity of the attack on Pearl Harbor, and by its scale, the boost to their morale that was so badly needed. Known as 'Bull' because of his rugged countenance and short temper, Halsey could also be something of a 'bull in a china shop' at times, and his aggressive stance could rebound on him.

In April 1942, Halsey was promoted to Commander of Carriers, Pacific Fleet. The US President, Roosevelt, wanted Japan bombed, but the only way a bomber could reach a target in Japan was if it was launched from an aircraft carrier. Although it was a US Army Air Force officer, Colonel James 'Jimmy' Doolittle, who led the famous raid against Japan on 18 April 1942, flying sixteen North American B-25 Mitchell twin-engined bombers (the maximum number that could be ranged on the flight deck as they were too big for the carrier's deck lifts) from the aircraft carrier USS *Hornet*, the carrier was attached to Halsey's Task Force 16, and the operation was under his overall command. The original intention had been to launch the attack at night to minimize the risk to the bombers, but Halsey's scouts detected the picket line of Japanese warships, set to provide early warning of an attack by air or by sea, by radar before daylight. Halsey managed to avoid the ships, but the attack was brought forward and one of the Japanese ships managed to radio a warning before it was sunk. The warning was ignored as the Japanese knew that the USN did not have any twin-engined carrier aircraft; twelve of the bombers duly arrived over Tokyo following an air-raid exercise, enabling them to escape unscathed, while the other four attacked other Japanese cities.

Strategically, the operation was a great success as it put the Japanese on the defensive and plans for a decisive engagement with the United States Navy off Midway were scrapped. In strict military terms, the operation had no impact on Japanese defences, war production or communications, and the small force of bombers was scattered over too many targets to make an impact (an attack on the Emperor's palace could have had tremendous benefits). Although a small number of Japanese civilians were killed, the main victims were Chinese, as the Japanese brought forward a planned advance on the mainland of China to seize airfields used by the bombers after they had overflown their targets, with heavy Chinese casualties and retribution visited on civilians. Nevertheless, the boost to American morale was considerable, as was the loss of face by the Japanese leadership.

The USAAF gave President Roosevelt credit for the idea, but the head of the USN, Admiral King, maintained in his memoirs that it came from a member of his staff.

Even Halsey was not immune to misfortune, missing the critical Battle of Midway in June 1942 due to illness. He was back in command of the USN in the South Pacific by October, however, and just in time! The Japanese believed that Henderson Field had been recaptured, meaning no shore-based air power for the American forces, while Admiral Halsey had just two aircraft carriers. Only the latter intelligence was accurate. Halsey had available the recently repaired USS *Enterprise*, with eighty-four aircraft in Task Force 16, led by Vice Admiral Kinkaid, and the *Hornet*, with eighty-seven aircraft, in Vice Admiral Murray's Task Force 17. Ashore at

Henderson Field, there were another sixty aircraft, mainly operated by the USMC. The rest of Halsey's forces were much weaker, with just one battleship, six cruisers and fourteen destroyers, most of which were heavily preoccupied blocking the 'Tokyo Express' resupply operation.

Against this busy force, the Japanese had 4 aircraft carriers, *Junyo*, *Shokaku*, *Zuikaku* and *Zuiho*, carrying a total of 212 aircraft, as well as 4 battleships, 10 cruisers and 29 destroyers.

Although they were aware of the approaching Japanese ships, when the Americans launched their first strike on 25 October, they failed to find their opponent. Despite this, early on 26 October, US reconnaissance aircraft found the *Zuiho*, and the Battle of the Santa Cruz Islands started in earnest when, at 0730, the USS *Hornet* sent a strike of torpedo-bombers and dive-bombers, escorted by Grumman Wildcat fighters. Slightly before this, at 0710, anticipating American action, one of the two Japanese admirals, Vice Admiral Nagumo sent a first wave of aircraft to attack the *Hornet*, with the aircraft reaching the ship shortly after 0900. Fifteen dive-bombers and twelve torpedo-bombers struck at the *Hornet*, with one bomb hitting the flight deck before a bomber flew into the island, although it remains unclear whether this was an aircraft out of control, or a suicide operation. Then two torpedoes hit the carrier on her starboard side, before three 500-lb bombs smashed their way through the wooden flight deck and into the hangar. Within ten minutes, the ship was ablaze and listing to starboard. Meanwhile, an American bomb had hit the *Zuiho*, causing serious damage.

At 0930, the *Shokaku* was hit and seriously damaged by five bombs, which ensured that she was out of action for nine months. In what was a major fleet operation, althought conducted by carrier-borne aircraft, a second wave of Japanese aircraft found the *Enterprise* and managed to hit her with three bombs, but failed to put her out of action. In addition to putting up combat air patrols to provide fighter cover, the Americans mounted an extremely effective curtain of anti-aircraft fire, and it was this that accounted for most of the Japanese losses, with the battleship USS *South Dakota* alone claiming twenty-six enemy aircraft shot down.

That afternoon, a third wave of Japanese aircraft returned to attack the *Hornet*, which was hit by a further torpedo and two bombs, eventually forcing the crew to abandon ship. The Americans then sent destroyers to sink the *Hornet* with torpedoes, but at this stage of the war American torpedoes were notoriously unreliable and all nine that hit failed to explode! The ship was finally sent to the bottom by torpedoes from a Japanese destroyer. All in all, it took four bombs and sixteen torpedoes, American as well as Japanese, to send *Hornet* to the bottom. She had been in service for just a year and seven days.

It finally dawned on the Japanese that they had not recaptured Henderson Field and they withdrew. The loss of the *Hornet* was a major blow to the Americans, but in intense fighting, they had lost just seventy aircraft compared to the hundred lost by the Japanese. Worse still were the aircrew losses as the Japanese lacked a training structure capable of quickly filling aircrew combat losses. They had also had two aircraft carriers badly damaged.

Halsey's aggression was matched by the Japanese, as was their obstinacy. In November, the Japanese sent a force of two battleships, two cruisers and fourteen destroyers under Vice Admiral Abe to Guadalcanal both to cover the landings and also to shell Henderson Field. This led to the naval Battle of Guadalcanal, one of the few in the Pacific War that did not include aircraft carriers. The battle started on 12 November when Rear Admiral Callaghan, with the two heavy cruisers *San Francisco* and *Portland*, three light cruisers and eight destroyers, heard of the Japanese approach. Callaghan had the advantage of radar, although not on his flagship, the *San Francisco*. The first phase of the battle ended with the Japanese losing one destroyer, *Ataksuki*, which was sunk, and having to abandon the *Yudachi*, while the Americans lost two light cruisers, *Juneau* and *Atlanta*, the former damaged in the battle and sunk later by the submarine *I26*, and five destroyers. During 13 November, aircraft from Henderson Field accompanied by carrier-borne aircraft from the *Enterprise* found the *Hiei* and sank her.

During the night of 13/14 November, the Japanese returned to bombard Henderson Field, destroying twenty aircraft. While a further surface vessel action did not materialize, aircraft from the *Enterprise* found the cruiser *Kinugasa* and sank her, after she had earlier been damaged, along with the *Izuso*, by aircraft from Henderson Field. *Enterprise*'s aircraft also damaged two Japanese destroyers. Aircraft from Henderson Field then sank seven out of the eleven transports under the command of Rear Admiral Tanaka taking troops to Guadalcanal, but the survivors continued to press on, expecting cover from a Japanese battle group.

Halsey ordered Rear Admiral Lee to the area, with the battleships *Washington* and *South Dakota* and four destroyers, after they were given the position of the Japanese battle group by the submarine *Trout*. Vice Admiral Kondo in the battleship *Kirishima*, with three heavy and one light cruiser and nine destroyers, started a night bombardment of Henderson Field, and as the Americans arrived, a further night battle was started on 14/15 November. In the opening stages, two American destroyers were crippled in a gunnery duel and later sunk, with another destroyer badly damaged and sunk later, while the *South Dakota* suffered a complete electrical failure, so that she was unable to use her guns, but was later fortunate to escape being hit in a Japanese torpedo attack. Unnoticed by the Japanese, the other American battleship, *Washington*, reduced the *Kirishima* to a wreck in a surprise bombardment, after which she sank. A Japanese destroyer also sank during the conflict. At 0030 on the morning of 15 November, Kondo pulled his forces out of the battle, but Tanaka pressed on regardless, running his ships aground and landing a further 2,000 men, as well as 250 cases of ammunition and 1,500 bags of rice. The transports were destroyed by American aircraft later that morning.

The one remaining success of the Japanese in the Solomons before they finally evacuated their troops from Guadalcanal was the sinking of the cruiser *Chicago* by a Japanese torpedo-bomber on 29 January 1943.

By late 1943, the Americans had redesignated their fleet for the Pacific, to be known alternatively as the US Fifth Fleet, under Vice Admiral Raymond Spruance, and the Third Fleet when under Vice Admiral 'Bull' Halsey. The exact composition of the two fleets could vary from time to time, but in essence the major fleet units were assigned to Halsey as the Third Fleet and Spruance as the Fifth Fleet, the concept being that while Halsey was at sea, Spruance was ashore planning his next campaign, and while Spruance was at sea, Halsey would be ashore. The respective task forces within the fleets would also change their designation, so that TF58, for example, would become TF38 whenever Halsey was in command.

For the assault on the Gilbert Islands, the Americans not only had their two new classes of aircraft carrier, but they also had the escort carriers – either converted merchant ships or carriers built on merchant hulls that could be converted to cargo ships once hostilities ended.

The initial landings were commanded by Spruance with the Fifth Fleet, starting on 19 November. Undoubtedly successful, the operation saw the loss of a light carrier on 20 November and an escort carrier on 24 November.

In 1944, between 15 and 23 September, as part of Halsey's command, Rear Admiral Wilkinson took Task Force 31 to land III Amphibious Corps on the Palau Islands, an important stepping stone between Guam, Saipan and the Philippines. Before the invasion of the Philippines, the issue of who was to take the lead arose once again, with General MacArthur, who had been in command of the defence of the Philippines when the Japanese invaded, pressing to be given command of the liberation force. On this occasion, the US Army won, and the ships and landing craft of the newly formed Central Pacific Command under Admiral Nimitz were placed under MacArthur's overall command, leaving Halsey's Third Fleet to operate independently. By this time Halsey's responsibilities ranged far beyond aircraft carriers, which, depending on whether Spruance or Halsey was in command, were largely grouped into what was known as TF58 or TF38, under the command of Vice Admiral Marc Mitscher. During operations prior to the landings in the Philippines, Halsey's Third Fleet kept Japanese airfields on Luzon and the central Philippines under constant attack, with Mitscher's TF38 having its carrier groups divided into four with a total of 8 fleet carriers and 8 light carriers, with a total of 1,000 aircraft between them, backed by 6 battleships, 15 cruisers and 60 destroyers.

This was a powerful and well-balanced force, but even so the Japanese managed to counter-attack and the cruiser *Honolulu* was hit by a torpedo, while a bomb hit the cruiser HMAS *Australia*.

Japanese desperation now reached its peak with a desperate plan involving 4 aircraft carriers – the recently repaired *Zuikaku* and the light carriers *Zuiho*, *Chitose* and *Chiyoda* – with just 116 aircraft, still commanded by Vice Admiral Ozawa, and a total force of 9 battleships, 19 cruisers and 35 destroyers. The primary objective was to bring the Japanese battleships finally into action, after they had enjoyed a quiet war as fleet clashes had become the preserve of carrier-borne aircraft. This was to be the Battle of Leyte Gulf, often described as the greatest battle in naval history. It was to be in four parts, with an air-sea battle in the Sibuyan Sea on 24 October followed by a night battle in the Surigao Straits on 24/25 October, which continued off Samar, and an air-sea battle off Cape Engano that same day. Every Japanese warship in the area was in action. Vice Admiral Ozawa, with four carriers, two battleships, three cruisers and nine destroyers, had the task of luring the Third Fleet to the north, away from Leyte. To the west of Luzon, Vice Admiral Shima was to head south from Japan with three cruisers and seven destroyers; Vice Admiral Kurita's First Striking Force of 5 battleships, including the giants *Yamato* and *Musashi*, 12 cruisers and 15 destroyers, would come from the west; and finally, Vice Admiral Nishimura with 2 battleships, 4 cruisers and 4 destroyers, was positioned to the south of Kurita. These forces suffered from limited air power.

Japanese desperation did not stop ambitious and increasingly unrealistic plans being prepared, with even more ridiculous names being coined for them. The grand design was called 'Operation Sho-Go', meaning 'to conquer'. Whatever impact this might have had on the hotheads, the more realistic amongst Japan's planners and senior officers knew that the best that could be managed would be to inflict such unacceptable casualties amongst the Americans and their Allies that some form of compromise could be negotiated between Japan and the Allies.

The action that the Japanese were anticipating was known to them as the Second Battle of the Philippine Sea, but to the Americans as the Battle of Leyte Gulf. Even at the outset, Halsey's opponents were pessimistic – one of them, Kurita, considered his chance for a victory after the sorties would be about fifty-fifty. The Japanese effort got off to a bad start when, on 23 October 1944, two American submarines, *Dace* and *Darter*, torpedoed three heavy cruisers including Kurita's flagship *Atago*, which sank almost immediately, as did the *Maya*. Kurita's orders were to be off Leyte on 25 October, but fighting had started the previous day when aircraft based on Leyte attacked the most northerly of the American carrier groups in the Battle of the Sibuyan Sea. This attack was intended to involve Ozawa's carrier-borne aircraft, so that the US Third Fleet would be drawn away and leave Kurita with a clear run at the transports, but the aircraft failed to find the American ships and, running short of fuel, attempted to fly to bases on Luzon; many of them were intercepted by American fighters on the way.

In fact, Kurita was forced to reverse course during the ensuing battle because of the strength of US air attacks. This was meant to be a tactical manoeuvre, but Halsey misread it as victory, and while carrier group 38.1 refuelled, he took the other three groups and gave chase. This was a mistake and against the plans prepared by the Americans before the battle, which called for Halsey's Third Fleet to guard the San Benardino Straits – with the San Benardino Straits open, Kurita was able to reverse course yet again and pass his ships through them under cover of darkness. The result was the Battle of Samar, which began early on 25 October, with Kurita's Centre Force battleships discovering and starting to shell the American escort carriers providing air cover for the troops ashore.

Kurita was convinced that he was heading into a trap as he mistook the escort carriers for standard fleet carriers. A second group of escort carriers ahead of him was also mistaken for further fleet carriers. Expecting other American carriers from Halsey's Third Fleet to approach from the north, he decided that it was safer to do battle in the open sea rather than in the confined waters of Leyte Gulf. Meanwhile, the escort carriers suffered the unwanted attentions of mass kamikaze attacks.

In fact, both Nimitz and Kinkaid believed that Halsey was working to plan and still safeguarding the San Bernardino Strait. They had to send signals demanding to know his true position once they realized that he had left the Strait open to the Japanese, and Halsey was ordered to return south. Had he sent part of his force northwards, Halsey could have covered the Strait with his remaining force.

Meanwhile an aircraft from the light carrier *Independence* had located the Japanese Northern Force at 0208, and Mitscher later discovered that this had divided into two. Halsey sent TF34 forward, with the battleships and cruisers ahead of the carriers.

The official US Navy report on the battle explained:

> The Commander Third Fleet's plan for pushing strong surface forces ahead of his carrier groups and toward the enemy was a logical piece of tactics. Our expectation, based on past achievements, is that in an exchange of carrier attacks between fleets, it will be our enemy's fleet that takes the worst of it, and starts retiring while still at a distance many times greater than gun range. The only possibility then of closing and capitalizing on our gun power is to overtake cripples or ships of naturally low speed.

In short, as with the Japanese plans for the battle, Halsey wanted to use his battleships and cruisers. It was not until later in the day that Halsey, aboard his flagship, the battleship *New Jersey*, turned his attentions to Kurita's Centre Force, which he should have encountered earlier. At first he was unlucky, but later that day and on 26 October, carrier aircraft from the Third and Seventh Fleets found the Centre Force and attacked, sinking two cruisers, including one that was not one of Kurita's ships but was instead escorting a Japanese transport to Leyte.

For the Japanese, the operation was a case of too little, too late – the Americans were now setting the agenda. Nevertheless, Halsey does not come out of this without criticism. His belief in not dividing his forces was a nonsense given the overwhelming strength at his disposal, and in disobeying orders and leaving the San Bernardino Strait unguarded, he had left the vulnerable escort carriers and transports at the mercy of Kurita's force – it was only the Japanese Admiral's bungling that saved the situation. If he had been determined to give chase, he could have at least communicated his decision to the Seventh Fleet and given its commander, Kinkaid, the opportunity to take the necessary measures to safeguard his flank. But, of course, this would have meant that Nimitz in turn would have got to know and would have ordered him to return to his position. Halsey was simply fortunate that his luck remained good and that Kurita failed, for all of his bravado before the battle, to press home his attack. The irony is that had Halsey stayed in position, Kurita would have brought about the naval battle that so many Second World War admirals on both sides were looking for, but it would have been even more conclusive as without air power Kurita's major surface units would have been at a disadvantage.

On 15 December 1944, US forces landed on Mindoro, a small island to the south of Manila, with three battleships, six escort carriers and seven cruisers providing support. The Pacific was not nearly as calm as its name suggests and three days later Halsey's Third Fleet was struck by a typhoon, often referred to as 'Halsey's Typhoon', while still providing support for the landings on Mindoro by mounting heavy air attacks on airfields on Luzon. The typhoon sank three destroyers and damaged three of the light carriers, and caused serious damage to the forward end of the wooden flight decks on two of the Essex-class fleet carriers, while also destroying 146 aircraft that were either washed overboard or smashed in their hangar decks. Halsey was subsequently criticized for failing to pay due attention to meteorological reports that would have given him warning of the impending storm.

Luzon itself was finally invaded on 9 January 1945, again with support from the US Third Fleet and with close support from Kinkaid's Seventh Fleet. As at Leyte, there were eighteen escort carriers providing close support, as well as six battleships and eleven cruisers. Once again, kamikaze attacks were launched at the invaders, with damage to several ships and the loss of an escort carrier, but by 12 January, the US Third Fleet's carrier-borne aircraft had destroyed all Japanese air power on Luzon.

Despite his recklessness, Halsey's luck held for the rest of the war, and it was aboard his flagship, the battleship *Missouri*, that the Japanese finally signed the surrender documents at a ceremony in Tokyo Bay on 2 September 1945. In December, he was promoted to the five-star rank of Fleet Admiral, the equivalent of the British Admiral of the Fleet. Nevertheless, many doubt his abilities as a strategist, planner and administrator, and indeed the fact that he succumbed to the temptation to give chase at Leyte Gulf, especially when he could have deployed part of his substantial force for this role, also calls into question his ability as a commander. Indeed, his actions at the Battle for Leyte Gulf have been considered to have been one of the biggest mistakes in naval history, compounded by his subsequent failure to avoid two destructive typhoons. He retired from active duty in March 1947 and died on 20 August 1959.

Chapter 6

Fighting on Two Fronts

Fleet Admiral Ernest J. King, USN (1878–1956)

The USN's Commander-in-Chief throughout the war and credited by the official US naval historian as the service's 'best naval strategist and organizer' as well as the 'Navy's principal architect of victory', King had to fight a war in two major theatres.

King was born in Lorain, Ohio on 23 November 1878, the son of Scottish parents. His father is credited with giving him an upright, but often inflexible character, and an austere and somewhat humourless outlook. As he matured, it soon appeared that his shortcomings were intolerance of weakness or inability in others, alcohol and other men's wives. He attended the US Naval Academy at Annapolis from 1897 until 1901, and was 4th in his class. He was Cadet Lieutenant Commander, the highest possible cadet ranking at that time, during his final year. He gained combat experience while still at Anapolis, serving in the USS *San Francisco* during the Spanish American War. On leaving, he became a junior officer on the survey ship *Eagle*, followed by the battleships *Illinois*, *Alabama* and *New Hampshire*, and then the cruiser *Cincinnati*. After returning to a shore posting at Annapolis in 1912, he received his first command, the destroyer *Terry*, in 1914.

During the First World War he served on the staff of Vice Admiral Henry Mayo, the Commander-in-Chief of the US Atlantic Fleet, which first brought him into contact with the Royal Navy, even seeing action aboard British warships. Many maintain that his pronounced Anglophobia developed during this period, although no one seems to know why. Certainly, it was already clear by this time that he had an ambitious, ruthless and driving personality, and this might not have endeared himself to British naval officers of the 'old' school. He was awarded the Navy Cross 'for distinguished service in the line of his profession as assistant chief of staff of the Atlantic Fleet'.

He ended the war with the rank of captain and was posted as commanding officer of the USN's Naval Postgraduate School. With two fellow captains, King prepared a report that recommended changes to naval training and career paths, most of which were accepted by the USN.

For himself, having served aboard surface warships between leaving Annapolis and the end of the First World War, when he returned to sea in 1921, as a captain close to the bottom of the seniority list, the best sea-going command he could get was the fleet supply ship *Bridge* (in the USN supply ships and oilers are part of the regular service, not Merchant Navy as is the case with the Royal Navy's Royal Fleet Auxiliary). Frustrated, he moved to submarines in 1923 as the still relatively new and unfashionable submarine fleet offered the prospect of advancement. Before taking command of a submarine division, or flotilla, King attended a short training course at the naval submarine base, New London, flying his commodore's pennant from *S-20*, and in 1923, he took over command of the submarine base itself. During this period, he directed the salvage of the submarine *S-51*, earning the first of his three Distinguished Service Medals, and he both proposed and designed the dolphin insignia for submariners, also since adopted by the Royal Navy.

It seems that King was developing a sound career path of his own, having made recommendations on that for other naval officers. In 1926, the chief of the Bureau of Aeronautics, Rear Admiral William Moffett, asked him if he would consider a transfer. King accepted the offer and took command of the seaplane carrier *Wright* with additional duties as senior aide on the staff of Commander Air Squadrons, Atlantic Fleet. His arrival coincided with the United States Congress passing a law stipulating that the commanding officers of all aircraft carriers, seaplane tenders and aviation shore establishments should be qualified naval aviators. King therefore reported to the naval air station at Pensacola for flying training in January 1927. He was the only captain in his class of twenty, received his wings as Naval Aviator No. 3368 on 26 May 1927 and resumed command of *Wright*. He frequently flew solo at first, and doubtless found this useful as he was able to fly to Annapolis for weekend visits to his family. Solo flying ended when a new naval regulation prohibited such flights for aviators aged fifty or more. Despite this, for the next ten years he flew an annual average of 150 hours.

King commanded *Wright* until 1929, except for a brief interlude commanding the salvage operations of another submarine, the *S-4*. He then became assistant chief of the Bureau of Aeronautics, BuAer, under Moffett. His first period at BuAer was cut short after the two men argued over future Bureau policy. King was replaced by Commander John Towers and transferred to command Naval Station Norfolk. Nevertheless, his connection with naval aviation was maintained when, on 20 June 1930, he became commanding officer of the carrier *Lexington* – at the time one of the largest aircraft carriers in the world. In 1932 he attended the Naval War College. In a war college thesis entitled 'The Influence of National Policy on Strategy', King expounded on the theory that America's weakness was representative democracy, writing:

> Historically . . . it is traditional and habitual for us to be inadequately prepared. This is the combined result of a number of factors, the character of which is only indicated: democracy, which tends to make everyone believe that he knows it all; the preponderance (inherent in democracy) of people whose real interest is in their own welfare as individuals; the glorification of our own victories in war and the corresponding ignorance of our defeats (and disgraces) and of their basic causes; the inability of the average individual (the man in the street) to understand the cause and effect not only in foreign but domestic affairs, as well as his lack of interest in such matters. Added to these elements is the manner in which our representative (republican) form of government has developed as to put a premium on mediocrity and to emphasise the defects of the electorate already mentioned.

This was hardly the stuff of a senior officer in the armed forces of a democracy, but many will recognize some truth in it. It also ties in with his advice to President Roosevelt that the public should be told nothing about the war – until it had ended and then only who had won.

Following the death of Admiral Moffett in the crash of the airship *Akron* on 4 April 1933, King became chief of BuAer, and was promoted to rear admiral on 26 April. As Bureau chief, King worked closely with the chief of the Bureau of Navigation, Rear Admiral William Leahy, to increase the number of naval aviators. At the conclusion of his term as Bureau chief in 1936, King became Commander, Aircraft, Base Force, NAS North Island. He was promoted to vice admiral on 29 January 1938 on becoming Commander, Aircraft, Battle Force – at the time one of only three vice admiral posts in the US Navy.

Ever ambitious, King hoped next to become either Commander-in-Chief of the USN, COMINCH, or Chief of Naval Operations (CNO), but his hopes were dashed when Admiral Harold 'Betty' Stark became CNO in 1939. King was posted on 15 June 1939 to the General Board, viewed by ambitious USN officers as a dead end where senior officers awaited retirement. When war broke out in Europe in 1939, the United States maintained strict neutrality at first, but this did not last for long and help was increasingly given to the Allies, and after the fall of France, to the United Kingdom. As it happened, Stark was one of King's few friends in the USN, and it was Stark who rescued King from the General Board. The Atlantic theatre assumed growing importance and in December 1940, Stark offered King command of the Atlantic Squadron, which he accepted despite it being a demotion to rear admiral. On going aboard his flagship, one of his first tasks was to assess the Squadron's war plans, but in his safe he found just one document: the plans for a possible war with Mexico! Nevertheless, the United States was increasingly waging undeclared war with Germany and in February 1941, the Atlantic Squadron became the Atlantic Fleet, and King was reinstated as a vice admiral, and Commander-in-Chief, Atlantic Fleet, but this time on a confirmed basis. In this position, he became well known to the US President, Roosevelt.

Despite the official US stance of neutrality as the war developed in Europe, the United States Navy had taken on the role of escorting convoys in the western Atlantic, ostensibly to ensure that neutral shipping was not engaged by German submarines. The rules of engagement were refined after a German U-boat attacked the destroyer USS *Greer* on 4 September 1941, while carrying mail and passengers from the United States to Iceland. The destroyer attacked with depth charges and although a second torpedo was fired, neither the destroyer nor the U-boat was damaged. For their part, the Royal Navy made facilities available to the United States Navy at Londonderry in Northern Ireland. When appointed commander of US naval forces in the Atlantic, Admiral Ernest King remarked that it was like being given a big slice of bread with 'damn little butter', reflecting on the shortage of ships. After the battleships *Idaho*, *Mississippi* and *New Mexico* had been transferred with the aircraft carrier *Yorktown* from the Pacific to the Atlantic, despite growing tensions with Japan, the President of the United States, Franklin Roosevelt, asked King how he liked the butter he was getting. King replied: 'The butter's fine, but you keep giving me more bread.' Promotion to Admiral followed almost immediately.

Being in an operational command was to prove a blessing when Japan attacked the US Pacific Fleet at Pearl Harbor on 7 December 1941. Stark was effectively blamed for this disaster and while he retained his rank and post, Roosevelt resurrected the old post of Commander-in-Chief, COMINCH, for King. Stark remained as CNO until March 1942, before being posted to London to command US naval forces in Europe, effectively a sidelined liaison post in which he remained until after the end of the war in Europe. When the findings of the court of enquiry into Pearl Harbor were later released in August 1945, King was to order that Stark should never again hold any post in which superior judgement was required. This was a harsh judgement, which King later admitted, but it was true that commanding officers in both the US services in the Pacific were still leading a pleasant peacetime existence while the threat from Japan was growing, and the lack of communication and coordination between the USN and the US Army was in itself a case of gross negligence.

After Stark departed for London, his old post of CNO was combined with that of COMINCH, although the staffs remained separate. This gave King considerable authority on paper, but despite a close working relationship with Roosevelt, the President prevented his naval chief from reorganizing the Navy Department, something which King regarded as so important that he returned to it time and again. Like all of the wartime leaders, Roosevelt also interfered with strategy against his service leaders' advice. King and Roosevelt disagreed over Task Force 57, the combined British Pacific Fleet and its fleet train, which King did not want but which Roosevelt had accepted when offered it by the British Prime Minister, Winston Churchill. King feared that coordination and communications between the two navies would be difficult and insisted that the Royal Navy did not make use of US facilities. In fact, TF57 did much useful work, especially off Okinawa and Formosa, as well as preventing the Japanese sending air reinforcements, and by the end of the war was attacking Japan.

On the other hand, while Roosevelt approved King's Pacific strategy, which was effectively to hold Hawaii, support Australia and drive north-westwards from the New Hebrides, King never objected to Roosevelt's 'Germany first' strategy. The rapid Japanese advance was stemmed as early as June 1942 with the great US victory at Midway, which saw four Japanese aircraft carriers lost in a single day, and by January 1943, the US victory at Guadalcanal showed that Japanese defeat was inevitable, given time. King ensured that 'Germany first' was not at the cost of the war in the Pacific. At the same time, his creation of the US Tenth Fleet, an anti-submarine command, in May 1943, was a significant contribution towards cutting Allied merchant shipping losses in the Atlantic.

After the great victory at the Battle of Midway, the Allies were well placed to attack the Japanese, but could still not neglect defensive measures. For King and to his Army counterpart, General George Marshall, this period was known as the 'offensive-defensive' and started with landings on the Solomon Islands on 7 August 1942. King advocated a step-by-step general advance through the New Hebrides, Solomons and the Bismarck Archipelago. In fact, both aspects of the strategy were interdependent since Japanese forces would be drawn away from their attempts to isolate Australia from the United States in order to ward off the American advance. This step-by-step approach, creating a number of strongpoints along the way, also recognized that it was the only way of bringing substantial forces within reach of the Japanese home islands.

King's approach was cautious and never underestimated the enemy. There were to be no short cuts, even when he was brought under some pressure by General Douglas MacArthur, Supreme Commander of the South-West Pacific Area, to support the capture of Rabaul, for which MacArthur wanted a naval task force including two aircraft carriers, a division trained in amphibious warfare and a very substantial number of land-based heavy bombers. King did not favour this plan, mainly because Rabaul would be exposed to a strong enemy counter-attack, and could be more of a liability than an asset, taking away forces that would be better used elsewhere. The order of priorities in the Solomons was to be the capture of the Santa

Cruz Islands and Tulagi, using a Task Force under the command of Admiral Chester Nimitz, followed by MacArthur taking Lae, Salamaua and the north-east coast of New Guinea – only then was Rabaul to be taken, along with other positions in New Guinea. This would mean that when it was finally occupied, Rabaul would no longer be exposed and its defence would not tie down unnecessarily large forces.

Nevertheless, in the Atlantic, whether it was because of his disdain for the Royal Navy or a simple inability to learn from others or to take advice, King suffered a steep learning curve after the United States entered the war. First, King decided not to request blackouts on the US eastern seaboard, then chose not to convoy ships, despite the lessons of the First World War when the British Admiralty had also delayed convoying ships until late in the conflict. Certainly both the convoys and blackouts were British proposals. At first King also refused, until March 1942, the loan of British convoy escorts when the USN had only a handful of suitable vessels. On the other hand, he was determined that US destroyer commanders should attack U-boats in defence of convoys. He also planned countermeasures against German surface raiders, although by the time the US entered the war this threat had diminished, except for ships on the Arctic convoys.

King had the USN and United States Coast Guard conduct regular anti-submarine patrols, which even followed a regular schedule that soon became obvious to the U-boat leaders, who coordinated their attacks to fit in between the patrols. Not having a blackout in coastal towns back-lit merchant ships for the U-Boats. The outcome was inevitable and a second 'happy time' for the U-boats followed, with appalling losses of merchantmen – 2 million tons were lost in January and February 1942 alone. Still King refused to instigate convoys because he maintained that he lacked sufficient escort vessels and, as with the Royal Navy in the First World War, that the formation of convoys with inadequate escorts would give the enemy larger targets.

In January 1942, King allowed a troop convoy, AT-10, to Iceland to take priority and allocated some of his limited number of escort vessels to escort it. He also allowed a strong destroyer force to remain moored in New York, even though U-boats were known to be near and ships were being sunk off Long Island. It was not until May 1942 that King started a coordinated convoy system between

Key West, off Florida, and Rhode Island, converting small cutters and other vessels to ensure that extra escorts were available.

By August 1942, the submarine threat in US coastal waters had been contained, and the 'second happy time' ended, a point that was driven home in no uncertain fashion with the loss of seven U-boats and a dramatic reduction in shipping losses. The same effect occurred when convoys were extended to the Caribbean.

In his role at any time, King would have had to have been not only a great leader, but one who could delegate. His time as COMINCH was not the best of times, and he found himself giving an estimated two-thirds of his time to the US Combined Chiefs of Staff and the Allied Combined Chiefs of Staff, so his ability to fight a truly global war depended in no small part on his ability to delegate, and to select outstanding staff officers and theatre commanders. He coped by not concentrating on details but instead handling the broad outlines of strategy and policy. This outstanding blend of abilities was marred by his contempt for civilians, which was hardly an asset in a democracy, and he maintained that they should be told nothing about the war until it was over, and then only who won. He might have got on well with Hitler or Hirohito! Even one of his own daughters described him as 'the most even-tempered man in the Navy. He is always in a rage.' On the other hand, if any officer could measure up to his demanding standards, he was treated with consideration and generosity.

On 17 December 1944, he was promoted to the five-star rank of fleet admiral, the equivalent of the Royal Navy rank of admiral of the fleet. After the Japanese surrender, he recommended that COMINCH should be abolished and remained in the service as CNO until he retired on 15 December 1945, at the age of sixty-seven years, but was recalled as an advisor to the Secretary of the Navy in 1950. This was despite suffering a debilitating stroke in 1947 and subsequent ill-health which eventually forced him to stay in naval hospitals, including Bethesda, Maryland, until he died of a heart attack in Kittery on 26 June 1956.

Highly regarded, but not loved, King was no Nelson, even though there are those who consider him to have been the twentieth century's greatest admiral, yet he never commanded ships or fleets at sea in wartime. There is no doubt that his Anglophobia led him to make decisions which cost many Allied lives. A true judgement is difficult, even with hindsight, as undoubtedly so much of the credit for winning the war in the Pacific, where the USN was the dominant and decisive force, was due to Nimitz. Rude and abrasive, King was loathed by many officers with whom he served and some maintain that he was the most disliked Allied leader of the Second World War – only the Free French leader, General Charles de Gaulle, might have had more enemies.

Chapter 7

Seeing Pearl Harbor as a Blessing

Fleet Admiral Chester W. Nimitz, USN (1885–1966)

The disaster at Pearl Harbor meant that the commander of the US Pacific Fleet, Rear Admiral Husband Kimmel, was relieved of his command. He was found guilty of dereliction of duty and retired, and although he was cleared by a naval court of inquiry in 1944, a post-war Congressional inquiry found him guilty of errors of judgement. His successor was Chester Nimitz, who became Commander-in-Chief US Pacific Fleet, and held this post throughout the war.

Chester Nimitz was born in Fredericksburg, Texas, to German immigrant parents. After his father died, an important influence in his life was his grandfather, a former merchant seaman. Despite this, Nimitz aimed to attend the United States Military Academy at West Point, but there were no vacancies. His congressman told him that he had one appointment available for the Navy and that he would award it to the best-qualified candidate. Nimitz felt that this was his only opportunity for further education and devoted extra time studying to earn the appointment. He was successful and entered the United States Naval Academy at Annapolis in 1901, graduating with distinction on 30 January 1903, placed 7th out of 114.

His first ship was the battleship USS *Ohio*, which he joined at San Francisco, before she cruised to the Far East. In September 1906, he was transferred to the cruiser *Baltimore* and on 31 January 1907, after spending two years at sea as then required by law, he was commissioned as an ensign. He remained on the Asiatic Station in 1907, where he successively served in the destroyers *Panay*, *Decatur* and *Denver*. It was while he was in command of the *Decatur* in the Philippines that his ship ran aground on a mudbank; Nimitz was court-martialled, found guilty of hazarding his ship and reprimanded.

Nimitz returned to the United States in the *Ranger*, a school ship. In January 1909, he started to receive training with the First Submarine Flotilla, of which he was given command in May with the flotilla leader *Plunger*. He commanded a succession of submarines including the newly commissioned *Snapper* and then *Narwhal*, followed by *E-1*. During this time he saved a naval rating from drowning.

He was sent to Germany and Belgium in the summer of 1913 to study at the diesel engine plants in Nuremberg and Ghent. Returning to the New York Navy Yard, he became the submarine *Maumee*'s Executive Officer and Engineer on her commissioning in October 1916. On 10 August 1917, Nimitz joined the staff of the Commander, Submarine Force, US Atlantic Fleet, becoming Chief of Staff on 6 February 1918. In September 1918, he joined the Office of the Chief of Naval Operations and in October became Senior Member, Board of Submarine Design.

Post-war, as a commander he became executive officer of the battleship *South Carolina*, before being promoted to captain, taking command of the cruiser *Chicago* in 1920 at Pearl Harbor. From the summer of 1922, he studied at the Naval War College, Newport, Rhode Island, before becoming aide and assistant chief of staff to Commander Battle Fleet in June 1923, and later to the Commander in Chief, US Fleet. In August 1926 he went to the University of California, Berkeley to establish the Navy's first Naval Reserve Officer Training Corps unit.

During this time, he lost part of one finger in an accident with a diesel engine, only saving it when the machine jammed against his Annapolis ring; he also suffered a severe ear infection, which resulted in him becoming partially deaf.

In June 1929, he was given command of Submarine Division 20. In June 1931, he assumed command of *Rigel* and the destroyers in reserve at San Diego, California. In October 1933, he became commanding officer of the cruiser *Augusta* on a deployment to the Far East, where in December the *Augusta* became flagship of the Asiatic Fleet. In April 1935, he returned to the USA to spend three years as assistant chief of the Bureau of Navigation, before becoming Commander, Cruiser Division 2, Battle Force after promotion to rear admiral. In September 1938, he took command of Battleship

Division 1, Battle Force. On 15 June 1939, he was promoted to vice admiral and appointed Chief of the Bureau of Navigation, coming into contact with President Roosevelt for the first time.

In contrast to King and Halsey, Nimitz was outgoing and affable, but this disguised a toughness matched by a talent for naval strategy, including the still emerging application of combined forces for amphibious landings.

Nimitz was one of the few who did not see Pearl Harbor as an unmitigated disaster, and indeed he even saw that the situation might have been far worse had the USN encountered the vastly superior Japanese forces in battle in the open sea, commenting: 'It was God's mercy that our fleet was in Pearl Harbor on 7 December 1941.'

In fact, the Japanese attack on the fleet had not been the masterstroke that it was expected to be. The aircraft carriers were at sea and within months this was to prove to be the theatre of war that was dominated by the aircraft carrier as much as by the amphibious assault. Most of the base facilities had suffered little or no damage. Even the battle fleet, that had borne the brunt of the Japanese attack and had several ships resting on the bottom of the harbour, was, for the most part, capable of being salvaged. The Japanese had sent two waves of attacking aircraft, but had they refuelled and rearmed their aircraft and sent a third and a fourth wave, the outcome might have been different. Despite having earlier expected to have to fight his way to Pearl Harbor, the Japanese commander, Nagumo, was in fact concerned that his fleet might be discovered by the American aircraft carriers, even though he outnumbered them in ships and aircraft. The head of the Imperial Japanese Navy, Admiral Yamamoto, knew that the war had been lost when he heard that further attacks had not been pressed home.

Nimitz knew that he had little time, a point that was driven home as news came in of incredible Japanese advances as island after island, territory after territory, was occupied. Only in the Malayan Peninsula, New Guinea and later in Burma did fighting continue for any length of time. The advance had to be stopped and then reversed. Nimitz quickly assembled a team of outstanding naval commanders, including Halsey and Spruance, with exceptionally capable subordinates such as Mitscher and Turner, as well as equally outstanding USMC commanders such as Alexander Vandegrift and Holland Smith. He also created a naval staff around him that was certainly equal to the task ahead.

One common thread amongst his senior officers was that they shared his passion for attack and all had strong aggressive instincts. Uniquely amongst naval commanders-in-chief he chose a submarine as his flagship, something which even Dönitz, another submarine officer who made it to the top of his navy, did not do. Halsey was sent with his carriers to raid Japanese-held islands early in 1942, and then in April, Nimitz launched the Doolittle raid on the Japanese home islands. Wrangling between the Navy and the Army over who should take the lead in the Pacific – which General Douglas MacArthur saw as the most important theatre of war and for which he pressed for priority against Roosevelt's 'Germany first' strategy – led to the theatre being divided. MacArthur was given the South-West Pacific Area, while Nimitz became Commander-in-Chief Pacific Ocean Areas, or CINCPOA, with overall command of all land and air forces in his area as well as naval forces.

The Battle of the Coral Sea in May 1942 was a tactical victory for the Japanese, whose losses were lower than those of the USN, but it was a strategic victory for the latter as damage to the Japanese fleet meant that desperately needed carriers were out of action for the Battle of Midway, and the Japanese advance on Port Moresby was stopped. Midway and Guadalcanal were the effective turning points in the Pacific War, after which Japanese forces were forced onto the defensive. Indeed, while Guadalcanal saw occupied territory recovered, Midway, in June 1942, showed that Japan could not hope to achieve victory with four aircraft carriers and their aircraft all lost in just a single day. Japan did not have the industrial capacity to cope with losses on such a scale, nor did the country have the training system to produce pilots and observers, or ground crew, fast enough to replace the loss of experienced men.

Nimitz was primarily responsible for the victory at Midway, helped by warnings of Japanese intentions from Ultra intelligence. While Ultra was untried and untested at this early stage in the Pacific War, Nimitz took the responsibility of deciding that it was valid and deployed his forces accordingly. He next chose to land forces on Guadalcanal in August 1942 before the Japanese could establish strong defensive positions and complete construction of an air-field. This was a risky strategy as time pressures meant that forces were hastily assembled, which led many to describe it as 'Operation Shoestring'; but it worked, although it was not until the following February that Guadalcanal was finally cleared of all Japanese forces.

Nevertheless, lessons were learnt and Nimitz was able to proceed with the strategy that saw islands in the Pacific recovered from Japanese occupation. Guadalcanal was the first stepping stone, and it was followed by Tarawa.

Many of the aircraft used to provide close air support at Guadalcanal were operated by the USMC, so it was all the more surprising that in 1943 Nimitz decided to omit carrier training from the syllabus, especially as the new escort carriers were starting to become available, many of which were used to cover amphibious assaults and could have been designed 'Marine carriers'. Nimitz was probably considering the extra time taken to train pilots in the difficult art of carrier-deck landings. The restriction was later removed in 1944.

After Guadalcanal and the start of the long island hop towards the Japanese home islands, Nimitz instigated the most successful submarine campaign ever – although the actual numbers of ships sunk and tonnages lost were lower than in the Atlantic and Mediterranean, it was far more effective than that overseen by Dönitz, cutting Japan off from fuel and raw materials, and also reducing food supplies so substantially that by the time of surrender, many were starving. The campaign under the sea was so persistent and daring that by the closing stages of the war, US submarines were operating in the Japanese inland sea, and one, the USS *Archerfish*, sank the largest carrier yet built outside the United States, the 65,000-ton *Shinano*, on 29 November 1944, before she could enter service.

While MacArthur and Nimitz were given their respective areas of command, the two came together for the invasion of the Philippines, with a massive USN presence supporting the landings on Leyte in October 1944. This led to the largest battle in naval history at Leyte Gulf, which has been described in Chapter 5, and which effectively destroyed the Imperial Japanese Navy.

As American forces advanced across the Pacific, Nimitz moved his headquarters closer to the front line, using Guam as his base for the costly assaults on Iwo Jima and Okinawa. When the Japanese were finally brought to surrender by the use of atomic bombs against Hiroshima and Nagasaki, and by the terrible plight of the country as a whole, it was Nimitz who signed the surrender document on behalf of the United States. By this time, he was a fleet admiral, having been promoted in December 1944.

Nimitz succeeded King as CNO, or Chief of Naval Operations, when the latter retired in late 1945.

Chapter 8

Decisive in Planning and Cool in Action

Admiral Raymond A. Spruance, USN (1886–1969)

Halsey's opposite number in the Fifth Fleet, which became the Third Fleet when commanded by Halsey, Spruance was engaged in some of the most decisive carrier operations and amphibious campaigns of the Pacific War.

He was born in Baltimore, Maryland, on 3 July 1886, but raised in Indianapolis, Indiana. He graduated from the US Naval Academy at Annapolis in 1906 and later underwent further training in electrical engineering. He spent a considerable amount of time at sea and during his career he was commanding officer of the USS *Osborne*, four other destroyers and the battleship *Mississippi*. Spruance also held several engineering, intelligence, staff and Naval War College positions between the wars. In 1940, he was commanding the Tenth Naval District which included what the USN described as the Caribbean Sea Frontier, and was based at San Juan, Puerto Rico.

In the first months of the Second World War in the Pacific, the then Rear Admiral Spruance commanded a cruiser division providing the surface screen for Halsey's aircraft carriers during the dangerous and uncertain days following the attack on Pearl Harbor. When Halsey fell ill, Spruance took his place and led Task Force 16, with two aircraft carriers, during the Battle of Midway in early June. His decisions during that action were important to its outcome, which changed the course of the war with Japan. After Midway, he became

Chief of Staff to the Commander-in-Chief, US Pacific Fleet and Pacific Ocean Areas, and later was Deputy Commander-in-Chief. He was promoted to vice admiral in mid-1943 and given command of the Central Pacific Force, which became the Fifth Fleet in April 1944. While holding that command in 1943–1945, with the USS *Indianapolis* as his usual flagship, Spruance directed the campaigns that captured the Gilberts, Marshalls, Marianas, Iwo Jima and Okinawa, and defeated the Japanese fleet in the June 1944 Battle of the Philippine Sea.

It would be easy to suggest that history has been kind to Spruance, but he was possessed with considerable ability, and both personal and professional qualities. The official US Navy historian described him thus: 'Power of decision and coolness in battle were perhaps Spruance's leading characteristics.' Crucial to his success was the ability not only to think clearly and plan, and then show strong leadership in battle, but also to be able to blend together a team, which included not only Rear Admiral Marc Mitscher, one of the ablest aircraft-carrier force commanders of the entire war, and Major General Holland Smith of the USMC, but also the British Pacific Fleet, which was attached to his command and which his superior, Nimitz, had not wanted. So many senior commanders, and not just naval men, suffered from vanity and delicate egos, but not Spruance. 'He envied no one, rivalled no man, won the respect of almost everyone with whom he came in contact and went ahead in his quiet way, winning victories for his country,' recorded the official historian.

Admiral Spruance held command of the Pacific Fleet in late 1945 and early 1946. He then served as President of the Naval War College until retiring from the Navy in July 1948. His diplomatic skills, honed in wartime, were put to good use, for despite not being a career diplomat, he was Ambassador to the Philippines in 1952–1955. He died at Pebble Beach, California, on 13 December 1969.

Chapter 9

The Royal Navy

The Royal Navy has always been the consummate blue-water navy, with a worldwide reach, while retaining the tasks that also fell upon a brown-water navy, such as fisheries protection and in times of war keeping ports open through minesweeping. For many years, the Royal Navy always aspired to the 'Two Power Standard', which meant that it was to be as large as any other two navies that it was likely to fight, but in 1922, the Washington Naval Treaty meant that the best the Royal Navy could aspire to was the 'One Power Standard', which meant that it would be limited to the size of the navy of one other nation, the United States. In addition to the Treaty stipulating not only a maximum tonnage of ships for the main navies, it also imposed restrictions on the total tonnage for each type of warship, and imposed maximum tonnages for individual vessels as well, with cruisers limited to 10,000 tons, for example, and capital ships to 35,000 tons, while aircraft carriers were limited to 27,000 tons, although the British were allowed two carriers of up to 33,000 tons each. Limited to a total warship tonnage of 525,000 tons, the situation was made more difficult by the determination of successive British inter-war governments to tighten the Washington restrictions, and drive down the tonnage of individual cruisers to a figure of around 8,500 tons for a heavy cruiser and 23,000 tons for an aircraft carrier.

By 1939, the Royal Navy had been through a number of re-organizations. The Grand Fleet of the First World War had become first the Atlantic Fleet and, later, the Home Fleet. The Inskip Award of 1937 had seen naval aviation handed back to the Admiralty, which formally took control of the Fleet Air Arm in May 1939.

In 1939, the distribution of the Royal Navy was:

1. The Home Fleet, which was the largest single administrative formation.
2. The Mediterranean Fleet, with its bases at Malta, Gibraltar and Alexandria.
3. The China Station, essentially meaning Hong Kong.
4. The East Indies Station, mainly centred on Singapore.
5. The American Station, meaning Bermuda.
6. The African Station, based on Simonstown, near Cape Town in South Africa.
7. The West Indies Station.

In 1939, the Home Fleet was the strongest element within the Royal Navy. Overall, the Royal Navy and Royal Marines totalled 129,000 men, of whom around 10,000 were officers. To bring it up to maximum strength in wartime, it could depend on recalling recently retired officers and ratings, as well as two categories of reserves, the Royal Naval Reserve (RNR) and the Royal Naval Volunteer Reserve (RNVR), which between them provided another 73,000 officers and men in 1939. Included in the 1939 total were 12,400 officers and men in the Royal Marines. By mid-1944, the RN had reached its peak strength of 863,500 personnel, including 73,500 of the Women's Royal Naval Service. The Royal Navy's wartime casualties amounted to 50,758 killed with another 820 missing, presumed dead, and 14,663 wounded. The WRNS lost 102 killed and 22 wounded, mainly in air raids.

The fleet in 1939 consisted of 12 battleships and battlecruisers, including HMS *Hood*, and 7 aircraft carriers, of which 4 were either in reserve or earmarked for early retirement; 2 seaplane carriers, of little use in the carrier age; 58 cruisers, 100 destroyers and 101 other escort vessels, as well as just 38 submarines, the lowest number of any major combatant nation, and 232 aircraft.

Chapter 10

'ABC'

Admiral of the Fleet Lord Cunningham of Hyndhope, RN (1883–1963)

Christened as Andrew Browne Cunningham, perhaps inevitably he was known affectionately as 'ABC' to his subordinates, not that many would have dared address him as such. His early career was typical of that of many British naval officers, graduating from the Britannia Royal Naval College at Dartmouth. Between the two world wars, he also suffered the inconvenience and insecurity of being 'rested' on half pay, even as a rear admiral. This was an old British naval tradition in peacetime for officers of the rank of rear admiral and below whenever there were more senior officers than posts, and one that did not end until the Second World War.

Andrew Cunningham was born at Rathmines, County Dublin, Ireland, on 7 January 1883 to Scottish parents. He was sent to Edinburgh Academy. The family had no maritime connections and Cunningham only had a vague interest in the sea, but he decided that he would like to join the Royal Navy and was sent to a Naval Preparatory School, Stubbington House, which specialized in sending pupils through the Dartmouth entrance examinations, in which he showed a particular ability for mathematics. Dartmouth at the time was organized and run much as a boarding school, which meant that parents had to pay fees.

At Dartmouth, Cunningham's introduction to the Royal Navy was as a cadet aboard the hulked training ship HMS *Britannia* in 1897, where one of his classmates was the future Admiral of the

Fleet James Fownes Somerville. He passed out 10th in April 1898, with first-class marks for mathematics and seamanship.

He joined HMS *Doris* as a midshipman in 1899 and was in South Africa at the start of the Second Boer War. By February 1900, he had transferred into the Naval Brigade ashore looking for action, which he saw at Pretoria and Diamond Hill. He returned to sea, still as a midshipman in *Hannibal* in December 1901, before joining the protected cruiser HMS *Diadem* the following year, during which he also took sub-lieutenant courses at Portsmouth and Greenwich. In 1903, he was a sub lieutenant in the battleship *Implacable* in the Mediterranean, but after six months he was transferred to *Locust* to serve as second-in-command. He was promoted to lieutenant in 1904, and in 1908 was awarded his first command, HM Torpedo Boat *No. 14*.

Cunningham's career spanned the end of the old Victorian navy with ships that, as Admiral Sir Jacky Fisher put it, 'could neither fight nor run away', and the twentieth-century navy in which the submarine and the aeroplane achieved overwhelming importance. He was a young officer when the all-big-gun battleship emerged, and took some time to appreciate the importance of air power, although he was to use this very effectively. He proved himself to be an outstanding commanding officer at sea during the First World War, winning the Distinguished Service Order (DSO) with two bars.

In 1911 he was given command of the destroyer *Scorpion*, which he commanded throughout the war. In 1914, his ship was involved in the shadowing of the German battlecruiser SMS *Goeben* and cruiser SMS *Breslau*, which were chased across the Mediterranean, but which passed through the Dardanelles to reach Constantinople. Cunningham stayed on in the Mediterranean and, in 1915, *Scorpion* was involved in the attack on the Dardanelles. Cunningham was promoted to commander and awarded his first DSO. In late 1916, he was engaged in convoy protection, a duty he regarded as mundane, probably because he had no contact with German U-boats during this time, later stating that: 'The immunity of my convoys, was probably due to sheer luck.' When *Scorpion* paid off on 21 January 1918, he had been aboard the ship for the unusually long period of seven years. He was transferred to Vice Admiral Roger Keyes' Dover Patrol in April 1918.

Post-war, Cunningham commanded another S-class destroyer, the *Seafire*, on duty in the Baltic. The British Government had recognized

Latvia's independence after the Treaty of Brest-Litovsk. Throughout several potentially problematic encounters with German forces trying to undermine the Latvian independence movement, according to his flag officer, Vice Admiral Cowan, Cunningham exhibited 'good self control and judgement', and 'Commander Cunningham ... has proved himself an officer of exceptional valour and unerring resolution.'

Afterwards, Cunningham was awarded a second bar to his DSO and promoted to Captain in 1920. On his return from the Baltic in 1922, he was appointed Captain of the British Sixth Destroyer Flotilla. Further commands followed including the destroyer base, *Lochinvar*, at Port Edgar in the Firth of Forth in 1926. Later, Cunningham became Flag Captain and Chief Staff Officer to Cowan while serving on the North America and West Indies Station. The late 1920s found Cunningham back in the UK participating in courses at the Army's Senior Officers' School at Sheerness, as well as spending a year at the Imperial Defence College. Afterwards, Cunningham was given command of the battleship *Rodney*. Eighteen months later, he was appointed Commodore of *Pembroke*, the Royal Naval barracks at Chatham.

In September 1932, Cunningham was promoted to rear admiral and became Aide-de-Camp to King George V, before being appointed Rear Admiral (Destroyers) in the Mediterranean in December 1933. He hoisted his flag in the light cruiser *Coventry* and used this time to practise fleet handling. There were also fleet exercises in the Atlantic Ocean where he learnt the skills of night actions that would prove their value at Matapan.

On his promotion to vice admiral in July 1936, further active employment seemed remote. However, a year later, due to the illness of Sir Geoffrey Blake, Cunningham assumed the combined appointment of commander of the British Battlecruiser Squadron and second-in-command of the Mediterranean Fleet, with *Hood* as his flagship. He retained command until September 1938, when he was appointed to the Admiralty as Deputy Chief of Naval Staff, although he did not actually take up this post until December 1938. He accepted this shore job with reluctance since he loathed administration, but the Board of Admiralty's high regard for him was evident. During a six-month illness of Admiral Sir Roger Backhouse, the then First Sea Lord, he deputized for Backhouse on the Committee of Imperial Defence and on the Admiralty Board.

The outbreak of war found Cunningham as an acting admiral and Commander-in-Chief of the British Mediterranean Fleet, which he regarded as 'the finest in the Royal Navy'. It was clear that the Mediterranean theatre would be crucial during the war, with the 'Med', in British naval slang, being part of the route from the British Isles to India, the Middle East and Australia. Italy's expansive plans in North Africa were clear from the Abyssinian crisis onwards and the close relationship between her Fascist dictator, Benito Mussolini, and the German Führer, Adolph Hitler, was all too obvious. The two countries had also sent forces to support the Nationalists in the Spanish Civil War. Italy was geographically positioned to cut the Mediterranean in half and also posed a threat to the Royal Navy's main base in the Mediterranean, Malta. All in all, everyone was surprised when the Italians did not declare war in September 1939.

The Mediterranean Fleet was one of the plum commands in the Royal Navy, second only to what was, at different times, termed as the Grand Fleet, Atlantic Fleet and, in 1939, the Home Fleet. It had a base at Gibraltar as well as at Malta, while Alexandria in Egypt was shared by the British Mediterranean Fleet and the French Marine Nationale, but Egypt was run almost as a British colony or protectorate, and the country's navy even had a British admiral in command.

Despite the importance of his command and of the three bases, there was no fighter defence for Gibraltar or Malta at the outbreak of war, while Cunningham had just one aircraft carrier in 1939, the converted light battlecruiser HMS *Glorious*, which was called to home waters for operations off Norway in spring 1940. The even older *Eagle*, a converted battleship, was recalled from the Indian Ocean as a replacement. The Royal Navy in the Mediterranean was outgunned by the Italian Navy, which had six battleships against the Royal Navy's three. It took the French Mediterranean Squadron to redress the balance.

The Fall of France

When Italy finally entered the war in June 1940, shortly before the fall of France, it was simply a matter of good luck for Cunningham that the Italians did not move swiftly to seize Malta. The island was bombed from the morning after the declaration of war, but not shelled by Italian battleships and cruisers, and no attempt was made to land troops. The Royal Navy possessed the ability to inflict serious damage on the Italian Navy and did so, especially at the Battle of Cape Matapan and at Taranto.

The fall of France had created an unexpected problem for the Royal Navy. The ships of their erstwhile ally were scattered at a number of ports, in the Atlantic from Portsmouth and Plymouth in the UK to Dakar in West Africa, and in the Mediterranean from Casablanca in French Morocco, Mers-el-Kebir and Oran in Algeria, to Alexandria in North Africa. While the Royal Navy was reluctant to take action against the French, the attitude of the new Vichy French Government was an unknown quantity, although it was known to include pro-Axis elements. It was important that the ships should not fall into German hands and it was the ships at Alexandria that posed yet another problem for Cunningham.

Cunningham had every sympathy with his French counterpart, Vice Admiral Godfroy, who was under orders from his Admiralty to sail, but was trying to confirm that the order was authentic. While de Gaulle was already in the United Kingdom intent on establishing the Free French forces, this move was not universally accepted by all French émigrés, and at this early stage of the war, with so few personnel available to de Gaulle, and the future policies of the Vichy regime not known, few were inclined to commit themselves. After all, the Germans had not occupied the whole of France, and they did not wish to be classed as traitors.

Naturally, most of the personnel involved wished to return home. Darlan had issued orders that ships were to be scuttled if there was a risk of them being seized by the Germans, but it was also clear that they were not to be handed to the British either. Cunningham later recalled:

> Though I had no doubts of the good faith of Vice Admiral Godfroy, it was impossible for the British fleet in Alexandria to go to sea for operations against the enemy leaving behind in harbour fully efficient units of the French Navy. Immediately we were out of sight they might . . . go back to France, where there was no assurance that they would not fall into German or Italian hands and be used against us.

Admiralty pressure on Cunningham to act decisively and quickly was considerable. It says much for his character that he refused to be hurried into taking action that could further affect Anglo-French naval relations.

Cunningham knew that his only alternatives were to intern the ships or risk unnecessary bloodshed on both sides by sinking them. After initially appearing to accept internment with the repatriation of most of his ships' companies, while the vessels would be relieved of their fuel and the warheads taken off their torpedoes, the Vichy Government's orders to sail forced Godfroy to change his mind. He instructed his ships to raise steam – a process that would take up to eight hours. Cunningham was alerted and, going on deck, saw not only that the ships were raising steam, but that their guns had been uncovered and they were ready for action, with the real possibility of a close-range gun battle in Alexandria harbour. The British warships immediately did the same, removing the tompions (muzzle covers) from their guns.

Cunningham immediately ordered his commanding officers to visit the French, while the flagship signalled each French warship in turn advising them of the British Government's offer of repatriation if the warships were put out of use. The visitors to the French warships were not unwelcome, but in many cases the decision was taken out of their hands as French ratings held meetings on deck, while the French commanding officers visited Godfroy on his flagship, *Dusquesne*. Later, Godfroy asked to see Cunningham and they agreed that all fuel oil was to be discharged from the French ships, their guns were to be disabled, and some 70 per cent of their crews were to be landed and eventually repatriated.

No attempt was made to press the French ships into the Royal Navy. Leaving small crews behind meant that the ships were maintained ready for the day of liberation.

By 7 July, the French fleet no longer presented a threat, allowing the British to leave Alexandria without any concern over possible French action to seize the port or the Suez Canal. Cunningham had shown considerable skill and diplomacy in a difficult situation – in modern terminology he had defused the situation.

Punta Stilo and Taranto

Soon afterwards, the first naval engagement between the British and the Italians occurred at the Battle of Punta Stilo, after the submarine HMS *Phoenix* had alerted Admiral Sir Andrew Cunningham, Commander-in-Chief of the Mediterranean Fleet, that the Italians had two battleships at sea. On 8 July 1940, the two ships were 200 miles east of Malta and steaming on a southerly course. Aerial reconnaissance later found that the two warships were supported by six cruisers and seven destroyers, escorting a large convoy. Cunningham planned to put his ships between the Italians and the major forward base at Taranto.

The following day, a Malta-based flying boat found the Italians 145 miles west of the Mediterranean Fleet at 0730. Further confirmation came from aircraft flown off from *Eagle*. By noon, the distance had closed to 80 miles and it was not until then that the Italian Admiral, Campioni, was alerted to the proximity of the Mediterranean Fleet by a seaplane catapulted from his own ship, the *Guilio Cesare*.

Other than Cunningham's flagship, *Warspite*, most of the British ships were outgunned. To slow the Italians down, two strikes by Swordfish armed with torpedoes were launched from *Eagle*, but failed to score any hits, missing the opportunity to slow the larger ships, or even sink a cruiser. Just before 1500 hrs, two British cruisers spotted four of the Italian cruisers, which responded with their 8-inch main armament, outgunning their British counterparts which only had 6-inch guns. Cunningham, ahead of his other two battleships in *Warspite*, raced to the rescue and opened fire at just under 15 miles, forcing the Italians back behind a smokescreen. While *Eagle* and the two older battleships tried to catch up, two Italian heavy cruisers attempted to attack the carrier, drawing further fire from *Warspite*, *Malaya* and *Royal Sovereign*. At 1600, the two fleets' battleships were within sight of one another and *Warspite* opened fire again at a range of nearly 15 miles, almost immediately after the second Swordfish strike. The Italians replied with ranging shots straddling the British ships, but a direct hit on the *Guilio Cesare* at the base of its funnels by a salvo of 15-inch shells persuaded the Italians to break off the engagement under cover of a heavy smokescreen. Cunningham also turned, aware that his ships would not be able to catch the Italian ships and that there was the risk of submarine attack. Italian bombers finally arriving to attack the Mediterranean Fleet bombed their own ships by mistake, to the delight of the crew of *Warspite*'s Swordfish floatplane, in the air since before the start of the action.

This was the only battle in the Second World War when two full battle fleets actually engaged.

An attack on the Italian fleet in its forward base at Taranto had been planned some years before the Second World War broke out at the height of the Abyssinian crisis in 1935, when the Mediterranean Fleet aircraft carrier was *Glorious*. The plan was revived in 1940. Originally it was intended that two carriers, *Illustrious*, newly arrived in the Mediterranean, and *Eagle*, should be used, giving a total of thirty Fairey Swordfish biplanes for the operation. A serious hangar fire aboard *Illustrious* delayed the operation, and then *Eagle*, having suffered extensive damage to her aviation fuel system as a result of near misses by heavy bombs, was not available. A number of aircraft were transferred from *Eagle*'s squadrons to those aboard *Illustrious*, giving a total of twenty-four aircraft for the operation, but before the operation could begin, two aircraft were lost. In the end, just twenty-one aircraft were available.

The operation eventually took place on the night of 11/12 November 1940, in two waves, with twelve aircraft in the first wave and nine in the second. Attacking against a heavily defended target, the first wave concentrated on the ships and the second wave on the shore installations. Three of the Italian Navy's six battleships were sitting on the bottom of the harbour when the raid ended, although two eventually returned to service, while other ships were damaged and fuel tanks ashore set on fire, while just two aircraft were shot down, with the crew of one of these being taken prisoner.

The Italians were forced to move their warships away from Taranto at first, although the next nearest port, Naples, was within reach of Malta-based Wellington bombers.

As the year ended, on 18 December, the Mediterranean Fleet was able to send two battleships, *Warspite* and *Valiant*, to bombard the port of Valona in Albania, being used by the Italians for their assault on Greece. Two days later, Cunningham visited Malta in *Warspite*, to a warm welcome. The Axis powers were soon to show, on 10 January 1941, that they were also capable of inflicting serious damage to the Royal Navy, when Malta's vulnerability was also brought home with a vengeance. The convoy code-named Operation Excess was escorted towards Malta by Admiral Somerville's Force H, and consisted of just four large merchantmen, three for Piraeus and one, carrying 4,000 tons of ammunition and 3,000 tons of seed potatoes, for Malta. Two other merchantmen, one with general supplies and another with fuel for Malta, came from Alexandria with the Mediterranean Fleet. Wellington bombers from Malta had raided Naples on the night of 8/9 January, damaging the battleship *Guilio Cesare*, and forcing her and the *Vittorio Veneto* to withdraw north to Genoa.

After initial skirmishes on 9 January, when Force H was bombed, *Ark Royal*'s Fulmars accounted for two bombers, but the real action came at the handover the following day. The Axis reconnaissance aircraft knew of the Mediterranean Fleet's presence in the area, but the bombers failed to find them until 10 January. Both carriers kept their Fulmar fighters on constant readiness.

On 10 January, the Luftwaffe and Regia Aeronautica attacked, with most of their bombs aimed at *Illustrious*. Luftwaffe Stukas quickly scored six direct hits and three near misses on *Illustrious*, whose deck was designed to take a direct hit of 500-lb bombs, but the hangar lifts were much weaker than this. The ship was forced to put in to Malta for repairs, where she remained prey to the attentions of the Luftwaffe and Regia Aeronautica until she was able to sail to the United States for repairs.

Matapan and the Fall of Greece

By this time, Cunningham had been confirmed in the rank of admiral, but he was to have little time to appreciate this vote of confidence by the Board of Admiralty. The Germans were preparing to attack Yugoslavia and Greece, and pressured their Italian allies to cut British seaborne communications between Alexandria and Athens. When Italian ships were sent into the waters south of Greece to attack British convoys, British aerial reconnaissance soon spotted the Italian ships. Cunningham intended to retain the element of surprise and considerable effort was put into making it seem that the Mediterranean Fleet was staying in port, convinced that Alexandria was awash with Axis spies. Then, under cover of darkness, the Mediterranean Fleet slipped out to sea late on 27 March.

The opening of the Battle of Cape Matapan started at daybreak the following morning when *Formidable* flew off aircraft for reconnaissance, fighter combat air patrol and anti-submarine patrols. They soon received two reports of cruisers and destroyers. In fact, Italian heavy cruisers were pursuing the British light cruisers and in order to rescue them from this predicament, *Formidable* flew off six Fairey Albacores escorted by Fairey Fulmar fighters to attack the Italian ships, which were being joined by the battleship *Vittorio Veneto*.

While the Fulmar fighters shot down one of two Junkers Ju88 medium bombers that attempted to attack the Albacores, and drove the other one off, the six Albacores dived down through heavy AA fire to torpedo the *Vittorio Veneto*. No strikes were made, but they did force the Italian battleship to break off the pursuit of the British cruisers.

A second strike of three Albacores and two Swordfish, again with Fulmar fighters, was sent off while two Italian bombers attempted to attack *Formidable*. *Vittorio Veneto*'s AA defences were surprised by the Fulmars machine-gunning their positions and the bridge as the Albacores pressed home their torpedo attack. As the AA fire started to hit it, the leading aircraft dropped its torpedo 1,000 yards ahead of the ship. The torpedo struck home almost immediately after the plane crashed and the battleship was hit 15ft below the waterline, allowing a massive flood of water to gush in just above the port outer screw, so that within minutes the engines had stopped. Hard work by damage-control parties enabled the *Vittorio Veneto* to start again, using just her two starboard engines, but she could only manage 15 knots. A third air strike was then mounted by *Formidable*. When this arrived over the ship at dusk, they attacked the Italians, diving down through a dense smokescreen and then being dazzled by searchlights and the usual colourful Italian tracer barrage in an unsuccessful attack. Then an aircraft flying from Maleme in Crete spotted a heavy cruiser, the *Pola*, successfully torpedoing it and inflicting such severe damage that she lost speed and drifted out of position. Once the Italian admiral, Iachino, realized what had happened, he sent two other heavy cruisers, *Zara* and *Fiume*, with four destroyers to provide assistance.

Although the Italians were not expecting a night action, Cunningham knew that they were weak in night gunnery and intended to take advantage of this. By this time, the opposing fleets were off Cape Matapan, on modern atlases usually referred to as Cape Akra Tainaron, a promontory at the extreme southern end of the Pelopponese peninsula. At first, Cunningham thought that the *Pola* was *Vittorio Veneto*. As his ships prepared to open fire, the Italian rescue force of *Zara* and *Fiume* sped across Cunningham's path and were illuminated by a searchlight from a destroyer. In the battle that followed, *Zara* and *Fiume* and two destroyers were sunk by the 15-in guns of the three battleships, while *Pola* was sunk in a torpedo attack from two destroyers.

The next morning, Cunningham had his ships pick up 900 Italian survivors before the threat of air attack stopped the rescue. Nevertheless, before leaving he relayed the position of the remaining survivors to Rome, saving many more lives. Although this was not the only time he did his best for a defeated enemy, he could seem harsh and unyielding to those around him. He considered that the naval airmen who attacked Taranto were only doing their duty, although he later admitted that he had not realized at the time what a 'stroke it had been'. The effect on morale aboard *Illustrious* was bad, with angry sailors tearing down the notices announcing the awards which included nothing higher than a DSO. He maintained a small staff, which undoubtedly meant that there was less overlap and duplication, but it put them under pressure. Cunningham simply retorted that he had never known a staff officer die from overwork, and if he did, he could always get another one.

By 23 April, the Greek Army had surrendered and the Mediterranean Fleet found itself evacuating British forces to Crete. Had Crete been used simply as a staging post, all might have been well, but the mistake was made of attempting to defend the island, despite the shortage of aircraft and the fact that the British had left most of their heavy equipment and their communications behind in Greece. In both the evacuation of Greece and then of Crete, Cunningham prolonged the operation for longer than his orders required, saving many soldiers from PoW camps.

Leaving the Mediterranean

Cunningham left the Mediterranean in June 1942 and served in Washington as head of the British naval delegation until October. It was his turn to realize that he did not enjoy staff work and it was no doubt with considerable pleasure that he found himself as Allied Naval Commander Expeditionary Force for the North African landings in November 1942. Early the following year he was promoted to admiral of the fleet, and became C-in-C Mediterranean; as Eisenhower's naval deputy he was responsible for the naval aspects of the landings in Sicily in July and at Salerno in September.

Meanwhile, the First Sea Lord at the Admiralty, the Royal Navy's most senior officer, Admiral of the Fleet Sir Dudley Pound, had been increasingly unwell for some time. He was overworked and had to cope not only with the normal strains of running a major part of the armed forces, but the fact that the Admiralty was also an operational headquarters. When he resigned in September 1943, before dying in October, Cunningham was appointed as his successor. As the alliance with the United States grew ever closer, he also became a member of the Combined Chiefs of Staff committees.

In his new role, Cunningham was quickly accepted by the other British service heads, and especially by the head of the Army, the Chief of the Imperial General Staff, General Sir Alan Brooke, later Field Marshal Lord Alanbrooke. Cunningham is credited with the success of the Normandy landing in June 1944, and the formation of the new British Pacific Fleet, the largest and most balanced fleet the Royal Navy ever created and which operated under the overall command of Nimitz. Not for nothing has the official Royal Navy historian described Cunningham as standing 'unique amongst the leaders of fleets and sailors'.

When the war ended, Cunningham was entitled to retire, but he resolved first to pilot the Navy through the transition to peace. There was a large reduction in the Defence Budget which proved to be a challenge for Cunningham, who later remarked in his memoirs: 'We very soon came to realise how much easier it was to make war than to reorganise for peace.' At the end of May 1946, Cunningham retired to Bishop's Waltham in Hampshire. Ennobled, he attended the House of Lords irregularly but campaigned for justice for Admiral Dudley North, who had been relieved of his command of Gibraltar in 1940, and obtained a partial vindication in 1957. Cunningham died in London on 12 June 1963 and was buried at sea off Portsmouth.

Chapter 11

Victor of the North Cape

Admiral Sir Bruce Austin Fraser, RN (1888–1981)

Fraser was most famous for his victory in the Battle of the North Cape, one of the few naval engagements during the Second World War that did not involve aircraft or submarines, and which saw the end of the battlecruiser *Scharnhorst*, Hitler's favourite warship.

Born in Acton, Middlesex, on 5 February 1888, he joined the Royal Navy as a cadet at Dartmouth on 15 January 1904. After graduating and then gaining sea time as a midshipman, Fraser obtained first-class passes in all his sub lieutenant's exams, which he took during 1907. Promotion proved rapid as his ability was soon recognized and, after being promoted sub lieutenant on 15 March 1907, he became lieutenant exactly a year later. During this period he served in the Channel and Mediterranean Fleets. He returned to the Home Fleet in August 1910 and remained there serving in HMS *Boadicea* until the end of July the following year. On 31 July 1911, Fraser joined *Excellent*, the Royal Navy's school of Gunnery at Whale Island in Portsmouth harbour, where he commenced the 'long course' to qualify as a specialist gunnery lieutenant.

Admiral Sir Bruce Fraser was Third Sea Lord on the Board of Admiralty from 1939 until 1942, being knighted in 1941. His role was to control the Royal Navy's finances and handle its procurement, but given the time needed for warship design and construction, most of the ships in the Royal Navy during the first three or four years of the war had been specified and ordered before the outbreak of hostilities. He was whisked away from Whitehall in 1942 to become the second-in-command to Admiral Sir John Tovey, Commander-in-Chief of the Home Fleet. When Pound resigned, shortly before his death in 1943, Fraser took over as C-in-C of the Home Fleet in the inevitable reshuffle of the most senior officers. In fact, he had been offered the post of First Sea Lord by the British Prime Minister, Winston Churchill, but Fraser, modest to the last, declared that while he would serve wherever he was sent, and believed that he had the confidence of his own fleet: 'Cunningham has that of the whole navy.'

Fraser was soon on the way to gaining the confidence of the entire Navy, however. The German battlecruiser *Scharnhorst* had fled from France and eventually ended up in Norwegian waters, where she posed an ever-present threat to the Arctic convoys from Scotland and Iceland to Murmansk and Archangel. On 26 December 1943, the *Scharnhorst* and five destroyers attempted to attack Arctic convoy JW55B, escorted by fourteen destroyers, but with a close-support cruiser squadron including *Belfast*, *Norfolk* and *Sheffield*, while a long-range protection group included the battleship *Duke of York* with the cruiser *Jamaica* and four destroyers. The convoy was missed in bad weather which also separated *Scharnhorst* from her destroyer escorts, whereupon the German ship was confronted by the British cruisers. After a second attempt a twenty-minute battle broke out with each side scoring two hits; *Scharnhorst* attempted to withdraw but ran into the *Duke of York* and *Jamaica*, ending up bracketed by the two British support groups. *Duke of York* scored several hits, and the cruiser *Jamaica* and British destroyers mounted a torpedo attack, after which British gunfire resumed as the battle-cruiser lost way and eventually capsized with the loss of all but thirty-six of her crew of more than 2,000 men.

In November 1944, Fraser was accorded the distinction of becoming the first Commander-in-Chief of the new British Pacific Fleet, which also had the dual identity of Task Force 57 when it was supporting the US Pacific Fleet. The British Pacific Fleet was the largest and most balanced naval force ever assembled by the Royal Navy. Nevertheless, Fletcher's was not a seagoing command and he was based ashore in Sydney, Australia. While the USN's senior officer in the Pacific, Admiral Nimitz, objected to the British presence, the fleet served an invaluable role, especially off the islands of the Sakashima Gunto, where it successfully stopped the Japanese from sending reinforcements, and by the end of the war it was attacking targets on the Japanese home islands.

At the end of the war, Fraser was accorded the honour of being the United Kingdom signatory of the instrument of Japanese surrender aboard the battleship USS *Missouri* in Tokyo Harbour. In 1948, he became First Sea Lord and Chief of the Naval Staff. He retired in 1951 with the rank of Admiral of the Fleet. When elevated to the peerage later, he took the title of Admiral of the Fleet Lord Fraser of North Cape, after his most famous victory.

Chapter 12

Poacher Turned Gamekeeper

Admiral Sir Max Horton, RN (1883–1951)

During the First World War, Horton had been one of Britain's ablest submarine commanders. There could therefore have been no one better to lead the fight against the German U-boat menace as Commander-in-Chief Western Approaches from 1942. His overriding responsibility was for the safety of the convoys crossing the North Atlantic, a role that became increasingly important as the content of the convoys started to include US and Canadian troops coming to the UK for the invasion of Europe.

Horton joined the Royal Navy as an officer cadet at Dartmouth on 15 September 1898. By the outbreak of the First World War, he was already a lieutenant commander in command of one of the first British ocean-going submarines, the 800-ton HMS *E9*. Surface ships rather than other submarines were the more usual victims of submarine attack. On 13 September 1914, Lieutenant Commander Max Horton was in command of *E9* when she surfaced 6 miles south of Heligoland to find the German light cruiser *Hela* only 2 miles away. Closing to a range of about 600 yards, *E9* sent two torpedoes towards the enemy ship before diving. As the submarine dived, an explosion was heard. Surfacing, Horton found that his prey had stopped, but enemy gunfire forced him to dive again and to stay down for an hour. Surfacing again, he could see nothing other than trawlers searching for survivors. On his return to his base at Harwich, Horton flew the pirate flag, the 'Jolly Roger' skull and crossbones, establishing a tradition in the Royal Navy's submarine service for boats returning from a successful operational cruise. Horton's next success came on 6 October while patrolling off the Ems, when he torpedoed and sank the destroyer *S-126*.

In the face of growing German U-boat activity, it had been decided to take the offensive, sending British submarines to the Baltic, where they could in turn wreak havoc on German shipping, in effect giving the enemy a taste of his own medicine. The idea had first been floated at a conference with Jellicoe aboard the *Iron Duke* on 17 September 1914. By the time implementation was in hand, the proposed flotilla had become just three boats, *E11*, *E9* and *E1*, with three hand-picked commanders, Lieutenant Commander Martin Nasmith, Lieutenant Commander Max Horton and Lieutenant Commander Noel Laurence respectively. Laurence was the senior officer.

Submarines were the only warships that could hope to enter the Baltic unobserved, at least in theory as the charts showed that there was not enough depth for submarines to submerge in the Kattegat, between Denmark and Sweden. Horton, commander of *E9*, suggested that the way to enter the Baltic was to run on the surface, but with the submarine trimmed down as low as possible in the water in the hope that at night the small conning tower of these early craft might not be noticed. His first patrol in the Baltic was nearly his last as he only narrowly missed being seen and rammed by a destroyer. German patrols were not the only hazard awaiting him. On one occasion his boat was frozen in port, and although he managed to get an ice-breaker to get out into the Gulf of Finland, once in the open sea *E9* started to ice up, and frozen slush clogged vents and valves froze solid. Spray froze on the rigging wires, the torpedo-tube caps and the periscope. Horton was determined to discover whether or not *E9* could still dive and to everyone's surprise, once she submerged, the warmer water soon melted the ice and the submarine was able to operate normally. The other major problem was that the British submarines were using Russian ports, but as the Russian forces fell back before the German advance on the Eastern Front, they had to change bases constantly. Operations were finally abandoned in 1917 because of the Bolshevik Revolution.

Between the wars, Horton, now a captain, served as commanding officer of first HMS *Conquest* and of the battleship *Resolution* during the 1920s. He was promoted to rear admiral on 17 October 1932, flying his flag aboard the Queen Elizabeth-class battleship

Malaya. Three years later he took command of the First Cruiser Squadron, flying his flag aboard *London*. Promoted to vice admiral in 1937, he commanded the Reserve Fleet.

Northern Patrol

At the outbreak of the Second World War, Horton was put in command of the Northern Patrol enforcing the distant maritime blockade of Germany in the seas between Orkney, Shetland and the Faeroes. In 1940, he was made commander of all home-based submarines, even though he was far more senior in rank than the C-in-C Submarines had traditionally been, due to a new Admiralty regulation that the C-in-C Submarines had to be an officer who had served aboard submarines in the First World War. Many believed that this regulation was forced through for the sole purpose of ensuring that Horton was on a very short list of qualifiers for the post, in order to ensure his rapid transfer to submarine headquarters at Aberdour, so great was the desire of some within the Admiralty to have him revitalize the submarine arm. Horton also had his own ideas and moved his headquarters from Aberdour, where he was subjected to the whims and prejudices of the fleet commanders at Scapa Flow, to Northways in north London. He claimed that this was because he wanted a freer hand in running his command, but many feel that it was because Northways was located near some of his favorite golf courses (he is said to have played a round of golf almost every day during the war).

He was promoted to the four-star rank of admiral on 9 January 1941 and was appointed Commander-in-Chief, Western Approaches Command on 17 November 1942. He took up his role as C-in-C Western Approaches at the most critical time of the war, with heavy losses to merchant shipping. Nevertheless, by May 1943, the situation had been transformed. He put in hand a series of changes in the way the escort ships were to be used. In addition to the escort group system, he oversaw the introduction of support groups, which would accompany the convoys but have the freedom to pursue submarines to destruction, being allowed to leave the convoy for long periods. These support groups proved to be decisive in the crucial spring of 1943, taking the battle to the U-boats and crushing the morale of the U-boat arm with persistent and successful counter-attacks.

Horton is widely regarded as one of the most crucial figures in the Allied victory in the Atlantic. The use of merchant aircraft carriers, the MAC-ships, and then escort carriers, helped close the Atlantic Gap – that section of the crossing that was beyond shore-based air cover – while the longer-range of aircraft such as the Consolidated Liberator also ensured greater security for the convoys. The increased number of purpose-built escort vessels, together with the Ultra intelligence that gave Horton the position of the U-boat wolf packs, all contributed to the Allied success. While much of this was the work of others, Horton was responsible for the overall control and coordination, and has been credited with showing untiring zeal, shrewdness and good strategic sense in the disposition of his forces. Perhaps his secret was that this successful submariner understood the workings of the minds of the U-boat commanders.

After the war, in August 1945, and at his own request, Max Horton was placed on the retired list in order to facilitate the promotion of younger officers. He was in any case past the peacetime retirement age. He was awarded the Knight Grand Cross in the Order of the Bath. He died on 30 July 1951 at the age of sixty-seven.

Chapter 13

'Catnapping at meetings'

Admiral of the Fleet Sir Alfred Dudley Pound, RN (1877–1943)

One of the most experienced British naval officers in 1939, Pound had commanded a battleship at the Battle of Jutland in 1916. Knighted in 1933, he held the prized position of Commander-in-Chief Mediterranean in 1936, and when the post of First Sea Lord had to be filled in June 1939, the first choice fell ill and the position was offered to Pound, who was promoted to the five-star rank of admiral of the fleet in July.

Born on the Isle of Wight on 29 August 1877, Pound did not come from a naval family, although his home was not far from the major Royal Navy base at Portsmouth. In 1891, at the age of fourteen, Pound entered the Navy as a cadet at Dartmouth. He advanced rapidly and by 1916 was a captain commanding the battleship HMS *Colossus*. He led her at the Battle of Jutland with notable success, sinking two German cruisers, beating off two destroyers and eluding five torpedoes.

After the war, Pound was posted to naval planning and became head of the planning division in 1922. During Roger Keyes' tenure as Commander-in-Chief of the Mediterranean Fleet in the late 1920s, Pound was his Chief of Staff. In 1936, he became Commander-in-Chief of the Mediterranean Fleet, serving until 1939, which meant that he was in the Mediterranean when Italy invaded Abyssinia and the League of Nations refused to take action, largely because of

French objections. His elevation to First Sea Lord came at a time when he was already showing the first signs of failing health.

Unusually shy for a very senior naval officer, Pound avoided publicity, even after he was appointed First Sea Lord on 31 July 1939. His health was already poor, but other experienced British admirals were also in bad shape. An incipient brain tumour was diagnosed by a naval medical officer, who did not tell the Admiralty. In addition, Pound also suffered problems with his hips, which kept him awake at night and so caused him to doze off at meetings.

There are sharply divided opinions of Pound from this time. Although his staff at the Admiralty found him easy to work with, admirals and captains at sea accused him of interference with their operations, which resulted in a number of serious clashes with Admiral John Tovey, the Commander-in-Chief of the Home Fleet. Winston Churchill, with whom he worked from September 1939, found him fairly easy to dominate, but he was able to frustrate Churchill's dramatic idea of sending a battle fleet into the Baltic early in the War. In this, he undoubtely saved the Royal Navy from the embarrassment of having ships bottled up in the Baltic where the Luftwaffe and German U-boats could have picked them off one at a time.

Perhaps Pound's greatest achievement was his successful campaign against German U-boat activity and the winning of the Battle of the Atlantic (1939–1945). On the other hand, his most criticized decision was ordering Arctic Convoy PQ17 to scatter, against the advice of his senior commanders, with disastrous results. He has also been blamed for allowing the two German battlecruisers, *Scharnhorst* and *Gneisenau*, along with the heavy cruiser *Prinz Eugen*, to make the Channel Dash in February 1942, steaming through the English Channel on their way home from France to Germany virtually unopposed, other than by a flight of six Fairey Swordfish torpedo aircraft. But this was unfair as it was an inter-service problem compounded by excessive secrecy. At the same time, he could claim many successes, at Taranto and Matapan, in the sinking of the German battleship *Bismarck*, and it was under his control of the Royal Navy that the Battle of the Atlantic began to be won. Perhaps his greatest strength was his ability to appoint outstanding commanders, with Horton at Western Approaches and Ramsay at Dover, while he confirmed Cunningham in his appointment in the Mediterranean.

Nevertheless, it cannot be denied that he also failed to delegate adequately. Uniquely amongst British service ministries, the Admiralty was, and remains, also an operational headquarters and Pound could not resist interfering in operational matters, helped by the use of radio. He was badly overworked and increasingly seriously ill from his brain tumour, but it was not until 1942 that he appointed a Deputy First Sea Lord. In the meantime, much damage was done to his reputation by keeping the seriousness of his illness and of his painful hip to himself, so that his opposite number in the British Army, the then General Alan Brooke, Chief of the Imperial General Staff, doubted his abilities because he would often doze off, or 'catnap', during meetings, even of the War Cabinet chaired by the Prime Minister himself.

Just one of the crosses which Pound had to bear was that of the Prime Minister, Winston Churchill, who had been brought back as First Lord of the Admiralty, its political head, in 1939, having held the same post for the first part of the First World War. The impetuous Churchill was subject to having a surfeit of ideas, only a few of them really good ones and many of which were conceived late at night after imbibing considerable quantities of alcohol, which led some senior officers to describe his ideas as 'midnight follies'. Some saw Pound as a moderating influence on Churchill, others blamed him for being too deferential. Nevertheless, there were limits to what Pound could accept and when, in March 1942, Mountbatten was promoted to vice admiral and allowed to join the Chiefs of Staff committee, he resigned the chairmanship of the committee in protest.

Early in 1943, he was offered a peerage, but declined it. He accompanied Churchill to the Quebec Conference in August 1943, by which time the effects of the tumour were increasingly serious and, after suffering two strokes, he formally resigned on 5 October 1943. The next day, the King's Private Secretary called at the Royal Masonic Hospital and gave the dying admiral the insignia of the Order of Merit. He died on Trafalgar Day, 21 October 1943. After a funeral in Westminster Abbey, his ashes and those of his wife, who had died the previous July, were scattered at sea.

Few senior naval officers can have failed to make some serious mistakes during their time in command, and Pound was no exception. The Royal Navy was short of very experienced senior officers in 1939, many of those who were available being elderly, ready for retirement and often in poor health. For Pound, and anyone else with serious hip problems, hip replacement surgery was simply not available at the time. His tendency to interfere was a serious weakness, but not an unusual one amongst senior commanders. He would in any case have been goaded into this on many occasions by Churchill who, initially as First Lord of the Admiralty, the Royal Navy's political master, and then as Prime Minister, found second-guessing his service chiefs, and the commanders below them, irresistable. The secret was, of course, that good communications should have been used solely to appraise commanders of the latest intelligence about a developing situation, something that was not done by the Admiralty at Jutland, for example, and not to 'back-seat drive'.

There had been a succession of First Sea Lords with failing health and it was not until the then Admiral Sir Andrew Cunningham replaced Pound that the Royal Navy once again had a robust leader.

Chapter 14

The Admiral who Evacuated the British Army from France, and Sent it Back Again

Admiral Sir Bertram Home Ramsay, RN (1883–1945)

A contemporary of Cunningham, Ramsay had a less illustrious career. He served in the Grand Fleet during the First World War, and also with the Dover Patrol, the force set up to protect British shipping supplying Allied forces in France. In 1938, he retired as a vice admiral. As war became increasingly likely, he was recalled in August 1938 and appointed Vice Admiral Dover.

Born in London into a family with Scottish origins on 20 January 1883, Ramsay joined the Royal Navy as a cadet at Dartmouth in 1898, when the service was still using the old hulk, HMS *Britannia*. He made rapid progress and became a midshipman within a year, on which he was posted to HMS *Crescent*.

He was given his first command during the First World War, the small monitor *M 25*, in August 1915, which was part of the Dover Patrol, keeping the English Channel clear of German warships, to enable reinforcements and supplies to be moved safely between the UK and France. In October 1917, he took command of another Dover Patrol vessel, the destroyer *Broke*. On 9 1918, his ship took part in the second Ostend raid, a follow-up to the Zeebrugge Raid, and he was mentioned in despatches. This operation, mounted on 10 May 1918, was the second attempt to block the port of Ostend, after the earlier attempt in April, timed to coincide with a similar assault on Zeebrugge, had failed. The cruiser *Vindictive*, which had been heavily modified for the Zeebrugge raid and badly damaged during the operation, was patched up and sent off again, this time to act as a blockship with another ship, the *Sappho*, which had to return with engine trouble, leaving it to *Vindictive* to block the port. The operation encountered further problems when it ran into thick fog but her commanding officer managed to place *Vindictive* right in the harbour mouth before he was killed by a direct hit whilst attempting to turn her across the channel. The first lieutenant took control but the ship had run aground and could not be moved. He blew up *Vindictive* and she settled, partially blocking the entrance.

Ramsay was a rear admiral when he retired from the Navy in 1938, but he was recalled in August 1939 to help deal with the Axis threat, and promoted to vice admiral. In making the appointment, the Admiralty undoubtedly held to the widespread belief that the Second World War would follow the pattern of the First World War. It was generally expected that British and French forces would continue to fight in France, and the cross-Channel supply routes would need to be protected from German warships – Ramsay's earlier experience of the Dover Patrol would therefore be invaluable. No one foresaw that the Germans would also invade the Netherlands as well as Belgium, or the speed of their advance through these countries and into France. French surrender that followed was not expected and came as a nasty shock. The desperate need to save as many British and French soldiers as possible was a responsibility placed firmly on Ramsay's shoulders.

Working in underground tunnels below Dover Castle with a small staff, which included Somerville, he organized and coordinated the evacuation of the British Expeditionary Force in 'Operation Dynamo'. The operation moved 338,226 British and French troops across the English Channel to the south of England, from whence a continuous stream of trains dispersed them throughout Great Britain. Inevitably, most of the ships used were civilian owned and manned, including not just merchant vessels and fishing boats, but private craft as well, many of which did sterling work moving troops from the beaches and the shallows out to ships moored in deeper water, although two-thirds of those evacuated were taken off the harbour's east mole straight onto ships. Meanwhile, other warships were used to keep German naval units, and especially

E-boats, from the evacuation fleet, and to provide anti-aircraft cover during the period of the evacuation. Nothing larger than a destroyer could get close enough to help, but the Fleet Air Arm also assisted by lending several of its Swordfish squadrons to RAF Coastal Command to provide short-range reconnaissance and anti-shipping measures.

'Operation Dynamo' officially started on 26 May, although by this time 28,000 rear-echelon personnel had already been evacuated. Part of the problem was that in order to avoid the many shallows and sandbanks in the English Channel, the safest route from Dover to Dunkirk entailed ships crossing from Dover to Calais and then sailing northwards along the coast to Dunkirk, exposing the rescue fleet to artillery fire and aerial attack. Two more northerly routes were also used, but one of these had to be abandoned as it was dangerously exposed to attack by U-boats and E-boats. The evacuation was not announced to the public until 29 May. The worst day for aerial attack was 1 June, after which Admiral Ramsay banned daylight sailings. The last sailings were on the night of 3/4 June, when most of the 53,000 French personnel were rescued.

The Dunkirk evacuation was costly, with nine British and French destroyers and eight troopships lost; out of the officially recorded 848 civilian vessels and small naval craft, no less than seventy-two were lost to enemy action and another 163 lost in collisions, with forty-five damaged. Yet, while Churchill rightly reminded the British people that 'wars are not won by evacuations', the loss of a third of a million British and French soldiers would have been a shock that could have completely undermined the ability to continue the war, and public morale might not have survived the trauma.

For his part in organizing 'Dynamo', Ramsay was knighted.

With 'Operation Dynamo' completed, Ramsay was in the unfortunate position of having the full might of the German armed forces on the other side of the Straits of Dover, just 22 miles away, and within German artillery range. Many of the civil population of Dover had to be evacuated, but as the port was of no immediate use for the cross-Channel packets of peacetime, many of them had to work elsewhere anyway. The general mood was that the Germans were unstoppable and likely to invade, which meant that Ramsay was faced with the enormous problem of defending the waters off Dover from the expected German invasion. For nearly two years, he commanded forces striving to maintain control against the Germans, gaining a second Mention in Despatches.

Ramsay was still at Dover when the two German battlecruisers *Scharnhorst* and *Gneisenau*, along with the heavy cruiser *Prinz Eugen*, made their Channel Dash in February 1942, steaming through the English Channel on their way home from France to Germany. He had substantial artillery at his disposal, but poor visibility meant that the gunners could not see the German ships. Thanks to German daring and British excessive secrecy, the three ships were not expected, and confusion over what to do allowed them to proceed virtually unchallenged.

Ramsay was appointed as Naval Force Commander and given responsibility for planning the amphibious assault phase of the invasion of Europe in April 1942, which at the time was expected to be later that year. But plans changed and when it was decided to invade North Africa instead, he was transferred to become deputy Naval commander of the Allied invasion of North Africa. Under the Allied Naval Commander of the Expeditionary Force, Sir Andrew Cunningham, Ramsay planned the landing efforts. Although many objected to a vice admiral on the retired list being given such responsibility, no doubt some of them wanting this role for themselves, Cunningham took Ramsay as his deputy, not only for the landings in North Africa, 'Operation Torch', but also for the landings in Sicily, 'Operation Husky'. During the Allied invasion of Sicily in July 1943, Ramsay was Naval Commanding Officer, Eastern Task Force and planned the amphibious landings.

No doubt the many lessons learned during these two successful operations were invaluable when Ramsay returned to London in December 1943 to begin planning 'Operation Neptune', the assault phase of 'Operation Overlord', the Normandy landings. In April 1944, he was promoted to admiral and restored to the active list. He proved to be the right choice yet again, with 'Neptune' running for the most part like clockwork, despite a 24-hour delay due to bad weather, this efficiency continuing in the no less vital follow-up of additional troops and supplies. The organization of the landings also meant that Ramsay had to resolve a potential conflict between Prime Minister Winston Churchill and King George VI. Churchill informed the King that he intended to observe the D-Day landings from on board the cruiser HMS *Belfast*, which was assigned to bombardment duty for the operation. The King, himself a seasoned sailor and a veteran of the Battle of Jutland in the First World War, then declared that he would accompany his Prime Minister.

Churchill thought this was too dangerous for his sovereign, but His Majesty disagreed. At a meeting with both of them, Admiral Ramsay defused the situation by simply refusing to take the responsibility for the safety of either man, pointing out the danger to both the King and the Prime Minister, as well as the risks for the planned operational duties of *Belfast*. He also made the point that both the King and Churchill would be needed ashore in case the landings went badly and immediate decisions were required. This settled the matter and both Winston Churchill and King George VI remained ashore in England on D-Day.

He was proving to be an efficient staff officer, regarded as tough and well liked by other senior officers in all three services. It was therefore a sad loss when he was killed in an air crash on 2 January 1945, flying to meet the then General Bernard Montgomery to discuss the Ardennes offensive. His record showed that he had saved the British Expeditionary Force and had planned three successful invasions.

It is difficult to fault Ramsay. True, the Allied losses on 'Operation Husky' were far worse than they need have been, but that was because bad weather intervened, and this was the first instance of a combined airborne and amphibious assault for Allied troops. Quite what he would have done next had he not been killed before the end of the war is virtually impossible to guess. While he could have helped organize the invasion of Japan, it is unlikely that the head of the United States Navy, Fleet Admiral Ernest King, would have allowed this. In any case, the USN and USMC had become expert at amphibious landings as they island-hopped across the Pacific. Fortunately, Japanese surrender intervened. He might well have overseen the liberation of British, Dutch and French colonial possessions and the repatriation of Allied prisoners.

Chapter 15

Dash and Daring

Admiral of the Fleet Sir James Fownes Somerville, RN (1882–1949)

Like Ramsay, Somerville was on the retired list but was not recalled until September 1939. He helped Ramsay organize the Dunkirk evacuation in May 1940, before being given command of Force H, based on Gibraltar.

Although he was born in Weybridge, Surrey, on 17 July 1882, James Somerville could easily have been born in New Zealand as his father had spent some time there farming. He joined the Royal Navy as a Dartmouth cadet on 15 January 1897, and by 15 March 1904 was already a lieutenant. During the First World War, Somerville became the Navy's leading radio specialist and served at Gallipoli, where he was awarded the DSO.

As a career officer, Somerville stayed in the service after the war, and on 31 December 1921 was promoted to captain and commanded HMS *Benbow*. With his radio experience, Somerville served as Director of the Admiralty's Signal Department from 1925 to 1927, and as a naval instructor at the Imperial Defence College from 1929 to 1931. He was promoted to commodore in 1932 and to rear admiral on 12 October 1933. Somerville commanded the British Mediterranean Fleet destroyer flotillas from 1936 to 1938, and during the Spanish Civil War his ships were often in Spanish waters protecting British subjects. From 1938 to 1939, he served in the East Indies Station, but in 1939 it was thought that he had tuberculosis and he was forced to retire on medical grounds, although it later turned out to be a false diagnosis.

Somerville was recalled for special duties by the Admiralty later in September 1939 with the start of the First World War. For the first winter of war, he did important work on naval radar development and in May 1940 was sent to Dover where he served under Admiral Ramsay, helping to organize the evacuation of Dunkirk.

He gained his own command when he was appointed as a vice admiral to command the newly formed Force H, based at Gibraltar, flying his flag on the battlecruiser HMS *Hood*. Force H was unusual inasmuch as its Gibraltar base meant that it could operate in both the Atlantic and the Mediterranean, where it often helped provide a strong escort for convoys as far east as Malta, as the Mediterranean became increasingly divided, with Force H confined to the western half and the British Mediterranean Fleet to the eastern. Somerville was given this exacting command, which was officially a powerful naval squadron, but in reality a small fleet, when Force H was formed on 28 June 1940. The idea was to fill the vacuum left by the fall of France and the loss of the French fleet, with its initial role being to stop this strategic asset falling into Axis hands.

After Henri-Philippe Pétain signed an armistice with Germany on 22 June 1940, Winston Churchill gave Somerville the task of neutralizing the main element of the French fleet, at Mers-el-Kébir in North Africa, attacking and destroying it if all other options failed. Churchill wrote to him: 'You are charged with one of the most disagreeable tasks that a British Admiral has ever been faced with, but we have complete confidence in you and rely on you to carry it out relentlessly.'

He felt privately that his orders to attack if all other avenues failed were a mistake, and that tackling the French fleet was an unwelcome task, as he and his men were all too aware that until recently France had been an ally. He was therefore anxious to avoid a battle with the French. On 3 July, he presented his opposite number at Oran, Admiral Gensoul, with an ultimatum, demanding that the French warships be handed over or neutralized, by which he meant that they should be non-operational. Force H included the aircraft carrier *Ark Royal*, commanded by Captain Holland, who was sent to meet Gensoul. The British ultimatum was rejected.

This left Somerville with no option but to attack the French fleet and the shore installations. A single burst of gunfire from one of his battleships blew an army barracks off the crest of a hill. Supported by an attack by aircraft from *Ark Royal*, it took just fifteen minutes for Force H to blow up the old French battleship *Bretagne*, and cripple the battleship *Provence* and the battlecruiser *Dunkerque*, both of which had to be run aground to prevent them sinking; the battlecruiser *Strasbourg* and six destroyers managed to escape to Toulon. Force H's ships were completely undamaged in this short action, although the thin flight deck of the British carrier would have been vulnerable to heavy shellfire.

Somerville's forces having inflicted severe damage on their erstwhile allies, the operation was judged a success, although he admitted privately to his wife that he had not been quite as aggressive in the act of destruction as he could have been.

On 27 November 1940, Force H, with the battleship *Ramillies* and battlecruiser *Renown*, as well as the aircraft carrier *Ark Royal*, was escorting three fast freighters from Gibraltar to Alexandria when Admiral Campioni was sent with the battleships *Vittorio Veneto* and *Guilio Cesare* to intercept them. When the Italians were spotted by British reconnaissance aircraft off Cape Teulada in Sardinia, Somerville moved Force H towards them. Both sides were supported by cruisers, with the British having five against the Italians' six, and these clashed first. The elderly *Ramillies* soon fell behind, but *Renown* followed closely on the British cruisers, and once they came under her fire the Italian cruisers withdrew behind their battleships, which then joined the Battle of Cape Teulada. *Ark Royal* sent her Swordfish to attack the Italians and although no torpedo strikes were made, this was enough to encourage Campioni to break off the battle, having no aircraft of his own. The outcome was that one Italian destroyer was badly damaged, as was the British cruiser *Berwick*. Nevertheless, the priority for Somerville was the protection of the convoy.

Force H continued to do its best to maintain the pressure on the Axis forces in the Mediterranean, despite being outnumbered and outgunned, not to mention having to face the combined forces of the Luftwaffe and the Italian Regia Aeronautica. On 9 February 1941, Somerville took the battleship *Malaya*, the battlecruiser *Renown* and the aircraft carrier *Ark Royal*, with a cruiser and ten destroyers as escorts, into the Gulf of Genoa, steaming into a relatively confined area close to the enemy's mainland. *Malaya* and *Renown* bombarded Genoa itself, while the *Ark Royal*'s aircraft bombed the port of

Leghorn and dropped mines off the naval base of La Spezia. The Italian battleships *Vittorio Veneto*, *Giulio Cesare* and *Andrea Doria*, with three cruisers and ten destroyers, were sent to intercept Force H, which they heavily outgunned and outnumbered. For a while, it looked as if Somerville was to have the decisive naval engagement for which Cunningham had longed, but the Italian ships failed to make contact. He was knighted that year for his successes with Force H.

It was this buccaneering spirit that probably inspired the Admiralty to send him to the Far East, and by February 1942 he was Commander-in-Chief of the Eastern Fleet. His force was ill-equipped to cope with a confrontation with Japanese forces. Between the wars, the British Government had sought to calm Australian and New Zealand fears about Japanese expansion by promising to send a large fleet eastwards in the event of war, but with war against both Germany and Italy in Europe, and France defeated, this was an impossible commitment. Having struck at the US Navy at Pearl Harbor, and covered landings in New Britain and the Netherlands East Indies, Admiral Nagumo took his carrier force into the Indian Ocean to attack Ceylon (now Sri Lanka). This was the furthest west Japanese warships reached, and while they did not attempt to invade the island, they brought considerable force to bear. Further north, Vice Admiral Ozawa took a smaller force to attack shipping in the Bay of Bengal and also bombed the Indian towns of Cocanada and Vizagatapan, causing little damage.

The Eastern Fleet had five elderly battleships, three aircraft carriers, and five cruisers. Two of the aircraft carriers were modern, but lacked high-performance aircraft and his battleships could not keep up with them, while the third was the elderly and small *Hermes*, the first aircraft carrier designed as such from the keel upwards. She was really only suitable for escort duties.

Alerted to Japanese intentions by Ultra intelligence, Somerville planned to use his carrier-borne aircraft for a pre-emptive strike at the Japanese fleet, planning a night attack to reduce the risk of his aircraft being shot down by the 300 aircraft aboard Nagumo's five carriers. Expecting an attack on 1 April, when the time passed, Somerville split his forces and sent most of his warships to his secret base at Addu Atoll (now Gan) in the Maldives, including his two modern, fast, armoured carriers, HMS *Formidable* and *Indomitable*.

This left him with just the elderly *Hermes* and her twelve or so Fairey Swordfish.

The Japanese fleet was discovered by a RAF Consolidated Catalina flying boat on 4 April, which radioed a report before being shot down by Zero fighters. On Easter Day, 5 April, Nagumo sent his aircraft to attack Colombo in what was intended to be a repeat of the raid on Pearl Harbor. The harbour was packed with merchant shipping, but the Eastern Fleet was absent. Although the RAF was able to put Hawker Hurricane fighters into the air, these were shot down by the faster and more agile Zeros. The Japanese aircraft caused severe damage to the harbour and shore installations, and hit an armed merchant cruiser and a destroyer, but their losses were heavier than on their earlier operations.

Aerial reconnaissance was mounted later in an attempt to find the Eastern Fleet, and a flight from *Soryu* discovered the two heavy cruisers, *Cornwall* and *Dorsetshire*, which were sunk in just twenty minutes.

On 4 April, *Hermes* was in harbour at Trincomalee – 'Trinco' to the Royal Navy – and was ordered to sea where it was thought she stood a better chance of surviving an attack. On 6 April, she was ordered to return to Trincomalee, but left again on 8 April after intelligence indicated that a Japanese attack was imminent. Spotted at sea on 9 April, she was ordered back to Trincomalee so that she could be protected by the harbour's AA defences. The Japanese attacked 'Trinco' at 0730 on 9 April, but again found the British Eastern Fleet absent. Nevertheless, out of eleven Hurricane fighters scrambled by the RAF, nine were shot down, while the Japanese attacked airfields and destroyed aircraft on the ground, as well as attacking the harbour and shore installations, and sinking a merchantman.

On learning of the presence of *Hermes* and her escort, the destroyer HMAS *Vampire*, an attack by eighty aircraft was ordered and the carrier was soon sinking, with the destroyer crippled by explosions from her magazines. Fortunately, the aircraft carrier was without her aircraft that day and many of the crew were able to swim the short distance to the coast of Ceylon.

Somerville's reaction to these setbacks was pragmatic. He realized that he could not protect his battleships and ordered them to Kilindini (now Mombasa) in Kenya, out of reach of the Japanese, who had still failed to find the Eastern Fleet. He signalled to the

Admiralty that he was reduced to creating diversions and 'false scents, since I am now the poor fox'. It was a matter of good luck for the British that the Japanese had no plans to invade Ceylon, but that was scant comfort as they were determined to take Malaya, Singapore and Burma.

Having managed to keep his fleet intact, Somerville was promoted to admiral, although still on the retired list, in May 1942, and later reinstated on the active list. He remained with the Eastern Fleet until August 1944, when Admiral Sir Bruce Fraser, who had sunk the German battlecruiser *Scharnhorst* in the Battle of the North Cape the previous December, was sent to relieve him. By November, the balance of power was changed when Fraser was given command of the newly formed British Pacific Fleet. Somerville was then sent to Washington to head the Admiralty delegation and was promoted admiral of the fleet in May 1945.

He famously signalled Cunningham when 'ABC' received his second knighthood: 'Fancy twice a knight at your age!' When Somerville died in 1949, Cunningham wrote: 'He was a great sailor and a great leader: shrewd, imaginative, determined and far seeing.'

Somerville was undoubtedly one of the most imaginative and inspiring of the Second World War admirals, and the impact of Force H in the Mediterranean was far in excess of its size. His period in the Far East was less successful, simply because his forces were outnumbered by the Japanese and he did well to husband his resources, which was often a braver decision than that of fighting and losing ships and men that were hard to replace. He was an aggressive commander in warfare, but lacked that certain arrogance or madness that was a flaw in Halsey's make-up. He possessed a sense of humour and of humanity, and left to his own devices might well have resolved the problem of the French fleet in North Africa without bloodshed, and without the appalling impact it inflicted on Anglo-French relations.

Chapter 16

Sinking the *Bismarck*

Admiral of the Fleet Sir John 'Jack' Cronyn Tovey, RN (1885–1971)

Famous for commanding the action in which the German battleship *Bismarck* was sunk before she could start her career as a commerce raider, this was only a small part of Tovey's distinguished career.

Born on 7 March 1885, Tovey entered the Royal Navy at the age of fourteen as a cadet at Dartmouth. At the start of the First World War, he was serving in the cruiser HMS *Amphion* and later commanded the destroyer *Onslow* during the Battle of Jutland, for which he was awarded the DSO.

Always known to his men as 'Jack', the name by which he signed himself, between the two world wars, Tovey attended an Imperial Defence Course in 1927 at the Imperial Defence College at Greenwich, HMS *President*, and afterwards was Assistant Director of the Tactical School until 1929. He was then stationed ashore at Portsmouth until April 1930, with further shore postings following until, in 1932, he was appointed commanding officer of the battleship *Rodney*, which must have been a welcome break as the inter-war Navy had too few sea-going posts for ambitious officers. After leaving *Rodney*, Tovey was promoted first to commodore and then to rear admiral and served as a flag officer in the Mediterranean from 1935 before becoming naval ADC to the King. He then returned to *President* to take the senior officers' war course.

On the outbreak of war with Italy in June 1940, Tovey was Vice Admiral Light Forces and Second-in-Command of the British

Mediterranean Fleet under Cunningham, and was present in the early engagements with the Italian Navy, including the first at the Battle of Punta Stilo. In November 1940, he was appointed Commander-in-Chief, Home Fleet in the acting rank of Admiral, leaving the Mediterranean before the Fleet Air Arm attack on Taranto. As commander of the Home Fleet he had several clashes with Dudley Pound, the First Sea Lord, and Prime Minister Winston Churchill, both of whom were strongly inclined to interfere in operational matters.

The Home Fleet had an extensive operational area, relieved only by the availability of Force H in Gibraltar which could sally forth into the Atlantic as easily as it could enter the Mediterranean. The Home Fleet had to try to keep the Germans blockaded in the Baltic as far as possible, look after the convoys in the North Atlantic and the Bay of Biscay, and also, closer to home, protect the coastal convoys that were so important to Britain's communications at the time. It was the Home Fleet that fought the Battle of the Atlantic. In 1940, when the fear of a German invasion was rife in the United Kingdom, the Home Fleet was the first line of defence. It also had to keep the major ports clear, both for its own use and for merchant shipping, although there were five home commands for this, each with its own C-in-C.

Despite this vast responsibility, Tovey was still a vice admiral, although he was knighted in 1941. His most famous action was the hunt for the German battleship *Bismarck*, which, because of the small number of German battleships, was intended as a commerce raider since a major fleet action, such as a rerun of the Battle of Jutland, was out of the question for the German *Kriegsmarine* given its inferiority to the Royal Navy's large surface fleet. Along with her sister *Tirpitz*, which was still completing, *Bismarck* was one of the two most impressive German warships. On 18 May 1941, in company with the heavy cruiser *Prinz Eugen*, *Bismarck* left the German port of Gotenhafen for a commerce-raiding operation, code-named 'Operation Rhine Exercise'. Soon after leaving Norway, the German ships were detected by the Royal Navy and shadowed by two heavy cruisers, HMS *Suffolk* and *Norfolk*, which tracked the Germans using their radar. Meanwhile, Vice Admiral Holland, with the battlecruiser *Hood* and the new battleship *Prince of Wales*, made plans to bring the Germans to battle. In the Denmark Strait on 24 May, the four ships met in what was to be a classic naval engagement. Only minutes into the battle, *Hood* blew up with the loss of 1,500 men, leaving just three survivors – this was generally believed to have been caused by a shell from *Prinz Eugen* penetrating one of her magazines. The *Prince of Wales*, still not fully worked up, was forced to retire after taking several hits from the German ships. The engagement was not completely one-sided, however, as *Bismarck* was hit three times, breaking the connections from the forward fuel tanks. *Bismarck* was forced to part company with the *Prinz Eugen* and head for St Nazaire, with Brest as an alternative, in occupied France.

The cruisers *Norfolk* and *Suffolk* continued to track *Bismarck* and at 2130 GMT (2230 British Summer Time), nine Fairey Swordfish from HMS *Victorious* found the *Bismarck* and launched a torpedo attack from different directions, so that to avoid one torpedo meant putting the ship in the way of another. The attack was followed by a brief gunnery exchange with the *Prince of Wales*, but this was broken off in the fading light.

The following day, 25 May, Force H left Gibraltar under the command of Somerville, who had the aircraft carrier *Ark Royal*, the battlecruiser *Renown* and two cruisers. Contact with the *Bismarck* was lost early on 26 May, until a RAF Consolidated Catalina flying boat rediscovered the ship. Early in the afternoon, in rough weather, fifteen Swordfish took off from the *Ark Royal*, while the cruiser *Sheffield* was ordered to maintain contact with the German ship. Unaware of the *Sheffield*'s presence, the Swordfish attacked her by mistake and she was only saved by her high speed, prompt evasive action and faults in the torpedo magnetic detonators. Tovey closed in on the *Bismarck* with the battleships *King George V* and *Rodney*, accompanied by a destroyer escort. He signalled Somerville that unless *Bismarck*'s speed could be reduced, he would have to withdraw *King George V* to refuel and leave *Rodney* on her own.

At 1915, again in low cloud and poor visibility, a further strike by fifteen Swordfish was launched from *Ark Royal* and on this occasion the torpedoes were fitted with contact detonators which required a direct hit. Flying low, the Swordfish pressed home their attack. Two torpedoes struck the ship, one immediately after the other, jamming the rudder and sending the ship into a continuous turn. A night torpedo attack on the *Bismarck* by destroyers caused little further damage. On the morning of 27 May, *King George V* and *Rodney* engaged the *Bismarck* in a final gunnery duel. The two British ships hit the *Bismarck* several times and after ninety minutes she was burning fiercely. Two cruisers then torpedoed the stricken ship, after which she was abandoned. The cruiser *Devonshire* started to rescue survivors before one of them told his rescuers that U-boats were coming, causing the cruiser to move away, as a result of which just 115 men survived from *Bismarck*'s ship's company.

After the *Bismarck* action, Tovey resisted moves to court-martial the *Prince of Wales*'s captain, John Leach, and Frederick Wake-Walker, the Admiral commanding *Suffolk* and *Norfolk*, who had broken off the battle with *Bismarck* after *Hood* had been sunk. Tovey was appalled and a row ensued between him and his superior, Pound, Tovey stating that the two officers had acted correctly in the circumstances. He threatened to resign his position and appear at any court-martial as 'defendant's friend' and defence witness. No more was heard of the proposal.

Tovey was promoted to admiral in 1942, by which time the Arctic convoys were a new responsibility. During 1942–1943, he was responsible for the safety of the convoys operating from Iceland to Archangel and Murmansk, but serious differences of opinion emerged between him and the Admiralty, which he criticized for its defensive strategy of protecting the convoys, when he saw the priority as being to bring *Bismarck*'s sister ship, *Tirpitz*, which spent most of its life after completion lurking in Norwegian fiords, to battle. He felt that removing this menace to the convoys was more important and a better way of ensuring their protection. This overlooked the fact that the convoys suffered heavy losses, despite never encountering the battleship, from submarine and air attacks, but that, of course, is with hindsight. He was later appointed Commander-in-Chief of the Nore, one of the five main home commands, based on Chatham. In May 1943, he was promoted to admiral of the fleet, and in June he became Commander-in-Chief, the Nore, with responsibility for controlling the East Coast convoys and organizing minesweeping operations.

Tovey retired from active service in 1946, although as an admiral of the fleet he remained on the active list for life. In the same year, Tovey was ennobled and took the title of Baron Tovey, of Langton Matravers, a title which became extinct on his death on 17 January 1971.

Always loyal to his subordinates, Tovey was responsible for much of the painstaking but unglamorous work of the Home Fleet at the height of the war, when the fate of the United Kingdom hung in the balance.

Chapter 17

The Royal Netherlands Navy

Dutch involvement during the Second World War was severely hampered by a strong pacifist lobby between the two world wars, while the nation genuinely expected to be able to maintain the neutrality that had saved it during the First World War. Neither Germany nor Japan was prepared to respect Dutch neutrality. The nation was quickly overrun when the Germans struck west on 11 May 1940, and although the better-equipped forces in the Netherlands East Indies escaped this initial conflict, they too were no match for the Japanese in the weeks that followed the attack on Pearl Harbor. Japan, faced with an embargo by the USA and the UK, desperately needed the oil and rubber, and other natural resources, of the Dutch East Indies, vast in extent and abundant in what would be Japan's war requirements, but weakly defended.

The Royal Netherlands Navy in 1939 was small, with just 8,000 personnel. Even so, it was effectively divided into two, with a small force in home waters to protect the relatively short stretch of Dutch coastline, and with a larger force deployed in the colonies, of which by far the most important were the Netherlands East Indies, a vast archipelago stretching some 3,000 miles east to west, rich in oil and natural resources. Many of the junior ratings aboard ships serving in the Far East were locally recruited.

The heaviest and most powerful ships in the service were in fact nothing more than light cruisers, and of these there were 4, all with 5.9-inch guns as their main armament (the Washington Naval Treaty defined a light cruiser as having an armament of 6-inch guns); there were also: 12 destroyers; a gunnery training ship; 5 sloops; 2 coastal defence ships of which one had 9.5-inch guns, but was very old, and described by a contemporary naval commentator as 'no longer of much fighting value'; 11 torpedo boats, of which 8 dated from the First World War; 3 gunboats; 7 minelayers and 7 minesweepers; 24 submarines mainly deployed to the East Indies, with only what was effectively a training fleet for home waters; and a submarine depot ship. Of these, the only ones that could have made any difference were the submarines, especially since Japanese anti-submarine warfare had progressed little since the First World War.

After the Netherlands were overrun by the Germans in May 1940, the local legislative bodies in the Netherlands East Indies remained loyal to the Dutch government-in-exile, but given the difficulty in communications and the inability of the government-in-exile to provide any assistance or strategic direction, the territory became virtually self-governing. The People's Council in Batavia, now Jakarta, on Java, bravely protested in January 1941 when the Japanese referred to the territory as part of the Great Asia Co-Prosperity Sphere, and resisted Japan's demands for its agricultural produce, unrestricted fishing rights, prospecting for oil and minerals and free access to all of its ports. Nevertheless, it did boost its exports to Japan for a while until ordered by the government-in-exile in August 1941 to cease supplying oil to Japan.

On 20 December 1941, elements of the Japanese Sixteenth Army, based in the Philippines, attacked Dutch territory in Borneo, Celebes and the Moluccas. On 11 January 1942, Japan used her paratroops for the first time for an airborne assault on an airfield in the north of Celebes. The oilfields in Borneo were soon under Japanese control, as were the airfields. The paratroops were used for an assault on Palembang in southern Sumatra, taking the oilfields and the major oil refinery.

After the fall of Singapore, the Allies attempted to curb the Japanese advance through the Netherlands East Indies. In January 1941, the British Prime Minister, Winston Churchill, appointed the then General Sir Archibald Wavell, Commander-in-Chief of British and Empire forces in India, to head the newly created ABDA (American, British, Dutch, Australian) Command in the NEI. But ABDA was an improvised command and, as in France and the Low Countries, consisted of allies who had not trained or exercised together, and was not only weak in manpower, but suffered from a shortage of equipment – what there was was of little worth. The Japanese advance could not be stopped.

Just two air raids, on 19 and 27 February, destroyed most of the air power available to ABDA. On 19 February, twenty-three Imperial Japanese Navy Mitsubishi Zero fighters shot down a mixed bag of forty Allied fighters, most of which were obsolete types. By 27 February, ABDA was dissolved. On 8 March, the Dutch surrendered and 93,000 men of the Royal Netherlands East Indies Army surrendered, as did those of other Allied armies who could not get away. Nevertheless, the Japanese failed to take all of the NEI as Dutch New Guinea remained under government-in-exile control.

The major naval engagement of the campaign was the Battle of the Java Sea, which started on the afternoon of 27 February. This was not only the first major fleet action of the war in the Pacific, but also the last in which both the opposing fleets did not rely on carrier-borne aircraft, for the simple reason that the Allies did not have any available in the area.

Chapter 18

Outnumbered, Outgunned and Outclassed!

Rear Admiral Karel Willem Frederik Marie Doorman (1889–1942)

By far the most junior of the admirals covered in this book, Karel Doorman was in the unenviable position of commanding Dutch, and then Allied, forces in the Netherlands East Indies after his own country had been overrun by German forces in May 1940. Worse, he had to command an improvised small force, hardly a fleet, in a major action without having had prior experience.

Born in Utrecht in 1889, Rear Admiral Karel Doorman began training as a naval officer in 1906, attending the Dutch Royal Institute for the Navy at Den Helder, the major Dutch naval base, from which he graduated in 1910. Since the Netherlands remained neutral during the First World War, he saw no action. His first command was the newly commissioned minelayer *Prins van Oranje* in 1932. He later commanded a destroyer before a staff appointment from 1934 to 1937. He then returned to sea with a cruiser squadron which consisted of the light cruisers *Sumatra* and *Java* in 1938, which he took to the Netherlands East Indies. In June 1940, he took command of the Dutch naval units stationed in the Netherlands East Indies.

After Pearl Harbor, his forces struggled to halt the Japanese invasion forces, but were outnumbered and overwhelmed. The major clash between the Japanese and the Allies came at the Battle of the Java Sea, which began during the afternoon of 27 February 1942 with an initial engagement known to the Japanese as the Battle of Surabaya. Doorman commanded a mixed ABDA force of two heavy cruisers, the USS *Houston* and the British HMS *Exeter*, while he flew his flag in the light cruiser *De Ruyter*, which was accompanied by the *Java* and the Australian HMAS *Perth*, together with nine destroyers. The Japanese force, which had been escorting the invasion fleet, included two heavy cruisers, two light cruisers and fourteen destroyers.

On paper, it looked as if the two forces were more or less evenly balanced, but the Japanese ships had superior firepower, including the highly effective 'Long Lance' torpedo. There was little communication between the Allied ships, and Doorman, although in command, had no experience of commanding a fleet action. Nevertheless, he saw his duty as getting around the Japanese warships to attack and destroy the transports carrying the invasion force. His major mistake was that he had anticipated a night action, so had left his reconnaissance aircraft ashore, which proved to be a serious drawback at the outset.

The opposing forces conducted a long-range gunnery duel, in which *Exeter* was badly damaged and a Dutch destroyer exploded after being struck by a torpedo. A destroyer action around *Exeter* saw a British destroyer sunk, and another one was lost in a minefield later. The battle continued after dark, albeit with intermittent bouts of savage fighting rather than sustained combat, during which both the Dutch light cruisers were torpedoed and sunk, with Doorman killed. At this stage, the remaining Allied ships withdrew.

The Japanese landed in Java at Bantam Bay the following day, with the landings covered by five aircraft carriers, cruisers and destroyers. When the cruisers *Houston* and *Perth* attempted to escape through the Sunda Strait they ran into the invasion force, sinking four transports before being destroyed by two Japanese cruisers supported by a number of destroyers.

On 1 March, *Exeter*, escorted by two destroyers, attempted to escape westwards, but was attacked by four Japanese cruisers and aircraft from the aircraft carrier, *Ryujo*, finally destroying all Allied sea power in the NEI. The only ships to get away were four US destroyers which managed to reach Australia.

Chapter 19

The French Navy

Known officially to the French as the *Marine Nationale*, and generally referred to simply as the 'Marine' by the man in the street, in common with most major navies the French Navy had expanded far beyond its Washington Treaty limits during the 1930s as a naval race began with neighbouring Italy – French naval planners had worked on the basis that the most likely opponent in a future conflict would be Italy. Parts of the South of France had been Italian territory in the past and given the arguments advanced by Hitler, similar moves by Mussolini could not be ruled out.

In 1939, the French had the fourth largest navy in the world and although limited to 175,000 tons of shipping by the Washington Naval Treaty, it had gone far beyond this by 1940, when it had a total tonnage well in excess of 600,000 tons. The 'Marine' had to wield a worldwide presence, but it operated large squadrons rather than fleets, so the Atlantic Squadron equated to the British Atlantic, later Home, Fleet, and the same relationship could be applied to the Mediterranean Squadron and the British Mediterranean Fleet. The main home bases were Brest on the Atlantic coast and Toulon on the Mediterranean coast, but just as the British had Gibraltar and Malta, the French had Oran and Mers-el-Kebir in Algeria, Bizerta in Tunisia, Casablanca in French Morocco and Dakar in West Africa. At the time, Dakar had the only dry dock between Gibraltar and Cape Town, so it was of immense strategic value.

There were also ships stationed in the Caribbean, in the Indian Ocean at Madagascar, and in French Indo-China, as well as at Beirut in the Lebanon.

It was not a balanced fleet. Although strong in battleships and cruisers, and far stronger than Germany in 1939 and 1940 in terms

In the Battle of the Coral Sea, Admiral Frank Fletcher stopped the Japanese advance on Port Moresby. He was known as 'Black Jack' by his men. He is seen here in the uniform of a vice-admiral, not being promoted to four star rank until his retirement. (US Naval Historical Records Centre)

Even posing, Admiral William 'Bull' Halsey seems forceful. His drive and aggression were welcome, but he could also be impetuous and at Leyte Gulf left US forces exposed. (US Naval Historical Records Centre)

A less flattering photograph of Halsey on the admiral's bridge of the flagship. (US Naval Historical Records Centre)

Ernest King in front of a map showing the North Atlantic, which was his responsibility on the outbreak of war before he became the USN's Commander-in-Chief for the rest of the war. (US Naval Historical Records Centre)

Another photograph of King, a leader of undoubted abilities, although his Anglophobia did on occasion mar his judgement. Nevertheless, contrary to popular opinion in the UK, he never objected to the policy of 'Germany first'. (US Naval Historical Records Centre)

Away from the battles and the ships, diplomacy was also a part of an admiral's duties. Here in the front row seated, second left, is Admiral of the Fleet Sir Dudley Pound, First Sea Lord; fifth left is Admiral H.R. Stark, USN, Commanding US Naval Forces in Europe, something of a sinecure after he was blamed for the disaster at Pearl Harbor, and next to Winston Churchill. The back row has seventh left Vice Admiral Sir Bruce Fraser, at the time Third Sea Lord. (IWM A 8486)

Commander-in-Chief in the Pacific, Nimitz is shown here (left) in tropical kit. He assembled a group of exceptionally able naval commanders, and six months after Pearl Harbor, inflicted a crushing defeat on the Imperial Japanese Navy at Midway. (US Naval Historical Records Centre)

Raymond Spruance was engaged in some of the most important carrier campaigns and amphibious assaults during the war in the Pacific as commander of the US Third Fleet. (US Naval Historical Records Centre)

Known as 'ABC' to his officers, Sir Andrew Cunningham was Commander-in-Chief of the British Mediterranean Fleet when Italy entered the war in June 1940. Under his command, the Royal Navy inflicted a crushing blow on the Italian Navy at Taranto. He later became First Sea Lord, the Royal Navy's service head. (FAAM PERS/315)

Admiral Sir Bertram Ramsay was in command at Dover, familiar territory as he had been a member of the famous First World War Dover Patrol, and not only rescued the British Expeditionary Force from France in 1940, but also played a leading role in planning the Allied invasion of Normandy in 1944. (IWM A 23440)

One of the Royal Navy's most successful submarine commanders during the First World War, Admiral Sir Max Horton turned from poacher to gamekeeper as Commander-in-Chief Western Approaches, protecting Allied convoys from the German U-boats. (IWM A 17422)

Sir John Tovey achieved fame for commanding the action in which the German battleship *Bismarck* was sunk before she could start commerce raiding. (Author's collection)

Seen here with Winston Churchill in northern France at a ceremony during the winter of 1939-1940, the French *Amiral de Flotte* Jean Francois Darlan had strong pro-German and anti-British feelings, so the British did not believe him when he maintained that the French fleet would be scuttled rather than handed over to the Germans, but the promise was kept. (IWM HU 86167)

No admiral rose as far as Karl Dönitz, for not only did he become head of the German Navy during the war, but he succeeded Adolf Hitler as Führer after his suicide. (IWM No HU 40271))

Grand Admiral Erich Raeder commanded the German Navy at the outbreak of war, and under him the overly-ambitious Plan Z was formed, but he actually believed that U-boats would be ineffective in the face of British anti-submarine measures. (IWM No A 14906)

Kondo was Koga's successor as commander of the Combined Fleet, and has come to be regarded as the most successful Japanese admiral at sea for, although he took command when Japanese fortunes were on the wane, earlier he had been in command off Malaya and Singapore during the heady days of Japanese advances and victories. (US Naval Historical Records Centre)

If anyone was responsible for the failure to complete the task at Pearl Harbor, it was Chuichi Nagumo, who let the commander of the Combined Fleet, Yamamoto, down by failing to send a third and even a fourth wave of aircraft to attack. (US Naval Historical Records Centre)

Yamamoto was Commander-in-Chief of the Combined Fleet at the time of Pearl Harbor, but he had been Japanese naval attaché in Washington as a captain and knew about American industrial superiority. He is seen here with the US Naval Secretary at the time. (US Naval Historical Records Centre)

The globe might be behind his right shoulder, but as he pondered over plans, Yamamoto knew that Japan could not hope to win an all-out war with the United States. (US Naval Historical Records Centre)

of submarines and destroyers, it had just one elderly aircraft carrier, the 22,000-ton converted battleship *Bearn*, and a seaplane tender, although two carriers of modern design were under construction. As France had expected its most likely adversary to be Italy, the need for aircraft carriers was not so obvious.

For France, the lack of a carrier fleet was a weakness once it found itself at war with Germany rather than Italy: aircraft carriers would have been very useful off Norway, and indeed for a nation with a far-flung empire such ships were invaluable. In some ways, the Italian and French fleets were almost mirror images of one another, except for the single French aircraft carrier and a seaplane carrier, while the French had also tended to produce a very distinctive ship type of their own in the *contre-torpilleur*, a large destroyer, almost of light cruiser dimensions and armament.

Given the permitted tonnage, the *Marine Nationale* had preferred to spend the 1920s building submarines and fast torpedo craft rather than exercising its right to build large battleships or a fleet of aircraft carriers, although the fleet included two fine modern battlecruisers. Nevertheless, in the naval race that developed between France and her old ally Italy, as the new Mussolini regime took the lead in rearmament, some significant differences developed in the ships chosen. The Italians favoured large and elegant cruisers with a high speed, against which the French had developed the large super destroyer, the *contre-torpilleur*, which were fast, but short on range.

In 1939, the French fleet consisted of: an elderly aircraft carrier and 3 modernized battleships; 4 old battleships that were of no operational value; 2 new battlecruisers, *Dunkerque* and *Strasbourg*; 7 heavy cruisers; 12 light cruisers; 32 large *contre-torpilleur* destroyers and 38 other destroyers; a seaplane tender and no less than 77 submarines. Ashore, while some naval air squadrons had been transferred to the new autonomous air force, the *Armée de l'Air*, the French Navy had never, unlike the British, lost control of naval aviation between the wars, and even shore-based maritime-reconnaissance aircraft remained in naval hands.

It could fairly be said that the French, with an extensive empire, nevertheless had naval squadrons where the British had fleets, in the Atlantic and the Mediterranean. In fact, these were very large squadrons that could even be described as small fleets. The British Mediterranean Fleet and the French Mediterranean Squadron combined were certainly a match for the Italian Navy. The real difference was that one was a traditional continental power and the other an island nation.

With their main trade routes being across the Mediterranean, the French Navy was not in action as soon as the Royal Navy. Both nations participated in the Norwegian campaign, initially covering the movement of 13,000 British and 12,500 French troops to Norway. The French Marine Nationale did not enjoy the spectacular successes experienced by the British, with the sinking of the German light cruiser *Konigsberg* by shore-based naval aircraft and then the two battles at Narvik, which accounted in total for a dozen German destroyers. Nevertheless, Admiral Derrien commanded the French naval contribution from the modern 7,600-ton light cruiser *Montcalm*, while the 5,900-ton light cruiser *Emile Bertin*, and the auxiliary cruisers *El Djezair*, *El Mansour* and *El Kantara*, which were converted merchantmen, escorted convoys with men and supplies, and suffered constant Luftwaffe attack. In fact the two navies were working well together, prompting the offical historians of the French navy, Auphan and Mordal, to write:

> Never in history had there been more cordial relations than those established in the battle area off Norway. Not merely was this collaboration in the technical field, but the far more important field of human relations – the spirit of *camaraderie* between the French officers and their brethren of the Royal Navy. Whether they sailed with the Home Fleet on escort duty off the fjords of Norway, French and British ships, side by side, learned to sustain and to parry the fierce attacks of Germany's formidable air force.

The French also suffered losses, losing the 2,400-ton super destroyer, *Bison*, while in one of those accidents that add to the losses inflicted by combat, another super destroyer, the Aigle-class *Maille-Breze*, also of 2,400 tons, was lost when one of its own torpedoes blew up while she was alongside at Greenock, on the Clyde.

Given the geography of Europe and the strategy adopted by Germany, there was nothing the French Navy could do to prevent German victory in the Battle of France in 1940. The Germans wanted the French Navy as their own was markedly inferior and plans to create a large fleet, known in Germany as Plan Z, were cancelled by Hitler on the outbreak of war in Europe except for ships that could be completed quickly. Germany didn't get the French ships, apart from a small number of submarines in 1942, but they got the bases, and from these their ability to wreak unrestricted submarine warfare against the British was boosted as no longer did the submarines have to sail from Germany, around the north of Scotland out into the Atlantic. From 1940, the Bay of Biscay was on the doorstep, and the wider reaches of the Atlantic just beyond. Meanwhile, the bulk of the French Navy was outside the grip of the Germans, with much of it at Toulon, in unoccupied Vichy France, and almost all of the rest at its bases in the Mediterranean, especially at Mers-el-Kebir and Alexandria, which it shared with the British Mediterranean Fleet, with a few ships at Dakar in French West Africa. There were a few that had escaped to the British naval bases of Portsmouth and Plymouth.

As France fell, the French Navy was undertaking acceptance trials of one new 35,000-ton battleship, *Richelieu*, and as surrender grew closer, all seaworthy units of the fleet were moved from their French ports, with the other new battleship, *Jean Bart*, completing at St Nazaire, being moved, even though uncompleted, to Casablanca.

What amounted to almost a Diaspora of the French Navy took place. Two old battleships, together with eight destroyers and three submarines, accompanied by a number of smaller vessels, made their way to the major British naval bases at Portsmouth and Plymouth. The two 26,500-ton battlecruisers, *Dunkerque* and *Strasbourg*, both fine modern ships, with two older battleships, six destroyers and a seaplane carrier, sailed to the naval base in Algeria at Mers-el-Kebir, near Oran. Six cruisers went to Algiers itself and many of the remaining submarines went to Bizerta, also in Algeria. The French squadron in the Mediterranean, under Vice Admiral Godfroy, which had been working closely with the British Mediterranean Fleet under Admiral Sir Andrew Cunningham, remained at Alexandria. This force had a battleship, four cruisers and three destroyers, which was a somewhat unbalanced formation as a far larger destroyer force would have been expected. Many smaller warships moved to Toulon, while there were also smaller vessels in the Caribbean and in French Indo-China, as well as a number of ships at Dakar.

The big problem was that although the French had promised to scuttle their ships rather than surrender them to the Germans, the British did not believe them and could not risk believing them. This was the crux of the problem. The British were scared that the French fleet would be taken and used against them by the Germans, but the Germans probably couldn't have made use of them as Hitler was soon to become disillusioned with surface warships, while the Germans lacked the fuel and munitions to sustain a large surface fleet at sea.

Meanwhile, in London, on 30 June, the Admiralty received a copy of a message telegraphed from the French Admiralty to Admiral Odend'hal at Portsmouth, advising him that the Italians had permitted the stationing of the French fleet at Toulon and in North Africa, with half crews aboard. The telegram continued to say that the Vichy authorities were optimistic about obtaining a similar agreement from the Germans, and ordered Odend'hal to insist on the British Government releasing both merchant and naval vessels in British ports. In fact, while the Germans did agree, there was no time to let Odend'hal know. What did happen was that the following day, both the Germans and the British demanded that they should have control over the French warships, with the Germans insisting that all French warships should be returned to France, or the armistice conditions would be changed.

The British immediately implemented plans to seize all French ships in British ports, with those anchored outside being called into port on a number of false, but seemingly real, pretexts.

At Portsmouth and Plymouth, 'Operation Catapult', the seizure of French warships, was implemented during the early hours of 3 July. British sailors and marines swarmed aboard the French ships, with armed men stationed at every hatch and in every passage, as British naval officers armed with pistols confronted the French commanding officers, demanding that the ships be handed over to the Royal Navy, while their crews would be detained. It was explained that the crews would shortly be taken ashore, after which they could either be repatriated to French territory, meaning North Africa, or could remain in the UK to continue to fight against the Germans.

In Alexandria, Cunningham had every sympathy with his French counterpart, Vice Admiral Godfroy, who knew that he was under orders from his Admiralty to sail, but was trying to confirm that the order was authentic. While de Gaulle was already in the United Kingdom intent on establishing the Free French forces, this move was not universally accepted by all French émigrés at this early stage of the war, with the future policies of the Vichy regime not known. After all, the Germans had not occupied the whole of France, and

French sailors did not wish to be classed as traitors. They were also still being paid.

In North Africa, after the fall of France, there were two elderly French battleships at Mers-el-Kebir, plus the modern battlecruisers *Dunkerque* and *Strasbourg*, as well as six large destroyers of the *contre-torpilleur* type, with seven smaller destroyers and four submarines at Oran. Since the declaration of war, the French Navy had been busy escorting convoys between metropolitan France and Algieria, seen as vulnerable to Italian attack. *Dunkerque* had only recently returned to Mers-el-Kebir, having visited Gibraltar.

After those French warships that had fled to British ports had been seized on 3 July, Force H was despatched to Mers-el-Kebir and Somerville attempted to open negotiations with the local French naval commander, Admiral Marcel Gensoul. This was easier said than done. In the confusion following the collapse of France, Gensoul was in a difficult position, not knowing the policies of his government and whether or not his country would expect him to continue the war or accept surrender and, perhaps, neutrality. He had a substantial part of his country's naval forces entrusted to his care and some excellent bases. Somerville's emissary was refused a meeting with Gensoul and so the negotiations had to begin in writing.

From this moment on, the die was cast. As described in Chapter 15, Somerville eventually had to open hostilities to try to destroy the French ships in North Africa, while at Alexandria, Cunningham, as we have seen, was able to use a show of strength combined with diplomacy.

Chapter 20

An Enigma

Admiral Jean François Darlan (1881–1942)

Between the two world wars, Darlan took much of the credit for building a modern French Navy. His achievement was recognized in 1939 when he was promoted to become France's first five-star admiral of the fleet, *amiral de la flotte*, the most senior in the service and a rank created especially for him, and put in command of the *Marine Nationale*.

Born in Nérac, Lot-et-Garonne, on 7 August 1881, Francois Darlan attended the *École Navale* from which he graduated in 1902. He commanded an artillery battery during the First World War, during which the French Navy, the *Marine Nationale*, saw little action at sea. He remained in the French Navy after the war and was promoted to rear admiral in 1929, and vice admiral in 1932. Darlan was made an admiral and Chief of Staff in 1936. In 1939 he was promoted to *amiral de la flotte* and given command of the entire French Navy.

After Paris was occupied in June 1940, Darlan supported the Premier and Head of State, Marshal Henri Philippe Pétain, for which he was rewarded by retaining his post as Minister of the Navy. He quickly ordered most of the fleet still in French home waters to French North Africa, which kept the ships out of German and Italian hands at first, but did nothing to quell British suspicions that it might be transferred later.

In February 1941, Darlan replaced Pierre Laval as Pétain's deputy. He was also named Minister for the Interior, Defence and Foreign

Affairs, making Darlan the *de facto* head of the Vichy Government. In January 1942, he took control of a number of other government posts.

Darlan has to be something of an enigma. British distrust of him was not without foundation. He was one of those Frenchmen who harboured strong Anglophobe tendencies and attitudes, and after the French surrender he also wanted a more equal relationship between France and Germany. He was as much a collaborator as Laval, and Darlan even proposed a political alliance between French Vichy forces and Nazi Germany through the Paris Protocols. Yet, at Dunkirk, his orders to Abrial, the French Admiral commanding the French warships providing assistance, and also the ground defence of the port, had been that the forces protecting the evacuation were to join the evacuation leaving as small a rearguard force as possible. French troops were expected to ensure that as many as possible of the British and Free Polish forces got away, before they could follow them. When the surrender happened and the German terms were known, Darlan proposed that the fleet should be allowed to proceed to North African ports. This was unacceptable to the British as they feared that the ships could then be seized by the Italians, and they demanded that the fleet should be removed from the Mediterranean, but Darlan, by this time in Bordeaux, the temporary seat of Government before it finally settled on Vichy, maintained that the French fleet would never be surrendered to the Germans or the Italians. Earlier, he had refused to send the fleet to the UK while French troops were still fighting implying that the situation would be different once France surrendered.

At the time of the armistice, Darlan went to great lengths to assure the United Kingdom that the French fleet, the *Marine Nationale*, would not fall into German hands, even ordering commanding officers to scuttle their ships should the Germans attempt to take them. Unfortunately, the British didn't trust Darlan, and seized or sank whatever ships they could, except at Alexandria.

The British attitude seemed to be justified for in May 1941, Darlan offered Hitler the use of French bases in Syria, and after a visit to Berchtesgarten he returned to France with plans for joint Franco-German operations in the Middle East. Pétain refused to agree to these proposals, which were undoubtedly of great appeal to the Germans, who had been unable to encourage their First World War ally, Turkey, to join them.

Meanwhile, Pétain had sacked Laval, but his successor, Pierre Flandin, did not meet with German approval, and neither did the next Vice-Premier, none other than Darlan. In April 1942, Pétain was therefore forced to reinstate Laval, who could not prevent the Germans from occupying Vichy France in November 1942. The problem was that the Germans had also become suspicious of what they regarded as Darlan's opportunism. In April, Darlan was made to surrender the majority of his responsibilities back to Laval, whom the Nazis considered more trustworthy, although Darlan retained the post of Commander of the French Armed Forces.

In the meantime, after the surrender of France until November 1942, the surviving units of the French Navy had been used to protect Vichy convoys between France and her North African colonies, an ever-present reminder to the British that here was a great naval asset that could be used against them. While the United States was still neutral, Darlan used the US embassy in Paris as an intermediary to warn the British not to interfere with French convoys, while reassuring the United States that the French colonies and the French Navy would not be offered to the Germans. Indeed, once the United States started to become more overt in its support of the United Kingdom, Darlan secretly offered the United States Navy free passage through the waters of France's Caribbean territories.

Darlan was in Algiers, visiting his son who was in hospital with polio, when the Allies invaded French North Africa on 8 November 1942. Initially, he assumed command of Vichy forces and resisted the British and American invasion forces, but after negotiations with Vichy and with the Americans, he surrendered his forces on 10 November, and agreed to work for the Allies, becoming High Commissioner for French North Africa. Undoubtedly his earlier courting of the United States had not been in vain, and indeed many senior US officers as well as the Government favoured Darlan to de Gaulle. Nevertheless, Darlan's appointment was short-lived, as he was assassinated on 24 December by a young Frenchman.

In fact, as it turned out, Darlan's assurances to the Allies were to be kept and the French fleet was scuttled, disabled or, in the case of a few ships, escaped. The official reason for the German occupation of the remainder of France was the Allied invasion of French North Africa, but even more important than this was the realization that if such a senior member of the Vichy regime as Darlan could, within two days, transfer his allegiance to the Allies, the entire regime could not be trusted.

Darlan's negotiation for a ceasefire after the invasion of North Africa had placed the Vichy regime in an awkward position, and in vain did they attempt to persuade the Germans that Darlan's actions were illegal. Despite Germany's heavy commitments on the Eastern Front, Hitler ordered the occupation of Vichy France on 11 November, sending large numbers of troops into the area. After difficult negotiations with the Vichy authorities, Hitler then ordered the seizure of the French fleet at Toulon on 19 November. At this time, French warships in Toulon numbered around eighty, with a total tonnage of 200,000, around a third of the 1940 tonnage, including the 22,500-ton battleship *Provence* and the two modern battlecruisers *Dunkerque* and *Strasbourg*. It took until 27 November before German forces finally moved to seize the vessels, encountering armed resistance from French forces that allowed five submarines to escape, and, even more important, gave the French crews aboard the warships time to scuttle them. These ships seem to have been fully or nearly fully manned, but there were others that had been decommissioned under the armistice terms and which simply had skeleton crews aboard. Apart from these, there were also minesweepers and other minor naval vessels and auxiliaries.

Darlan's qualities as a fighting admiral are impossible to quantify as he never commanded a fleet at sea under wartime conditions, although as mentioned earlier, the *Marine Nationale* did cooperate closely with the Royal Navy during the Norwegian campaign. It is also important to recognize the problems facing someone whose country has been overrun by a foreign power. The wholesale transfer of the French fleet to the Royal Navy in 1940 would undoubtedly have helped the British by giving additional ships for convoy protection and other duties, albeit at the cost of having to produce ammunition for the peculiar gun calibres favoured by the French in many of their warships. The question is, however, would all of the crews have supported this move? Many Frenchmen did indeed serve with the Free French forces, but many others were more interested in returning home to be with their families.

It would have needed a political decision for the country to continue fighting alongside the United Kingdom, operating from its colonies, especially those in North Africa, for the French armed forces to have settled in happily alongside those of the British.

This would have been a difficult decision to take given that the Germans had left much of France unoccupied at first, even allowing a small army of 100,000 men to continue and the Vichy regime being allowed to use warships to escort its convoys across the Mediterranean.

Darlan was undoubtedly opportunist, anti-British and even pro-German. Described by his contemporaries as 'impassive' and 'difficult to read', Darlan was unpopular with the Allies, who regarded him as pompous. He even asked Eisenhower to provide 200 Coldstream Guards and Grenadier Guards for the commemoration of Napoleon's greatest victory at Austerlitz in 1815. On the other hand, the same accusation could be levelled at another Frenchman, General de Gaulle, the head of the Free French, who was also extremely difficult to work alongside.

The question will always remain unanswered as to why the Germans kept Darlan at arm's length and did not encourage a closer relationship that could, eventually, have given them the prize of the French fleet. It could have been due to Hitler's increasing dissatisfaction with the *Kriegsmarine*'s surface fleet and what he saw as its poor performance, but another reason could have been both the increasing shortage of manpower in Germany and also the persistent problem over fuel supplies. German arrogance meant that they wanted those whom they had defeated to feel the fact and they did not want to share victory with those whom they regarded as racially inferior. They even had growing contempt for their Italian allies, whom they daubed 'the harvest hands' for coming into the war when the Battle of France was almost over and victory certain.

Chapter 21
The German Navy

The Treaty of Versailles in 1919 had determined that the then *Reichsmarine*, the post-First World War German Navy, would be small and primarily designed to provide coastal protection. It was the London Naval Treaty of 1935 that paved the way for the reconstruction of the German Navy, granting Germany a total tonnage equivalent to 35 per cent of that of the Royal Navy, although within this figure, what can only be regarded as an oversight or collective memory loss allowed Germany a larger percentage of submarines, with the option of parity with the Royal Navy! Before this, the name of the service had been changed from *Reichsmarine*, 'State Navy', to *Kriegsmarine*, 'War Navy', as a foretaste of German intentions. The Germans even managed to build extra ships once new tonnage was permitted, ordering the battlecruiser *Gneisenau* secretly.

Alone amongst the navies of the main combatants, the *Kriegsmarine* was weaker in 1939 than had been the *Kaiserliche Marine*, or Imperial German Navy, in 1914. That the London Naval Treaty accepted the prospect of the *Kriegsmarine* having parity in submarines with the Royal Navy even surprised many in Germany at the time; it also led others to believe that war with the United Kingdom was not imminent, with the commanders of the *Kriegsmarine* expecting that war would not break out until after 1942. The Luftwaffe had enjoyed priority in rearmament, then the German Army, but only belatedly did significant reconstruction appear imminent for the *Kriegsmarine*, but it was too late – crippled by shortages of raw materials and labour, its shipbuilding plans were dramatically cut back the day war was declared, with only those ships nearing completion exempted. The result was that Germany went to war with just 2 elderly battleships plus 2 modern ships, *Bismarck* and *Tirpitz* still building, 2 battlecruisers, *Scharnhorst* and *Gneisenau*, as well as 3 armoured cruisers, known to the British press as 'pocket battleships', and 3 heavy cruisers, 6 light cruisers, 22 destroyers and 20 torpedo boats and small destroyers, as well as a force of just 59 submarines, many of them small and confined either to coastal waters or to training duties.

The most obvious deficiency with the *Kriegsmarine* was its lack of aircraft carriers and the small number of destroyers. Its surface force was also vastly inferior in numbers. Nevertheless, the fall of France meant that E-boats were within hit-and-run range of British ports and coastal shipping, while the U-boats no longer had to leave German waters and take the hazardous passage north of Scotland to reach their hunting grounds in the North Atlantic and the Bay of Biscay.

It was not meant to be this way. A succession of plans had in fact been drawn up by the naval staff, starting with Plan X, which was in turn superseded by Plan Y, and then ultimately came Plan Z.

Plan Z was Raeder's dream. This was the plan for the big battleships and aircraft carriers, armoured cruisers and other vessels, including 249 U-boats. Formulated in late 1938, it received Hitler's approval in January 1939, and was due to be completed by 1947, although the bulk of it would be completed by 1945. The initial plan included: 4 aircraft carriers, 6 large battleships known as the H-class and three battlecruisers, the O-class; no less than 12 Kreuzer P-class  *Panzerschiff*; 2 Hipper-class heavy cruisers, which would be *Seydit*z and *Lutzow*; 2 improved M-class light cruisers; and 6 Spahkeuzer-class large destroyers, as well as 249 U-boats.

In fact, the Plan ultimately envisaged that by 1947, in addition to the above there would be another 4 aircraft carriers, albeit of a smaller type than the *Graf Zeppelin*, up to 12 battlecruisers and 8 heavy cruisers, 24 light cruisers, 36 light cruisers, 70 destroyers and 78 torpedo-boats; there would also be 162 Atlantic-type U-boats, 60 coastal U-boats and 27 special-purpose U-boats, almost certainly either minelayers or supply boats. The then head of the U-boat arm, Dönitz, started to lobby for a stronger U-boat arm, creating tension between himself and his superior, Raeder, but eventually Plan Z was amended to allow 300 U-boats.

The problem was that Germany did not have the shipbuilding capacity for this work, let alone the necessary materials. There had been no sustained new construction of major warships for many years and so the slipways were simply not available. Worse still, the fuel needed exceeded the total fuel consumption of Germany in 1938.

Construction had already started on the first German aircraft carrier, the *Graf Zeppelin*, in 1936, and after she was launched in 1938, plans were laid to begin work on a second ship, the *Peter Strasser*, but this never happened. During 1939, orders were placed for carrier versions of the Messerschmitt Bf109 fighter and the Junkers Ju87 Stuka dive-bomber, designated as the Bf109T and Ju87C. In mid-1939, the two battleships *Bismarck* and *Tirpitz* were both launched, and then the keels were laid for the first three of the giant H-class battleships.

Nevertheless, the Luftwaffe, or to be precise the Minister for Air, Hermann Göring, would not relinquish control of any aspect of military aviation. This was at a time when the British had realized their mistake in combining all service aviation in the Royal Air Force and were returning naval aviation, the Fleet Air Arm, to the Royal Navy. The lack of any earlier German interest in aircraft carriers also meant that the *Graf Zeppelin*'s design was obsolete even before she was launched. The best comparison was with the British Courageous-class and the French *Bearn*. Work never started on the second German carrier, the *Peter Strasser*, but at one stage, as a panic measure, conversion of a liner and two warships to aircraft carriers was considered before the idea was quietly dropped.

The problem in dealing with German admirals of the time was that they had few opportunities to show their abilities during the war. With the *Kriegsmarine* so weak other than in submarines, and even then that did not happen until well into the war, a major naval engagement with an Allied navy was out of the question. In fact, on the Führer's orders, Germany's major ships were harboured, literally as well as figuratively, and only allowed out to sea when there was no danger of them encountering either British carrier-borne aircraft or a superior British battle fleet. The fact that the crew of the Navy's second battleship, *Tirpitz*, spent most of the war aboard the ship hiding in a Norwegian fjord shows what a waste of manpower, scarce raw materials and opportunity these ships were. The most that could be said for it was that her presence was something those British naval planners coordinating the convoys to and from the Soviet Union could not overlook. She also caused the Fleet Air Arm and the RAF to spend much time, fuel, aircraft, munitions and lives in attempting her destruction, which was difficult given the high and steep sides of the fjords, and the heavy AA defences deployed around her. Nevertheless, using large 'earthquake' bombs, the RAF's No. 617 'Dambusters' Squadron eventually capsized the *Tirpitz*.

In 1939, the *Kriegsmarine* had 122,000 personnel, rising to 190,000 the following year, and peaking at 810,000 in 1944, after which its manpower figures plummeted as men were transferred to the Army to defend the Reich. In 1943, the year when war had originally been expected to break out, it had 780,000 men.

The *Kriegsmarine* lost 48,904 men due to enemy action, and 11,125 through other causes. Another 25,259 were wounded, while a staggering 100,256 were listed as missing.

Chapter 22

Advocate of Unrestricted U-boat Warfare

Grand Admiral Karl Dönitz (1891–1980)

No naval officer in any of the combatant nations during the Second World War rose as far as Dönitz, who ultimately became Hitler's successor as Führer. By the time he took over on 30 April 1945, the post had lost all of its authority and Germany was within days of surrender.

Dönitz was born in 1891 in Grunau-bei-Berlin, a suburb of the German capital. He joined the German Navy in 1910 as an officer cadet and in 1913 he was a midshipman aboard the light cruiser *Breslau* in the Mediterranean, with the ship acting as escort for the battlecruiser *Goeben*. Both ships were enforcing a blockade of the Balkans and were able to use the facilities of the British Mediterranean Fleet's main base of Malta. They were back the following year and *Breslau* narrowly missed being interned in Malta by the Royal Navy, but escaped and with *Goeben* was transferred to the Turkish Navy with her crew. Eventually, Dönitz returned to Germany and joined the still new U-boat arm, rising to command a succession of submarines in the Mediterranean. He was one of the pioneers of the tactic of a surface night attack, and in October 1918 he penetrated a destroyer escort unobserved to sink a merchantman.

In post-war Germany, he was one of the small band of young officers handpicked to remain in the much-reduced *Reichsmarine*, which itself had been riven by mutinies and Bolshevik uprisings. The Treaty of Versailles not only limited the size of the German Navy, but also banned U-boats. The Germans nevertheless immediately started planning for the future rebuilding of a U-boat arm, and Dönitz was posted to a torpedo-boat unit, which practised U-boat tactics, including the night surface attack. German designers had their submarines built abroad, particularly in the Netherlands, and won contracts from a number of nations, including Turkey, for their craft, and helped their client states with training.

Dönitz was the lucky recipient of a travel award instituted by the post-Versailles German President, Hindenburg, and chose to visit the British and Dutch colonies in the Far East. Leaving Germany in February 1933, he was away when the Nazis began their brutal campaign against their enemies, but Dönitz himself was also considered by some as being unbalanced. One of those who viewed him in this way was Canaris, under whom he had served during the early 1930s, a view shared by the US Consul General in Berlin. Even his own writings suggest that he was also something of a fantasist, and not only exaggerated his wartime actions, but also claimed to have such a high reputation that he was known to senior British commanders.

On his return to Germany, he met Hitler for the first time in 1934 after being appointed commanding officer of the light cruiser *Emden*, about to depart on a foreign cruise. While he was away, Hitler ordered Germany's first post-First World War U-boats in February 1935, and unknown to himself, Dönitz was selected as head of the new U-boat service, initially as commander of the 1st Flotilla. Despite recording that he was unenthusiastic at the prospect of a return to U-boats, during the time that passed between taking up his appointment in 1935 and the outbreak of war in Europe in September 1939, he worked hard to develop U-boat tactics and pressed for a substantial U-boat force. When conducting naval exercises, he was always careful to be with the fleet at sea, although usually in a surface vessel which he used as his command ship. By the outbreak of the Second World War, he was holding the rank of commodore.

The London Naval Agreement had conceded to Germany parity in submarine numbers with the Royal Navy, which at the time meant seventy U-boats, but by September 1939 only fifty-six had been built, and of these only twenty-two were of a size that could operate in the North Atlantic. While Hitler immediately banned the construction of further major surface units, and only allowed completion of those that could be commissioned within a year or two, Dönitz argued that a country short of manpower and raw materials should concentrate on submarine warfare in the hope of blockading the British Isles. While he was undoubtedly right in pressing for a U-boat campaign, not everyone in the German Navy agreed with him. Indeed, many senior officers felt that the day of the submarine was past and that British countermeasures such as Asdic made submarines vulnerable, and a waste of manpower and other resources. But Dönitz was realistic and logical enough to ensure that his U-boats knew when and how to attack and how to track a convoy.

Dönitz was a fervent admirer of Hitler, but there was friction with Raeder, the head of the Navy. Recognizing German naval weakness, neither man wanted war in 1939, and within minutes of the uncoded signal being sent to all units of the Royal Navy, 'Total Germany', on 3 September 1939, those around Dönitz saw his shock as he left the room briefly to prepare a message of encouragement to his staff.

It was Dönitz who planned and ordered the attack on the British battleship *Royal Oak* in the anchorage of Scapa Flow on Orkney, in October 1939, which was an early blow to British morale. For this, he was promoted immediately to rear admiral, or *Konteradmiral*, later in 1940 to vice admiral, or *Vizeadmiral*, and in 1942 to *Admiral*. During this time, he organized the growing number of U-boats, which he closely controlled and operated in wolf packs, causing severe Allied losses mainly in the North Atlantic and Bay of Biscay, but he also succeeded in causing heavy losses in the Mediterranean. Nevertheless, as the 'Atlantic Gap', the section of mid-ocean beyond air cover, steadily closed, the constant reporting of weather and ship movements by the U-boats and the orders radioed from Germany – broken by Ultra intelligence after the German Enigma codes were captured – worked against the U-boats and losses began to rise alarmingly. Construction of new boats continued apace and overall 1,168 were built by the time the war ended in 1945.

The surface fleet enjoyed no such success, although a chance shell fired by the heavy cruiser *Prinz Eugen* sank the pride of the Royal Navy, the British battlecruiser *Hood*, in spring 1941. When the battleship *Bismarck*, one of only two modern capital ships operated by the *Kriegsmarine* during the war years, was sunk in May with the loss of most of her crew, Hitler ordered that his major surface units be withdrawn from the Atlantic and severe restrictions were placed on their use. Worse was to follow in December 1942 when the

Panzerschiff (known to the British media as a 'pocket battleship') *Lutzow* and the cruiser *Admiral Hipper* failed to destroy a British convoy and the Battle of the Barents Sea developed, as a result of which Hitler demanded the decommissioning of all major surface units. Raeder resigned in protest.

Hitler promoted Dönitz as Commander-in-Chief of the German Navy in January 1943, with the rank of grand admiral, or *Grossadmiral*. Although there was no need for him to do so, Dönitz decided to continue as Commander-in-Chief of the U-boats.

Dönitz is generally regarded as having been promoted far beyond his abilities and experience at the time. He failed to reverse the fortunes of the U-boats in the Battle of the Atlantic and played a part in the mishandling of Axis naval forces in the Mediterranean. He has been described as having many hare-brained schemes, possibly a further manifestation of his being mentally unbalanced.

Throughout this increasingly desperate period for Germany, Dönitz remained loyal to Hitler, and after Hitler and Göring fell out, he was selected as Hitler's successor. He ruled Germany as Führer from 30 April 1945 until he was arrested by the Allies on 22 May. Before this, he negotiated the German surrender, but only after first attempting to ensure that his men remained at their posts, fighting to the death if necessary. Field police were given authority to hang any deserters they found.

During the Nuremberg war crimes trials, he was tried for issuing the order to sink the British liner *Laconia*, 250 miles north-east of Ascension Island, on 12 September 1942, with many of the victims being Italian prisoners of war. He was acquitted, but given a ten-year sentence for two other charges, which he survived to be released and spent a quiet retirement.

Dönitz lacked both judgement and experience, while he had never commanded a wartime fleet at sea. He was in fact a theorist and no doubt this fed his fantasies. He was right about the U-boats, but the wolf pack system was controlled centrally and this was its undoing as improved countermeasures and Ultra intelligence enabled the Allies to find and hunt down the U-boats, as well as diverting convoys away from the U-boat lines.

His admiration for Hitler meant that the Führer was unchallenged when he refused to send the major surface units to sea, and perhaps Dönitz himself felt that these ships were better held as a threat than actually used. In fact, the ships suffered from considerable weaknesses. The two battlecruisers, *Scharnhorst* and *Gneisenau*, were commissioned with just 11-inch guns, and although these were meant to be replaced later with 15-inch guns, this never happened. Larger-calibre guns not only provided a bigger punch, but also enjoyed a longer range. Without the higher-calibre weapons, such ships could have been destroyed by British battleships with their 14-inch, 15-inch and, even, in the case of *Rodney* and *Nelson*, 16-inch guns before they could even get the British ships within range. Perhaps such ships were better off in port.

Chapter 23

Builder of the *Kriegsmarine*

Grand Admiral Erich Johann Albert Raeder (1876–1960)

Erich Raeder was the very model of the Prussian naval officer, even more so than Dönitz. Beginning his career at a time when a still newly united Germany was intent on becoming not just the foremost continental power, but a world power as well, he lived through the period when the Kaiser declared that the German Army and Navy were on an equal standing, rather than the former being the 'senior' service.

Raeder was born on 24 April 1876, into a middle-class family in Wandsbek, a district of Hamburg, Germany. His father was a headmaster. He joined the *Kaiserliche Marine*, German Imperial or Royal Navy, in 1894 and rapidly rose in rank, becoming one of Tirpitz's staff officers before becoming Chief of Staff for Franz von Hipper in 1912. He served in this position during the First World War as well as in seagoing posts, taking part in the Battle of the Dogger Bank in 1915 and the Battle of Jutland in 1916. Like Dönitz, Raeder was one of those few officers selected to remain in the much-reduced post-First World War *Reichsmarine*. He continued to rise steadily in the peacetime Navy, becoming a *Konteradmiral*, rear admiral, in 1922 and a *Vizeadmiral*, vice admiral, in 1925. In October 1928, Raeder was promoted to *Admiral* and made Commander-in-Chief of the *Reichsmarine*, the Weimar Republic Navy, or *Oberbefehlshaber der Reichsmarine*.

The First World War actions had made a considerable impact upon him, and his ambition was to create a new High Seas Fleet that could fight and win a second Jutland, ensuring that it emerged victorious over the Royal Navy beyond all doubt. It must have rankled with him that Jutland, which on paper was a German victory, with the Royal Navy losing more ships and more men, was often presented as a British victory in that the High Seas Fleet never again sought an engagement with the Grand Fleet.

As a rear admiral, one of his duties included running training courses for staff officers. Nevertheless, despite holding this important role, he was also effectively an embarrassment to his superiors and had been moved aside. He had been close to von Trotha, who had been head of the Navy at the end of the war and had intended to send his ships on a 'death ride', rather than accept surrender. Later, on 21 June 1919, he issued the order to scuttle the ships interned at Scapa Flow. Von Trotha was one of the men who inspired the leaders of the infamous Kapp *putsche*, when Wolfgang Kapp, a Prussian official, had led a naval *Freikorps* in a march on Berlin late on 12 March 1919, protesting over Allied demands for 900 'war criminals' to be placed on trial, with those named ranging from the Kaiser and his ministers, through senior officers such as von Trotha, down to individual U-boat commanding officers. The German Army refused to confront the protesters, and the Government fled from Berlin.

In an atmosphere of chaos and anarchy, ratings revolted and arrested their officers at many naval bases, while the Government, which had re-established itself in Stuttgart, called for a general strike. The situation was only saved by Kapp resigning during the general strike and the Government was then able to reassert its authority.

Raeder was an able and very correct officer, a disciple and devotee of Tirpitz, who saw the future of the German people as being on the oceans, the policy of *Weltpolitik*.

Raeder became head of the German Navy in 1928 with the rank of admiral. At the time, the Weimar Republic was short of resources and Germany was crippled by the reparations demanded by the United Kingdom and France. Just as the Army was limited to 100,000 men, the Navy was limited to being a coastal defence force, its largest ships three elderly coastal battleships and some light cruisers, while for the most part the fleet included torpedo-boats, but no submarines. The first new light cruiser, the *Emden*, was launched in 1925, and in 1931 came the first of the powerful long-range *Panzerschiffe*, or armoured ships, known to the British media as 'pocket battleships', which were presented to the former Allies as being replacements for the coastal battleships.

When Hitler took power in 1933, he found much support in the armed forces. Like many senior German naval officers, Raeder was an admirer of the Nazis and of Hitler. He was later to claim that he agreed with Hitler on the need for a strong navy, but nothing else, but this is difficult to reconcile with the early collaboration between the two men. His support for Hitler went beyond a simple yearning for order and stability within Germany, but a desire to achieve what Tirpitz had failed to do – create a dominant navy – which was why he strongly supported Adolf Hitler's attempt to rebuild the *Kriegsmarine*. This was far from easy as Nazi Germany continued to be short of resources.

Hitler repudiated the Treaty of Versailles in March 1935, opening the way to the unveiling of an air force and the announcement of reconstruction of the German Army and Navy. The London Naval Agreement gave the Germans far more than they expected, for while they were held to a proportion of British naval strength in most categories of warship, they were allowed parity in submarines. A battleship and an aircraft carrier had already been ordered secretly, while the first submarine flotilla was being readied with Dönitz as its first commander.

On 20 April 1936, shortly before his sixtieth birthday, Hitler presented Raeder with the rank of *Generaladmiral*, or General Admiral. Nevertheless, his desire to rebuild the German Navy was hampered by constant challenges from Hermann Göring's demands for money and raw materials to create the Luftwaffe. Raeder was forever attempting to gain the Führer's ear, away from the heads of the other armed services.

Raeder soon had his staff preparing plans for a new German Navy, Plan X, which was soon superseded by Plan Y and, in its final form, appeared as the famous Plan Z. This was a longer-term plan that would not be completed until 1947. This was in itself a weakness, as Hitler had assured Raeder that there would be no war with the British until 1944, although this date kept being brought forward, and even these dates meant that the planned fleet would be far from complete. Raeder did not tackle the fleet expansion programme systematically. Decisions were taken in an arbitrary way and because the fleet was developed piecemeal it was unbalanced, lacking, for example, sufficient destroyers. Ships were completed with armament of insufficient calibre with, for example, the battlecruisers *Scharnhorst* and *Gneisenau* having only 11-inch guns. It was also the case that Raeder, in common with many of his contemporaries in every major navy, was a big-ship, big-gun officer. Despite the successes of the U-boats in the First World War, he only reluctantly accepted Dönitz's plans for a larger U-boat arm, and placed no urgency on aircraft-carrier construction at all. The *Kriegsmarine* was behind the Luftwaffe and the Army in order of priority for rearmament, but Raeder did not manage to obtain Hitler's support for an all-out programme of warship construction until the end of January 1939, although, as we have seen, on war breaking out in Europe, Hitler cancelled the plan except for ships nearing completion and the U-boats. Although promoted to grand admiral, the equivalent of the British admiral of the fleet or the US fleet admiral, in April 1939, Raeder's position was weak. Earlier, in an attempt to obtain Göring's support, he had backed down on plans for the *Kriegsmarine* to have its own organic air power. When war broke out he was shaken and concluded that his men 'would only be able to show that they knew how to die with honour'.

Nevertheless, he had been promoted to *Grossadmiral* in 1939, and later that year suggested 'Operation *Weserübung*', the invasions of Denmark and Norway, in order to secure sheltered docks out of reach of the Royal Air Force, as well as providing direct exits into the North Sea. Another reason for the invasion of Norway was that the Gulf of Bothnia froze in winter, which meant that iron ore from Sweden had to be transported by rail to a Norwegian port and then shipped along the coast to Germany. These operations were eventually carried out, but with relatively heavy losses. Invading Denmark was easy with a land frontier with Germany, but the long Norwegian coastline meant that Norway was more difficult, especially since a spirited defence at Oslo not only sunk the cruiser carrying the headquarters and its staff, but enabled the country's leaders to escape and organize armed resistance while British and French forces hastened to stop the invasion.

Raeder was not a strong supporter of 'Operation Sealion', the planned German invasion of the United Kingdom. He felt that the war at sea could be conducted far more successfully via an indirect strategic approach, by increasing the numbers of U-boats and small surface vessels in service – in addition to a strategic focus on the

Mediterranean, with a strong German presence in North Africa, plus an invasion of Malta and the Middle East.

With too few submarines to conduct an effective campaign right from the declaration of war, Raeder did well at first with his surface raiders, including auxiliary merchant cruisers. The loss of the *Graf Spee*, a *Panzerschiff*, was the first setback. The next, the high cost of the invasion of Norway, was won at a heavy cost to the Navy in terms of the loss of a light cruiser to British naval air power, albeit land-based, and of several destroyers in two battles at Narvik.

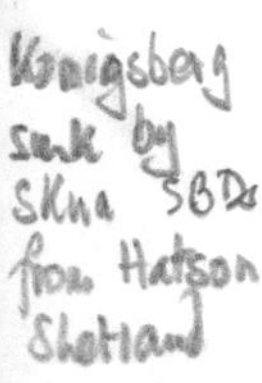

Nevertheless, Norway was his last success. Rivalry with Göring meant that Navy-Air Force collaboration was spasmodic. Maritime-reconnaissance was patchy and there was no real equivalent of the British minelaying operations by the RAF and Fleet Air Arm. He failed to persuade Hitler that victory in the Mediterranean and North Africa should precede the invasion of the Soviet Union, 'Operation Barbarossa'. Indeed, it was Göring who encouraged Hitler that Germany should invade Crete using paratroops and air-landed troops, leaving the Navy on the sidelines. The follow-up landings by sea suffered heavy losses at the hands of the British Mediterranean Fleet.

The policy of 'Mediterranean before Russia' advocated by Raeder was logical. Indeed, as soon as Italy had entered the war, the Axis powers should have made the invasion of Malta their objective. The islands were poorly defended and could only manage an improvised fighter cover using three Gloster Sea Gladiator fighters 'borrowed' from the Royal Navy. Had the Italians sent their six battleships to bombard the main island of Malta itself, on the day after Italy had entered the war, and followed this up with an invasion, they would have cut the Mediterranean in two, solved their problems of resupplying their forces in North Africa, and then could have tackled the Soviet Union next, leaving the Balkans alone for the time being, if not altogether. As it was, the preoccupation with Yugoslavia and Greece, and then Crete, delayed the start of 'Operation Barbarossa' so that there was not enough time to secure the objectives before the harsh Russian winter set in. There would also have been more troops available without the need to garrison Yugoslavia and Greece. Whereas Raeder understood this, Hitler refused to see it. On the other hand, Raeder wanted to see the UK defeated first before the Soviet Union was invaded, but Germany's need for fuel, raw materials and food all dictated the thrust eastwards. Germany could not afford to continue to pay Stalin for fuel and raw materials, even though the Soviet dictator was prepared to supply Germany right up to the time of the invasion.

The U-boat war in the Atlantic was highly successful and cost-effective at first, at least until the tide began to change in favour of the Allies in 1942. The results from the surface fleet were far less impressive. The early loss of the *Panzerschiff*, *Graf Spee*, in the Battle of the River Plate was an early warning, especially as she had heavier guns with a longer range than those of her opponents. In 1941, destroying the British battlecruiser HMS *Hood* was down to sheer luck, but the loss of the *Bismarck* that followed was a serious blow to German morale and meant that for a short time, until *Tirpitz* was completed, the *Kriegsmarine* was without a modern battleship. Hitler then began to guard his remaining heavy ships carefully, bringing them home, as happened to the battlecruisers *Scharnhorst* and *Gneisenau*, and the heavy cruiser *Prinz Eugen*. In December 1942, after *Lutzow* and the cruiser *Admiral Hipper* failed to destroy a British convoy, Hitler demanded the decommissioning of all major surface units. This prompted Raeder to resign, although he was given the sinecure of Inspector of the Navy. As he left, he asked Hitler to protect the *Kriegsmarine*, and his successor, from Göring.

Raeder did not escape being put on trial at Nuremberg, where he was sentenced to life imprisonment for 'waging aggressive war'. Nevertheless, he was released in 1956, the year after the Allies had allowed the then West Germany to start to rebuild her armed forces.

Chapter 24

The Italian Navy

On entry into the Second World War, the Italian Navy, the *Regia Marina*, had six battleships and seven heavy cruisers, as well as fourteen light cruisers – a powerful force for a nation with few maritime pretensions. Although an aircraft carrier was under construction, this was never finished. Lighter forces included 122 destroyers and torpedo-boats, and, something usually overlooked, there were 119 submarines, twice as many as Germany's *Kriegsmarine* possessed in 1939! Manpower was 168,614 officers and men at the time of Italy's entry into the war in June 1940, and by August 1943, this had risen to 259,000, despite the size of the fleet having shrunk and growing problems over fuel supplies.

While a modern fleet, the *Regia Navale* suffered from many shortcomings. Warship designers had placed more emphasis on style and speed than on effective armament and armour protection, but, more important still, they lacked radar. The main bases were in the south at Taranto in Italy's 'instep': Genoa in the north-west and La Spezzia, slightly further south, as well as Trieste at the northern end of the Adriatic, close to the border with Yugoslavia. Of these, only Taranto was well placed as a forward base as the war developed, being close to Malta with the shortest mainland shipping route to North Africa, where Italian ground and air forces needed to be kept supplied. Ships based on Taranto could effectively cut the entrance to the Adriatic, or indeed could have cut the Mediterranean in half.

On paper, major units of the Italian fleet sounded impressive enough. The Andrea Doria-class of battleships, which included the *Conte di Cavour* and the *Caio Duilo*, were vessels from the First World War that had been reconstructed between the wars, nevertheless, their relatively low displacement of 22,964 tons and light main armament made them obsolescent, despite a reasonable speed of 27 knots. More impressive were the two ships of the Impero-class, under construction just before the outbreak of war and intended to make full use of the maximum dimensions permitted by the Washington Treaty.

Domination on paper was not the same as domination in reality. The Italian Navy had not been faced with a serious conflict since the Balkan Wars thirty years earlier and had not engaged the Austro-Hungarian Navy during the First World War.

Training was poor, and so too was the study of naval warfare by the officers. Many believe that naval personnel were better trained than those of the other two services, certainly better than the Army, but this is open to question. There was also a wide gulf between the ratings and the officers, with little movement upwards from the ranks. In terms of gunnery, the Italians placed more emphasis on muzzle velocity than on accuracy, which in any case was usually confined to static gunnery exercises rather than exercises at high speed in the open sea. A similar problem arose with their ships, which were fast, but only in ideal conditions, and suffered from poor sea-keeping. Night fighting was regarded as unlikely, even impossible, which, lacking radar it probably was.

On the other hand, it would be wrong to overlook the fact that the Italian Navy, and the other Italian armed forces, did excel in using small specialized forces, such as the two-man crews of the human torpedoes. These were ridden by their operators who sat on top, and once inside an enemy harbour and under the target ship, the warhead could be detached and fastened to the hull. The intrepid crew could then make their escape on the torpedo.

The Italian Navy faced the prospect of war with even less enthusiasm than did the Germans. For the latter, it was a case of war, long expected, coming too soon before their ambitious plans were anywhere near fulfilment. They went into action painfully aware of their relative weakness compared to the Royal Navy, even though that service was stretched due to the United Kingdom's global commitments. For the Italians, entering a war that had already started meant that they had no element of surprise and their opponents were already on a war footing.

What both Axis navies had in common was that they lacked the ear of the dictator. The Italian air force, the *Regia Aeronautica*, was as much the apple of Mussolini's eye as the Luftwaffe was of Hitler's.

Unlike the Germans, the Italians had a convoy problem from the outset, something the Germans only gained with the invasion of Norway. Italian forces in North Africa had to be kept supplied, but little could be done for those in Abyssinia, present-day Ethiopia, as long as the Royal Navy controlled the Suez Canal. Even in North Africa there was a problem. The limited experience of warfare of the Italian military meant that the army in North Africa badly underestimated the volume of supplies needed under combat conditions, putting the Navy under still greater pressure.

The *Regia Marina*'s commanders were concerned that they could be bottled up in the Mediterranean, but the strategy they followed was ill suited to modern warfare. Their ships had not developed properly since the First World War so that they sent cruisers without Asdic as escorts for convoys, which simply gave the British submarine commanders a better choice of targets and did nothing for the safety of the convoy. None of their ships had radar or Asdic. There was no pressure on Mussolini, not even advice, from his admirals for action against Malta, other than leaving the *Regia Aeronautica* to attempt to bomb the islands and the British garrison into submission. An early invasion could have succeeded and made the conduct of the rest of the war in North Africa so much easier. As it was, Mussolini embarked on an unsuccessful invasion of Yugoslavia and Greece, his forces had to be rescued and the invasions completed by his German allies.

At Taranto, the Italians concentrated their six battleships on 11 November 1940 but failed to ensure that torpedo nets were properly rigged, having removed them earlier in the day. The Royal Navy airmen who mounted the attack that night from the fast armoured carrier HMS *Illustrious* couldn't believe their luck. There was still luck clinging to the Italians at this stage, as none of the bombs or torpedoes hit a magazine, which kept the number of casualties low compared with the Japanese attack on Pearl Harbor. Nevertheless, half of Italy's battleships were out of action the next morning. Even after the attack, when the major fleet units were moved from Taranto, they were only taken as far as Naples, easily within range of the RAF's Malta-based bombers.

The Battle of Cape Matapan was a complete success for the British Mediterranean Fleet and its Commander-in-Chief, Cunningham. While the Italians showed great courage in mounting an armed attack by fast motor launches on the Grand Harbour at Valletta, and then again using human torpedoes at Alexandria, such operations barely had an impact. The attack on Malta failed and in any case there was little in the Grand Harbour worth sinking. At Alexandria, the attack was successful, but the 'charioteers', as the British would later describe the crews of human torpedoes, were captured and taken prisoner, while the British battleships were able to be repaired.

All in all, the Italian naval commanders were taken by surprise by the outbreak of war, had no contingency plans for executing a naval war and were uncertain over the role the Navy should play in supporting the other services. Even more than the Germans, they did not get the cooperation they needed from their Air Force, and like the Germans, inter-service rivalry and the arrogance of the Air Force commanders meant that creating a naval air arm was impossible. An aircraft carrier was laid down and the Germans even sent the catapults that would have been used in the *Graf Zeppelin* had she been completed, but like the German ship, the *Aquila*, a conversion of the passenger liner *Roma*, was never completed.

It need not have been this way. The head of the *Regia Marina*, Admiral Domenico Cavagnari, was both Chief of Staff and under-secretary of his department, a true one-man head, who served for seven years, which was an exceptionally long time by any standard, but especially so under Mussolini who, like most dictators, had his favourites, but usually only for a limited period. Nevertheless, Italian inter-war naval planning was based on just one premise: that any future war would be with France and that any future naval engagement would follow the pattern set at the Battle of Jutland. The changes that were taking place in Europe seem to have almost completely passed the Italian Navy by, and Jutland was to prove to be a one-off, with no naval battle afterwards even remotely like it.

Fuel proved to be a problem from the start, with just 1.7 million tons stockpiled, which was topped up monthly by supplies from Romania, for as long as the Germans could spare it.

Political interference was similar to that experienced by the Germans, with a political reluctance to put ships at risk. The over-whelming fear was the war might end with Italy no longer having a navy!

After the Fleet Air Arm's successful attack on Taranto, Cavagnari ordered his fleet to avoid confrontation with the Royal Navy. Nevertheless, with the war going badly for Italy, especially at sea, Taranto was the final straw and heads had to roll. On 11 December

1940, he was dismissed and Admiral Arturo Riccardi was appointed as his successor, with Admiral Angelo Jacchino taking the new post of Commander of the Fleet at Sea. Despite this emphasis on combat leadership, the fortunes of the Italian Navy did not improve, as the Battle of Cape Matapan was to prove.

Chapter 25

The New Broom

Admiral Arturo Riccardi (1878–1966)

Riccardi had the unfortunate task of taking over from a predecessor deemed to have failed in the eyes of Italy's dictator, Benito Mussolini. Evidence of the failure was not hard to find, with three out of Italy's six battleships sitting on the bed of the major naval base at Taranto.

Born in Pavia in 1878, Riccardi saw action with the marines in China during the Boxer Rebellion in 1900–1901 and also further action during the First World War, although this would have been relatively limited. Post-war, he spent a period as a staff officer before being promoted to rear admiral in 1932, and after joining the Fascist Party in 1934, he was later promoted to vice admiral in 1935. His responsibilities included naval personnel, making him the equivalent of the Royal Navy's Second Sea Lord. Succeeding the disgraced Admiral Domenico Cavagnari as Chief of Staff of the *Regia Marina* on 11 December 1940, Riccardi also held the position of the Navy's Under-secretary of State.

His duties included liaison with the *Kriegsmarine* over the defence of Italy, but despite Riccardi forcing a more aggressive strategy at sea, Italian failures continued with the Battle of Cape Matapan, the big clash between the Italian and British navies, covered earlier in Chapter 10, where the Axis air power was not provided by the Italian *Regia Aeronautica* but by the German Luftwaffe.

Riccardi had taken up his new post at a time when Italy had proved incapable of subjugating Yugoslavia and Greece, but the Germans pressed him to cut British maritime communications between

Alexandria and Athens. Italian ships were sent into the waters south of Greece to attack British convoys, but British aerial reconnaissance soon spotted the Italian ships. This was a marked contrast to the situation with the Italians, which lacked their own naval air power and relied upon the Air Force to provide reconnaissance as well as air strikes, but cooperation between the two services was so poor as to be virtually non-existent.

The Battle of Cape Matapan exposed a major weakness in Italian battle plans, which was that they did not expect to engage an enemy at night. Lacking radar, night gunnery would have been difficult, but not impossible given training and suitable optical instruments.

Mussolini had boasted that the Mediterranean was 'Mare Nostrum', which meant 'our sea', but while Italy effectively cut the sea in two, it never controlled it. It was only a matter of time after the Allies invaded North Africa in November 1942, followed by an amphibious and airborne assault on Sicily the following spring. When Benito Mussolini was overthrown, Riccardi also fell from grace and was replaced on 25 July 1943.

While some maintain that Riccardi was a specialist in naval air power, the truth was that he, and other Italian naval officers, had precious little experience of air power. His failure to ensure that the fleet under his command at Taranto was adequately protected was unforgivable, but he was promoted further. It was not his fault that Italian aerial reconnaissance was so bad that the presence of the British Mediterranean Fleet was not detected, but even so, there was complacency at *Supermarina*, the Italian Admiralty, which took it for granted that British forces would be detected in time for Italian warships to leave harbour and engage them.

It is, perhaps, not surprising that Riccardi did not face charges of being a war criminal.

Chapter 26

The Imperial Japanese Navy

The only Axis navy to be prepared for war and the only one aware in advance of just when it would enter hostilities, the Imperial Japanese Navy knew that it had little time in which to destroy the US Navy in the Pacific and then seize its opportunity before American seapower could reassert itself. The senior commanders knew that they could not counter the industrial might of the United States, but that expansion westwards to seize the Malayan Peninsula and the Netherlands East Indies was essential if Japan was to have the raw materials, fuel and food necessary to sustain combat. Despite its large carrier fleet and its submarine force, which was not used to its full potential, the Imperial Japanese Navy suffered from severe limitations: it lacked a training programme capable of replacing combat losses; senior officers did not understand and were not interested in the unglamorous role of convoy protection; discipline amongst senior commanders was poor and coordination always missing so that the best-laid plans were not always fulfilled, especially later as the tide turned decisively against Japan.

Japan had been one of the First World War Allies, but the Imperial Japanese Navy had seen little action, even though at one stage it did send warships to bolster the Royal Navy in the Mediterranean. When the war ended, the country had the world's third largest navy. The Washington Naval Treaty of 1922 allowed the IJN 60 per cent of the warship tonnage permitted to the United States and the United Kingdom – something that Japan subsequently objected to, seeking naval parity. In one sense, the objections were there simply for show, a flourish of diplomacy, as the country actively sought to breach the Washington limits while at the same time pursuing an aggressive policy of expansion in China.

In common with the Royal Navy, the Imperial Japanese Navy was the senior service, but there was no autonomous air force, with both services maintaining their own army and navy air forces, with that of the IJN usually referred to as the Japanese Navy Air Force. The Japanese had modelled themselves on the Royal Navy to a great extent, and even accepted the services of a British Naval Mission in the early 1920s before Japanese plans for colonial expansion were fully understood outside the country.

On 7 December 1940, the day of the attack on the US Pacific Fleet at Pearl Harbor, the IJN had: 10 battleships with another 2 under construction; 10 aircraft carriers with 4 under construction; 18 heavy cruisers and 20 light cruisers, with another 4 of the latter still being completed. These ships were supported by a comparatively small destroyer force of 112 ships, with 12 still building, but there were also just 65 submarines, of which 21 could be considered as obsolete, while another 37 were being built. There were, in addition, 9 elderly river gunboats, doubtless of some use in China, 12 minesweepers and at least 4 submarine depot ships, as well as seaplane carriers. There were around 1,750 combat aircraft, plus another 530 flying boats and floatplanes for reconnaissance.

This was an impressive fleet and set to become more impressive still, but action had to be taken before the naval shipbuilding programme could be completed as sanctions imposed by the UK and the USA meant that Japan was in danger of becoming short of fuel, raw materials and even food. Unlike the British, the Imperial Japanese Navy had an impressive range of aircraft to operate from its carriers, notably the Mitsubishi Zero fighter, an agile aircraft that could outfight anything deployed by the Royal Navy and the Royal Air Force in the East. Other aircraft included dive-bombers and torpedo-bombers, all of modern design and high performance.

While the aircraft were good, the other notable item in the Japanese inventory was the 'Long Lance' torpedo, an effective and accurate weapon. In general, gunnery was better than in most of the combatant navies, aided by excellent optical equipment.

Although it was a large fleet with its own aircraft carriers and naval air power, nevertheless, the Imperial Japanese Navy's warships were often based on obsolete design concepts and this was especially true of the aircraft carriers. Anti-submarine warfare was no more advanced than it had been during the First World War. An unusual feature of the IJN was that it included a substantial number of aircraft-carrying submarines, some of which could carry two aircraft – the only other aircraft-carrying submarine was the French *Surcouf*. There is little evidence of these unusual boats being used to their full potential, and indeed, just a few recorded incidents of them being used at all. The Japanese did not make good use of their submarines generally, as the doctrine was that they should operate with the surface fleet to help reduce the odds before a naval battle – again this was a doctrine that had failed the test of the First World War, when the concept of the 'fleet' submarine had exercised British naval planners and designers, often with results that were completely impractical. The problem was, of course, that in the Pacific, all of the battles that mattered were between carrier-borne aircraft with the opposing fleets seldom seeing one another.

The IJN lacked an experienced and capable naval leadership as a purge during 1934 had seen many of the Imperial Japanese Navy's best officers dismissed. The Navy's leaders in 1941 were Admiral Oikawa Koshiro, the Navy Minister, and Nagano Osami, the Chief of the Navy Staff, both of whom have been described as second-rate admirals. While the IJN was much less hawkish than the Imperial Japanese Army, it was the Army that dictated the pace of events. Even so, after the purge, there was a notable increase in the number of younger and more hawkish officers, with major commands from 1934 onwards being given to militant officers who cultivated an aggressive and arrogant sense of superiority. After the victories at Pearl Harbor and Singapore, many senior Japanese officers felt that the IJN was invincible, sweeping all before it, but Pearl Harbor wasn't the victory it appeared to be at first.

The IJN provided close support for army operations in China during the 1930s, and so it was probably the Navy in 1941 that had the most recent experience of combat, especially of providing support for amphibious operations. This role continued once Japan entered the Second World War, even to the extent that the IJN suffered from an inability to assume an independent strategic role as the war progressed, in complete contrast to the United States Navy. It was also the case that the Imperial Japanese Navy had no experience of fleet actions after the Battle of Tsushima in 1905, and in combat against the Chinese, the Japanese invariably had superior numbers and equipment.

Imagination was lacking amongst the naval leadership in making the best of its assets, apart from the attack on Pearl Harbor. Had this been accompanied by an aggressive submarine campaign, especially around the Pacific end of the Panama Canal, the United States would have had considerable problems in rebuilding and then expanding the Pacific Fleet. The aggressive mentality of many officers also meant that convoy protection was overlooked until it was too late, and then far too little was done.

The strategic plan revolved around reducing the disparity in size between the USN and the IJN. This was the logic behind the attack on Pearl Harbor, and afterwards was the logic behind what the IJN planners assumed would be a war of attrition. The idea was to draw the USN closer to the IJN's bases and, once the difference in sizes between the two fleets had been whittled away, seek a major engagement with the Americans, the 'decisive battle' that would leave Japan free to win the war. It says much for the IJN that these policies were followed even though many senior officers, including Admiral Yamamoto, believed that at best Japan would have a year of unchallenged naval superiority after Pearl Harbor before the Americans could re-establish themselves in the Pacific.

The major problem with Japanese planning for warfare was that the country lacked the resources to sustain a major fleet through a long conflict. It did not have the industrial might of the United States that would enable it to replace its losses quickly or easily, and it did not have the training system in place that would do the same for personnel, so that as the war progressed, standards of training and the experience of those in the front line dwindled rather than improved, as with the Allied navies. At the outset, standards of gunnery were high, but this was not a big-gun naval war. Intelligence was poor and remained so throughout the war, with appalling ship recognition that played its part in the failure at Leyte Gulf. Japanese observers could not tell the difference between a large fleet carrier and an escort carrier, or even at times between a tanker and a carrier.

In 1941, the average experience of a Japanese naval officer and especially an airman was far superior to that of his British or American counterparts, but by 1944, the edge had been lost and during 1945 experience was a rarity as losses could not be replaced. On the lower deck, the level of training and experience was higher than in most navies, with only around 20 per cent of ratings conscripted.

A fleet was maintained off China, but the rest of the warships were grouped into the Combined Fleet, under the command of

Admiral Yamamoto initially, but later commanded by Koga and then Toyoda. The Combined Fleet's constituent parts were: the First Fleet, consisting of battleships and aircraft carriers; the Second Fleet, which provided reconnaissance; the Third, providing amphibious forces and undertaking blockades; the Fourth Fleet, which covered the conquered territories; the Fifth Fleet which stayed in northern waters as a reminder that relations between Japan and the Soviet Union were uneasy; and the Sixth Fleet, which had most of the navy's submarines. There were two air fleets: the First for carrier-borne aircraft and the Second for land-based aircraft.

These fleets were changed and reformed into task forces as the need arose. At Pearl Harbor, Yamamoto headed the Main Body while Vice Admiral Nagumo led the Strike Force which carried out the attack. There was also a Southern Force which covered the landings in Thailand and Malaya. New fleets and air fleets followed as the Japanese advance rolled westwards and southwards.

By August 1943, a further reorganization saw the First Fleet become the battleship force; the Second a diversion attack force; the Third, the striking force mainly operating aircraft carriers; the Fourth, the Inner South Seas Force; the Fifth remained as the northern force; the Sixth became the Advance Expeditionary Force, which was strange at a time when Japanese forces were defending rather than attacking; and the Eighth, the Outer South Seas Force. There were later changes, although as the number of ships and aircraft dwindled, many of these became increasingly irrelevant.

The passion for aggressive operations had one overwhelming drawback that contributed to defeat. There was no appetite for the important but tedious task of convoy protection and this only came late in the war, when the escorts provided were inadequate for the number of merchantmen that needed to be escorted. While the Japanese had excellent weapons and good optical aids for gunnery direction, especially at night, they lacked Asdic – when an Allied submarine was in the vicinity of their warships, the technique used was to race down the track of a torpedo, dropping depth charges. No attempt was made to introduce escort carriers, even though the Japanese Army Air Force had aircraft transports that might have been suitable.

The war did not go as the Japanese had expected. They swept through most, but not all, of the Netherlands East Indies and through Thailand, Malaya and Singapore, but came to a halt in Burma where they were increasingly put on the defensive, and in New Guinea. At sea, in April 1942, they were victorious over the British Eastern Fleet off Ceylon (now Sri Lanka), but in May, although the Battle of the Coral Sea was a tactical victory for the Japanese, it left them weakened for the Battle of Midway in June, which saw the IJN lose four aircraft carriers in a single day, along with experienced air crew. Just one victory was left to them in the battles off Guadalcanal, on 26 October 1942, in the Battle of the Santa Cruz Islands. The long war of attrition as US forces island-hopped towards Japan saw the IJN worn down, without the capability to rebuild itself. As the war drew to a close, the only means available to it was that of kamikaze attacks, usually using senior ratings and junior officers with little strategic sense, whose sacrifice was, more often than not, a complete waste. The kamikaze were not only suicide aircraft, sometimes using manned bombs which were disposable but did not give the pilot the option of returning to base if he did not find a target, there were also explosive-filled motor launches and human torpedoes.

Out of 451 surface ships either in commission at the outbreak of the war or commissioned during the war, only thirty-seven were operational when Japan surrendered. Some 2,000 kamikaze aircraft had been held back ready to repel an invasion of Japan, but by the time of the surrender, the people were starving and there was insufficient fuel to continue the war other than by kamikaze sacrifice.

Chapter 27

An Overcautious Commander

Fleet Admiral Minechi Koga (1885–1944)

At the outbreak of war, as a vice admiral, Koga had been criticized for being overcautious, but he took command of the Combined Fleet in April 1943 at a time when Japanese fortunes were on the wane and the fleet had not recovered from the Battle of Midway only ten months earlier. A combination of circumstances had in any case forced the Japanese to become more defensive in their approach as the 'Doolittle' raid on Tokyo and other cities had shown that they were vulnerable, something that was soon borne out at Midway.

Born in Arita in 1885, Koga entered the Imperial Japanese Naval Academy and graduated in 1906, coming 14th out of 176 cadets. Afterwards, he served as midshipman on the cruiser *Matsushima* on its long-distance navigational training cruise to Hawaii, New Zealand and Australia, the Netherlands East Indies, Singapore and China. On the ship's return, he was commissioned as an ensign and posted to the *Katori*, followed by *Otowa* and *Suma*. As a sub lieutenant he served in the *Soya* and *Aki*, and as a lieutenant from 1911, he served in *Kashima*.

After taking a course at the IJN's Naval War College, Koga was given a staff posting during which he was promoted to lieutenant commander in 1917. In common with most Japanese naval officers, he saw no action during the First World War. In 1920, Koga worked at the Japanese Embassy in Paris. He returned in 1922 and was promoted to commander, becoming executive officer on the *Kitakami*. Promoted to captain on 1 December 1926, Koga returned to France as naval attaché until 1 November 1928. After his return to Japan, he took command of the Yokosuka Naval Station before commanding the heavy cruiser *Aoba* from 31 December 1930, and the battleship *Ise* from 31 December 1931. Exactly a year later he was promoted to rear admiral and appointed Chief of the Imperial Japanese Navy General Staff's Intelligence Division.

On 31 December 1936, he was promoted to vice admiral, before succeeding Kondo as Vice-Chief of the Naval Staff in December 1937, a post that he held until October 1943. Despite the positions he held, Koga was the complete opposite of the pro-war faction and shared Yamamoto's misgivings about war with the United States.

He had an agreeable and calm personality, and had considerable experience of staff work. Combining the staff role of Vice-Chief with the operational role of Commander of the IJN's Second Fleet in 1939 must have been an onerous task, although afterwards he was placed in command of the China Area Fleet on 1 September 1941.

He suffered from a lack of imagination and disagreed with Yamamoto regarding the use of naval aviation, remaining a firm battleship advocate until events later in the Pacific War proved his position outdated. In short, he was another wartime admiral who not only lacked an understanding of the role of air power, despite Pearl Harbor and the Battles of the Coral Sea and Midway, but also underestimated what it had achieved and what it could achieve. He continued the tradition of failing to use the large Japanese submarine fleet effectively.

Early in the war in the Pacific, Koga commanded naval operations during the capture of Hong Kong in December 1941. Following the death of Admiral Yamamoto on 19 April 1943, Koga succeeded him as Commander-in-Chief of the Combined Fleet in his flagship, the battleship *Musashi*. Belatedly, Koga attempted to revitalize Japanese naval operations by reorganizing the Combined Fleet into task forces built around aircraft carriers in imitation of the United States Navy, and even formed a land-based naval air fleet to work in coordination with the carriers. This was preparatory to mounting an aggressive counter-offensive in the Aleutians to dilute American forces and to lure the American fleet into a major naval engagement in 1943. However, the losses of Japan's land and carrier-based aircraft based in the central Pacific eventually forced a Japanese withdrawal from the Gilbert Islands and Philippines by the end of the year. Forced to adopt a more cautious stance, he attempted to conserve his remaining forces to inflict maximum damage on the Americans when they closed toward the Philippines.

Despite his reorganization of the Combined Fleet, Koga still sought the decisive 'all-big-gun' battle between the opposing fleets, even though he was forced to concede that if it did occur, the chances of a Japanese victory were slim. This was known to the Japanese as Operation Z, but the planning was not completed until 8 March 1944. He was to have no chance to see it happen, for he was killed in a plane crash on 31 March when his aircraft, a Kawanishi 'Emily' flying boat, crashed during a typhoon between Palau and Davao while overseeing the withdrawal of the Combined Fleet from its Palau headquarters on 31 March 1944. His death was not announced until May 1944 when he was formally replaced by Admiral Soemu Toyoda. He was promoted to Fleet Admiral posthumously and was accorded a state funeral.

Operation Z survived, but the plans were being carried by his chief of staff, Vice Admiral Shigeru Fukudoma, when his aircraft landed at Cebu in the Philippines and he was captured by guerrillas, the plans ending up in the hands of the US Army commander in the Pacific, General Douglas MacArthur.

Chapter 28

Japan's Most Successful Commander at Sea

Fleet Admiral Nobutake Kondo (1886–1953)

Kondo was Koga's successor as Vice-Chief of the Naval Staff, taking over in October 1939 and remaining until October 1941. He later succeeded Koga as commander of the Combined Fleet.

Nobutake Kondo was born in 1886 and graduated from the Imperial Japanese Naval Academy in 1907, too late to see action in the Russo-Japanese War. His career included extensive service at sea and ashore. After commanding the battleship *Kongo* in 1932, his posts included President of the Naval Staff College, Chief of Staff for the Combined Fleet, and Deputy Chief of the Naval Staff.

After Yamamoto, the then Vice Admiral Nobutake Kondo was the most important Japanese fleet commander in the first year of the war. As a vice admiral at the outset of the war in the Pacific, Kondo was the commander of the Southern Force which sank the Royal Navy's Force Z, HMS *Repulse* and *Prince of Wales*, off Malaya in December 1941. As commander of the Second Fleet, the IJN's principal force for independent operations, Kondo was in overall command of the naval forces supporting the invasion of Malaya, Sumatra and Java in the great opening offensive, and also overall commander for the foray into the Indian Ocean shortly thereafter in April 1942. He also conducted a number of successful attacks on Allied merchant shipping with Nagumo and commanded the Midway Occupation Force while Nagumo commanded the strike force with four aircraft carriers.

When operating independently of the main battle fleet, the Second Fleet's composition varied depending on the mission and the ships available – at Midway it included two battleships, a light carrier and six heavy cruisers. In the Guadalcanal fighting of November 1942, the Second Fleet comprised the small fleet carriers *Junyo* and *Hiyo*, the battleships *Kongo* and *Haruna*, four cruisers and nineteen destroyers.

Kondo came closer to a decisive naval battle than most of his contemporaries during the campaign for control of the Solomon Islands. He was ordered to lure the US fleet into a conventional naval battle and set a trap for them, which the Americans avoided but which did, nevertheless, lead to the Battle of the Eastern Solomons on 24 August 1942. He provided naval support for the Japanese forces ashore at Guadalcanal and on 26 October 1942, he scored Japan's last victory at sea in the Battle of the Santa Cruz Islands. In both engagements he also took command of an element of the fleet. In the Santa Cruz battle he was with the 'Advance Force' of two battleships, four cruisers (flying his flag in the heavy cruiser *Atago*) and a destroyer screen, accompanied by the carrier *Junyo*, which, however, operated independently with its own destroyer escorts.

Following the first Battle of Guadalcanal in November 1942, Kondo decided to lead the battleship *Kirishima* along with cruisers *Atago*, *Nagara*, *Sendai* and *Takao*, in what was intended to be a decisive attack to knock out Henderson Airfield with a massive night naval bombardment. For this operation, the Japanese had no less than four aircraft carriers once again, with a total of 212 aircraft. Vice Admiral Kondo in the van of the fleet had *Junyo* with 55 aircraft, supported by 2 battleships, 5 cruisers and 14 destroyers, while the main fleet under Vice Admiral Nagumo had the other 3 carriers, *Shokaku*, *Zuikaku* and *Zuiho*, with 157 aircraft, as well as 2 battleships, 5 cruisers and 15 destroyers. This resulted in the Battle of the Santa Cruz Islands, covered in more detail in Chapter 5, which was the last occasion in which the Imperial Japanese Navy could claim a victory.

Nevertheless, Kondo next suffered a defeat on the night of 14/15 November covering another admiral, Tanaka, who was attempting to run transports to Guadalcanal. With the battleship *Kirishima* as his flagship with three heavy cruisers, a light cruiser and nine destroyers, Kondo started a further night bombardment of Henderson Field, and as the Americans arrived, a night battle ensued. In the opening stages, in a gunnery duel, two American destroyers were crippled and later sunk, with another destroyer badly damaged and sunk later, while the *South Dakota* suffered a complete electrical failure so that she was unable to use her guns, but was later fortunate to escape being hit in a Japanese torpedo attack. Unnoticed by the Japanese, the other American battleship, *Washington*, used her radar and in a surprise bombardment reduced the *Kirishima* to a wreck after which she sank. A Japanese destroyer also sank during the conflict. At 0030 on the morning of 15 November, Kondo pulled his forces out of the battle, but Tanaka pressed on regardless, running his ships aground and landing a further 2,000 men, as well as 250 cases of ammunition and 1,500 bags of rice. The transports were destroyed by American aircraft later that morning.

Kondo's defeat meant that the Allies were able to save the important air base at Henderson Field.

Later, Kondo served as Deputy Commander of the Combined Fleet, and took over briefly as acting commander on Yamamoto's death in April 1943. Nevertheless, he was still tainted by the Guadalcanal failures and was soon removed from seagoing commands or any positions of real authority until appointed to the Supreme War Council in the shake-up of May 1945; he was there while the Supreme War Council directed Japanese policy in the last months of the war.

An able staff officer and a gunnery expert, despite his earlier victories Kondo has been described as being too cautious to be a successful fighting admiral, although this seems unfair. His weaknesses were his inability to use air power effectively and his failure to appreciate the threat it posed to his forces. In short, he was too 'old school' for a war in which air power had taken over from firepower. The problem was that while his ships survived the Battle of the Santa Cruz Islands, his airmen did not, and already the Japanese were suffering from falling levels of experience amongst the naval aircrew. Kondo did, however, survive the war.

Chapter 29

Snatching Defeat from the Jaws of Victory

Vice Admiral Chuichi Nagumo (1887–1944)

Few senior naval officers had a better opportunity to make a decisive impact on an enemy fleet during their careers than Vice Admiral Chuichi Nagumo, and few failed so badly. Given command of the largest carrier fleet assembled at the time, he gives the impression of not fully understanding the potential of aviation, yet failed to take advice from the leading naval aviator under his command.

Nagumo had somehow acquired a reputation in peacetime for being a daring naval officer, but events were to prove that he was in fact overcautious. He was a torpedo specialist and in December 1941, he was the officer selected for the prestigious appointment of the *kido butai*, the Combined Fleet's aircraft carrier striking force, charged with the attack on the US Pacific Fleet's forward base at Pearl Harbor on Hawaii.

Chuichi Nagumo was born on 25 March 1887 in Yonezawa, northern Japan. He attended the Imperial Japanese Naval Academy and graduated in 1908, 8th out of 191 cadets. As a midshipman he served on the cruisers *Soya*, *Nisshin* and *Niitaka*. Promoted to ensign in 1910, he was posted to the cruiser *Asama*. After attending torpedo and gunnery schools, he was promoted to sub lieutenant and served on the battleship *Aki*, followed by *Hatsuyuki*. In 1914, he was promoted to lieutenant and was assigned to the battleship *Kirishima*, followed by the destroyer *Sugi*. On 15 December 1917, he became commanding officer of the destroyer *Kisaragi*.

Like most Japanese naval officers, despite the country being one of the Allies, Nagumo had an uneventful First World War. Post-war, he attended the Naval War College, and in 1920, on leaving, he was promoted to lieutenant commander. From 1920 to 1921, he was captain of the destroyer *Momi*, but was then posted to the Imperial Japanese Navy General Staff, becoming a commander in 1924. In 1925 and 1926, Nagumo accompanied a Japanese mission to study naval warfare strategy, tactics and equipment in Europe and the United States, a reflection of the country's recent status as a wartime ally.

On returning home, Nagumo served as an instructor at the Imperial Japanese Naval Academy from 1927 to 1929, specializing in torpedo warfare and destroyer tactics. He was promoted to captain in November 1929, assumed command of the light cruiser *Naka* and from 1930 to 1931 was commander of the 11th Destroyer Division. After returning to staff positions between 1931 and 1933, he became commanding officer of the heavy cruiser *Takao* from 1933 to 1934, then the battleship *Yamashiro* from 1934 to 1935, before being promoted to rear admiral on 1 November 1935.

He next commanded the 8th Cruiser Division, supporting Imperial Japanese Army operations in China from the Yellow Sea. As a supporter of the militarists, he found favour with the dominant political factions in Japan. From 1937 to 1938, he was commandant of the Torpedo School, and from 1938 to 1939, he was commander of the 3rd Cruiser Division. Nagumo was promoted to vice admiral on 15 November 1939. From November 1940 to April 1941, he was commandant of the Naval War College.

On 10 April 1941, Nagumo was appointed Commander-in-Chief of the First Fleet, the Imperial Japanese Navy's main carrier battle group, largely due to his seniority and his association with the pro-war faction. Many then and since have doubted his suitability for this command, given his lack of experience with naval aviation.

While the attack on Pearl Harbor had been war-gamed by the Japanese to prove its practicality – that such an attack was indeed feasible had already been confirmed by the Royal Navy's success at Taranto in November 1940. The Japanese had far greater resources at their disposal for the attack on Pearl Harbor, with more ships and more aircraft, and the aircraft were far superior to anything the Fleet Air Arm had available at the time. Nevertheless, they were expecting to have to fight their way to the target, and Nagumo expected to lose between a third and a half of his ships.

The initial attack on Pearl Harbor could be presented as a great Japanese victory. The Japanese attacked on a Sunday morning, in the well-justified belief that this would find the defences at a low ebb, with most, if not all, commanders away from their posts, and their subordinates at rest. In fact, the Army and Navy commanders were spending the morning playing golf together. They also had the advantage of surprise, sailing through a tropical storm and launching their aircraft in conditions that would have seen exercises cancelled. Even though the Americans knew that the Japanese fleet was at sea, they had convinced themselves that it was headed for somewhere in South-East Asia. When a radar operator at the radar station on the northern tip of Oahu reported blips, the duty officer was expecting a flight of B-17 bombers. The radar station itself was about to close down for the day.

Even if the alarm had been sounded, the attack could not have been stopped, but the defences would have been prepared and those men aboard their ships or at their shore stations could have gone to action stations; fighter aircraft could have got off the ground. The Japanese had expected to have to fight their way to the target and were surprised to find that they reached it unscathed. Despite the rising tension between the two countries and Japan's known friendliness towards the Germans and Italians, the ships in the harbour did not even have torpedo nets in place – which the Japanese had expected to find.

There was nothing new about American suspicions over Japanese intentions. Japanese aggression in China had not been conducive to stability in the Far East. At first the Americans had been reluctant to act, with many advocating isolationism, but to many Japanese it had seemed that war with the United States was inevitable. American opinion changed as the extent of Japanese ambitions became clear. Japanese atrocities in China could not be ignored, especially after the rape of the former Nationalist Chinese capital of Nanking, which fell to Japanese forces in December 1937.

The signing of a non-aggression pact between China and the Soviet Union highlighted Japanese ambitions and put Indo-China under threat. In December 1940, the United States imposed an embargo on the sale of scrap metal and war materials to Japan. This was followed by the freezing of Japanese assets in the United States in July 1941, after Japan invaded Indo-China. The United Kingdom followed, denying Japan the currency with which to purchase oil and raw materials. Japan was left with a strategic reserve of 55 billion barrels of oil, enough for eighteen months of war. The only way to extend this was for Japan to find another source of oil, by invading the Netherlands East Indies.

The government of Japan was in the hands of the Army dominated pro-war faction. The Allied embargo meant that Japan had either to abandon its plans for what amounted to an Asian empire, the so-called 'Greater Asia Co-Prosperity Sphere', or go to war and achieve its needs by conquest. Japan had few friends since the Soviet Union and the United States saw her as a dangerous rival; the British Empire also viewed her as a threat, and Germany and Italy were too far away to be able to provide any worthwhile assistance.

In the end, the commander of the Combined Fleet, Admiral Yamamoto, decided to strike a crippling blow at the US Pacific Fleet by attacking its main base at Pearl Harbor, on the Hawaiian island of Oahu. If Pearl Harbor could be knocked out and major units of the Pacific Fleet were destroyed at the same time, it would take time for the United States to re-establish a significant naval presence in the area. Given the vast distances involved in the Pacific, control of the seas had to take precedence over everything else.

The Japanese were able to devote far greater resources to the operation than the British had managed at Taranto. Instead of one aircraft carrier with twenty-one obsolescent biplanes, they were able to use six aircraft carriers with 423 aircraft – and not a single biplane amongst them. The aircraft were modern monoplanes, including the famous Mitsubishi A6M, the 'Zero', but this was a fighter, and the real work was to be done by dive-bombers, torpedo-bombers and the so-called 'level bombers', aircraft which dropped bombs in the conventional manner.

Unlike Taranto, where Britain and Italy had been at war for some months by the time of the attack, Japan intended to attack without first declaring war on the United States.

Circumstances aided the Japanese. The fleet approached the flying-off position through a tropical storm, so remained undetected. The United States Pacific Fleet had its battleships and cruisers in harbour, off-duty on a Sunday morning. The radar watch was lacking in many respects and was not maintained continuously. Contrary to Japanese fears, the fleet did not even have torpedo nets around those ships that could have been vulnerable to such attack. There were no standing fighter patrols or ships on picket duty.

The Japanese sent 353 of their aircraft to Pearl Harbor. Expecting that they might have to fight their way to the target, the first wave of 183 aircraft was unopposed and even had the benefit of the local weather forecast from a radio station at Hawaii. Flying at 10,000 feet, the first wave passed over the northernmost point of Oahu at 0730 hrs. At 0749, the attack began.

There was no anti-aircraft fire at this stage and the sky was completely clear of fighters. Freed from any need to defend the bombers, the Zeros dived down and raced across the dockyard and the airfields, firing at anything in their sights. Dive-bombers swooped on Ford Island, their bombs causing fires and sending debris into the air. Torpedo-bombers flew so low when attacking Battleship Row that those watching thought that they would never clear the towering superstructures. To many senior Japanese naval officers, who like their counterparts in other navies were still adherents of the 'big-gun' navy, success was to be measured by the scale of the losses suffered by the Pacific Fleet.

When it was time for the second wave to mount its attack, the Zeros had to attack American fighters as they struggled into the air. The strike aircraft in the second wave consisted entirely of bombers and dive-bombers, as torpedo-bombers were seen as being too vulnerable once the defences had been alerted; later experience at the Battle of Midway was to prove correct this assessment of the dangers facing torpedo-bombers. As it was, almost all of the twenty-nine Japanese aircraft shot down over Hawaii that morning belonged to the second wave.

The Japanese airmen could see the battleship *Arizona* blazing, while the *Oklahoma* had capsized, along with the target ship *Utah*, counted by Japanese intelligence as an active battleship, while both the *California* and *West Virginia* were settling; the light cruiser *Helena* had been crippled; the *Pennsylvania* and two destroyers, all in dry dock, were all damaged.

The commanding officer of another battleship, *Nevada*, decided that his ship would be safer at sea than sitting as a target in Battleship Row. The Japanese dive-bomber pilots realized that this was their chance of sinking the ship in the harbour mouth, thereby blocking the port, and dived down onto the ship in the face of heavy

AA fire. The commanding officer did well to beach his ship, keeping the base functional and saving her.

When the leader of the attack, Mitsou Fuchida, was asked whether the Pacific Fleet would be able to operate from Pearl Harbor for six months, he confirmed that the main force would not be able to operate for that period of time, but that many smaller vessels and the shore installations were still functional. He urged a further attack, at least a third wave, if not a fourth. The targets would be the remaining ships, and, even more important, the shore installations and airfields.

Meanwhile, the hangar and flight-deck crews were rearming and refuelling aircraft, including the torpedo-bombers that would be needed should American warships give chase. The Japanese were all too well aware that the big disappointment of the morning had been the absence of the American aircraft carriers among the ships assembled at Pearl Harbor. Torpedoes were more effective than bombs in the open sea, while there was often the problem that bombs would bounce off the heavy armour of a battleship. This work continued while the aircrew had lunch.

While the airmen were feeding, the decision was taken not to make a further strike. Nagumo ordered a withdrawal to the north-west and in so doing lost any chance of victory for the Imperial Japanese Navy by failing to send a third and even a fourth wave of aircraft to Pearl Harbor. The only possible justification would have been an attack on the Panama Canal to delay reinforcement of the Pacific Fleet. As a result, at no time was Pearl Harbor unavailable to the United States Navy, while the airfields ashore were quickly repaired. The US Pacific Fleet's carrier force remained at sea until it was safe to return and then started the series of attacks that brought the Japanese to battle, and ultimately, to defeat.

Nagumo's mistake was noticed immediately by Yamamoto. Nevertheless, over the next few months, it seemed as if Nagumo was the greatest admiral in history. His fleet took part in the invasion of the Netherlands East Indies, attacked Darwin in Australia's Northern Territory, and sank British warships in the Indian Ocean. The next objective was to secure Japan's position in mid-Pacific by seizing Midway.

The Battle of Midway in June 1942 was to prove to be a disaster. It was marred from the outset by over-optimism and the selection of an island as an objective that hardly justified the attention. These problems were compounded by poor reconnaissance, and then finally settled by indecision and poor management of their carrier flight decks and hangars on the part of the Japanese. Even many Japanese were divided over whether or not Midway was worth the risk. Amongst those at Imperial Headquarters in Tokyo, many favoured isolating Australia from the United States. Others were taking a more defensive line, following the Doolittle raid on Japanese cities. The objective at Midway was twofold: to occupy the island and lure the US Pacific Fleet beyond the atoll so that it could be destroyed.

Midway is a coral atoll and two islands, some 1,300 nautical miles north of Honolulu, with a total area of just 2 square miles. Although annexed by the United States in 1867, a naval air base was not established until 1941, just in time for the outbreak of war in the Pacific.

Nagumo's chief-of-staff, Kusaka, objected to the operation because the ships were not ready – they needed to refit and retrain new aircrew to combat readiness.

One of the most experienced airmen in the Imperial Japanese Navy also objected. The veteran of Pearl Harbor, Mitsuo Fuchida, felt that the base on Midway was not worth taking. He knew that too many experienced aircrew had been removed from the carriers after a campaign in the Indian Ocean, and that they needed to recover from their losses off Ceylon. In addition, the carrier force was to be divided, with a raiding force and two carriers sent to the Aleutians, leaving four for the Midway operation. Many objected to this splitting of the available forces.

What the Japanese did not realize was that the Americans had already broken their codes and were aware of their plans.

The Japanese were hoping for a decisive victory, despite having sent two carriers, the *Ryujo* and *Junyo*, to attack Dutch Harbour, in the Aleutian Islands, close to Alaska. The Midway force was under the command of Nagumo.

The Battle of Midway

Unknown to the Japanese, the Americans were concentrating their naval forces to defend Midway Island, on which the United States Army Air Force also had a base, with fighters and heavy bombers, including the new Boeing B-17 Flying Fortress.

It was at this stage that a combination of good intelligence and a sound grasp of strategy began to tell. The Americans were not distracted when Japanese carrier-borne aircraft attacked the Aleutians on 3 June. Instead, their energies were concentrated on finding the main Japanese fleet, including not just the inevitable aircraft carriers, but the troop transports as well. Having located the Japanese forces, Boeing B-17s were despatched from Midway on the afternoon of 3 June to bomb the landing fleet, but without scoring any hits on the ships. A ship underway at sea is a difficult target, especially for high-altitude bombing.

The Japanese were to open their attack on 4 June, intending that it would be led by Mitsuo Fuchida, who had led the raid on Pearl Harbor. After he was confined to the sick bay of the carrier *Akagi*, having had an operation for appendicitis, another officer took his place. Fuchida was determined to be present for the attack and had refused the offer of a destroyer to take him to hospital. This determination led him to rise from his sick bed on the morning of the attack and make his way to the flight deck. Although Fuchida had remained with the fleet so that he could help with the planning of the operation, he had been overlooked. This led to the first mistake as the search patterns being flown by the fleet's reconnaissance aircraft were badly planned, leaving large areas of sea uncovered, so that an American force could approach undetected.

At dawn, Nagumo sent a hundred aircraft to Midway to destroy the island's defences. Almost immediately, the fleet came under heavy attack from USAAF and shore-based USN aircraft from Midway. The attackers managed to disrupt the formation of the fleet and were able to strafe the carriers' decks, killing and injuring many crewmen, before being chased off by the fleet's Zero fighters for the loss of seventeen American aircraft.

By this time, the aircraft from the Japanese carriers were over Midway, inflicting heavy damage to the shore installations. The airfield and anti-aircraft defences were still operational and the attack leader passed this information back to the fleet by radio. Nagumo realized that a second strike was necessary. The problem was that this would need bombs and the remaining aircraft aboard the four carriers had been loaded with torpedoes, expecting an attack on American warships. The order went out for these to be taken off and exchanged for bombs, quickly!

The armourers were engaged in this task when a reconnaissance aircraft reported that it had seen ten American warships. Nagumo changed his mind – the American warships posed the more serious threat to his ships and to the troop transports – and the order was reversed, so that the bombs had to be taken off the aircraft and torpedoes put back on again.

The hangar decks of the carriers were by this time the scenes of frantic activity, with each aircraft having what amounted to two warloads on or near the aircraft, with bombs for the attack on Midway and torpedoes for the strike against the American warships. Rather than scramble those aircraft which now had torpedoes fitted, Nagumo decided to hold these back until the aircraft of the first strike, now returning from Midway and short of fuel, had been recovered aboard the carriers.

It was at 0900 hrs, while the Japanese were still waiting for the first strike to return, that one of their reconnaissance aircraft reported sighting an American aircraft carrier, thought to be the *Yorktown*. This came as a surprise to the Japanese, who had assumed that there were no American carriers in the vicinity because of the lack of fighter cover for the earlier attack on their ships. But it was too late to change the orders – the first wave had returned. All they could do was wait for these aircraft to land, move them down into the hangars as quickly as possible and get the second strike aircraft away.

The second strike of aircraft were on the Japanese carrier decks, ranged ready for take-off, when the first wave of American carrier aircraft attacked. The entire force of aircraft from two carriers, the *Enterprise* and *Hornet*, had been put into the air, while the *Yorktown* had sent half of her aircraft. This meant that a total of 156 aircraft were sent to attack the Japanese fleet.

The first wave consisted of forty-one Douglas Devastator torpedo-bombers, which suffered heavy losses as they ran in to make their attack, flying low over the waves towards the Japanese carriers. No less than thirty-five of these aircraft were shot down by heavy anti-aircraft fire from the fleet and by the few fighters which had managed to get airborne from the carriers. Whole squadrons disappeared. Many of the aircrew had no time to escape from their low-flying aircraft before they crashed into the sea. The ease with which this attack was fought off, combined with their earlier successes against the aircraft attacking from Midway, put the Japanese into a jubilant mood. After the setbacks at the Battle of the Coral Sea, they were confident that they were now on the verge of yet another victory.

The paradox was that, had the Japanese carriers been depending on radar, they might not have spotted the low-flying Devastators until it was too late, but they would have noticed the second wave, which consisted of high-flying dive-bombers, in good time.

At 1022, the first of the second wave of Douglas Dauntless dive-bombers plunged down from 19,000 feet towards the first of the carriers. Each carried a 1,000-lb bomb. The Japanese were still preoccupied with the torpedo-bombers and the aftermath of their ill-starred attack. Eyes were therefore cast down to the sea, rather than looking into the air, and the Zero fighters were still flying around at sea level. Aboard the ships, the flight decks were still full of armed aircraft ready to strike at the American ships. In the hangars, aircraft were being refuelled, while the bombs for the Midway attack lay on the hangar deck, for there had been no time to return them to the magazines.

The first bombs hit the *Kaga*, which took four direct hits from the twelve bombs aimed at her. Four direct hits were more than enough. The bombs crashed through the flight deck and exploded in the hangars, amongst the aircraft being refuelled and rearmed, and the bombs left on the hangar deck. The ship was abandoned almost immediately.

The first bomb aimed at the flagship *Akagi* missed, but only just as it exploded and black water was washed over everyone on the ship's bridge. Then the ship was hit by two 1,000-lb bombs. The first bomb crashed through one of the lifts, while the second penetrated through the flight deck. Both bombs exploded on the hangar deck, hitting stacks of 1,750-lb bombs intended for the airfield at Midway and setting these off in a chain reaction. Fully armed aircraft exploded in flames, again in a chain reaction as one aircraft exploded and set the one nearest to it ablaze, before that also exploded. The hangar became a blazing inferno and soon flames were sweeping across the flight deck. Those working below, in the engine rooms and in the sick bay, were cut off.

A third carrier, the *Soryu*, was also on fire by this time. Three 1,000-lb bombs had hit her flight deck in a straight line and again crashed into the hangars. Only *Hiryu*, ahead of the rest of the fleet, was still operational. The dive-bombing raid was over in just four minutes.

Faced with a crushing defeat, Nagumo wanted to go down with his flagship but was persuaded to transfer his flag to a cruiser, the *Nagura*.

In an attempt to strike back at the Americans, a strike was mounted from the *Hiryu*, but just eight Japanese dive-bombers managed to penetrate the *Yorktown*'s fighter screen and AA fire to drop three 500-lb bombs on the carrier. The first of these bombs exploded amongst parked aircraft on the carrier's deck, setting these on fire. The second went down the funnel, a lucky shot for the Japanese, and blew out five of her six boilers. The third penetrated three decks to ignite the carrier's aviation fuel. These hits could have been fatal for the carrier, but prompt damage control and effective fire-fighting smothered the aviation fuel with carbon dioxide, while as a precaution the magazines were smothered in foam.

Early in the afternoon, *Hiryu* sent a further strike against the *Yorktown*, consisting of just ten Nakajima Kate torpedo-bombers and six Zero fighters. Once the Japanese aircraft were sighted, the *Yorktown* stopped refuelling aircraft and drained her aviation fuel system – a precaution against pipelines being ruptured during an attack. Although very short of fuel, six Grumman Wildcat fighters were scrambled to intercept the attackers and managed to shoot down five of the torpedo-bombers.

The Japanese believed that they had attacked two different carriers and that neither ship was operational. They also believed that the Americans had just two carriers in the Pacific leaving them without a strike capability, and that they could therefore inflict a crippling blow on the rest of the American fleet, using aircraft recovered from the other Japanese carriers and now embarked aboard *Hiryu*.

With the Japanese preparing for a final all-out attack on the American fleet, with the surviving aircraft ranged on the flight deck of *Hiryu*, the ship was attacked by more Dauntless dive-bombers. As she turned sharply to avoid their bombs, the Americans scored four direct hits and four near misses. Near misses can sometimes be as fatal as hits, the reverberation causing damage inside the hull, especially to fuel lines, and to plating. These ones set off aviation fuel fires.

The Japanese carrier force had been destroyed.

Had the reconnaissance from the carriers been more thorough, defects in Japanese intelligence could have been corrected. With four carriers, Nagumo could have ensured that one ship was always ready with a free flight deck ready to launch fighters, and he could have maintained fighter patrols which would have caught the American dive-bombers.

After Midway, final defeat was a matter of time for the Japanese, for whom the battle ended any hope of victory, or even of a stalemate with a negotiated compromise.

For Nagumo, Midway was the beginning of the end. He was involved at Guadalcanal and at the Battle of the Santa Cruz Islands, but his forces were steadily eroded and so too, it seems, was his self-confidence. On 11 November 1942, he was reassigned back to Japan, where he was given command of the Sasebo Naval District. He transferred to the Kure Naval District on 21 June 1943, and from October 1943 to February 1944 was again Commander-in-Chief of the IJN 1st Fleet, although this was preoccupied with training duties by that time.

In March 1944, Nagumo was once again given a combat command, being sent to the Mariana Islands as Commander-in-Chief of the short-lived IJN 14th Air Fleet, and simultaneously Commander-in-Chief of the equally short-lived Central Pacific Area Fleet. The US invasion of Saipan began on 15 June 1944. Within days the IJN under Vice Admiral Jisaburo Ozawa was overwhelmed by the US Fifth Fleet in the decisive Battle of the Philippine Sea costing Japan approximately 500 aircraft. Nagumo and his Army peer, General Yoshitsugu Saito, were then left on their own to defend Saipan against the American assault. On 6 July, during the last stages of the Battle of Saipan, Nagumo committed suicide, not in the traditional method of seppuku, but rather a pistol to the temple. He was posthumously promoted to admiral.

Chapter 30

The Last Japanese C-in-C

Vice Admiral Jisaburo Ozawa (1886–1963)

Jisaburo Ozawa had a distinguished naval career and succeeded Toyoda as the last Commander-in-Chief of the Combined Fleet in May 1945, when the end of the fleet and surrender of his country was simply a matter of time. A modest man, he refused promotion to admiral because he believed that serving his country was more important than rank.

He was born on 2 October 1886, in rural Koyu County on the Japanese island of Kyushu. Like his contemporaries at the head of the Imperial Japanese Navy, he attended the Imperial Japanese Naval Academy, which he left in 1909, not especially highly placed amongst that year's graduates. He served as a midshipman on the cruisers *Soya* and *Kasuga* and battleship *Mikasa*. Promoted to ensign, Ozawa served on the destroyer *Arare*, battleship *Hiei* and cruiser *Chitose*, and as a lieutenant, on *Kawachi* and *Hinoki*. He specialized in torpedo warfare. He attended the Japanese Naval War College in 1919, afterwards being promoted to lieutenant commander, and was given his first command, the destroyer *Take*. He subsequently commanded *Shimakaze* and *Asakaze*. He served as chief torpedo officer on *Kongo* in 1925.

Except for a twelve-month visit to the United States and Europe in 1930, he served in staff positions from 1925 until 1933. On 15 November 1934, he was given command of the *Maya* and of the *Haruna* in 1935. On 1 December 1936, he was promoted to rear admiral. He continued to serve in various staff positions, including

Chief of Staff of the Combined Fleet in 1937 and Commandant of the Imperial Japanese Naval Academy. He was promoted to vice admiral on 15 November 1940.

After the attack on Pearl Harbor, Ozawa became responsible for Japan's naval operations in the South China Sea as Commander-in-Chief of the Southern Expeditionary Fleet, providing support for the invasion of Malaya. Between January and March 1942, his fleet was involved in the invasions of Java and Sumatra. Despite his conventional naval background, Ozawa was one of the leading advocates of naval aviation in the Imperial Japanese Navy – he was the first high-ranking officer to recommend that the Japanese aircraft carrier forces be organized into an air fleet so that they could train and fight together. No doubt if he had commanded the attack on Pearl Harbor, the outcome would have been different, but he did not replace Chuichi Nagumo as commander of Japan's carrier forces until 11 November 1942. It was too late, for while Ozawa proved an aggressive and skilled commander, he was overwhelmed by the numerical and technological superiority of the United States at the Battle of the Philippine Sea. After the battle, he offered his resignation, but it was was not accepted.

The remnants of his fleet were present at the Battle of Leyte Gulf against the forces of Admiral William Halsey. Despite being the senior admiral there, the overall Japanese battle plan was to sacrifice his force as a decoy so that Kurita's Centre Force could attack MacArthur's invasion forces on the Leyte beaches. Nevertheless, Ozawa commanded his forces well and many believe that he was the foremost amongst Japan's wartime admirals. Despite this, his fleet ended its career off of the Philippines with flight decks empty for lack of aircraft and pilots. Afterwards, he succeeded Toyoda as the last Commander-in-Chief of the Imperial Japanese Navy from 29 May 1945. He refused promotion to full admiral and remained as vice admiral until the final dissolution of the Imperial Japanese Navy.

He died in 1966 at the age of eighty.

Chapter 31

Commanding Defeat

Admiral Soemu Toyoda (1885–1957)

Soemu Toyoda was in the unfortunate position of in effect stepping into a dead man's shoes. Commander of the major naval base at Yokosuka, he replaced Vice Admiral Koga as Commander-in-Chief of the Combined Fleet in March 1944.

Born in Oita on 22 May 1885, he seems to have acquired the ambition of joining the Imperial Japanese Navy in childhood and when he was old enough he joined the Imperial Naval Academy. After graduating in 1905, he subsequently specialized in gunnery. His early postings were aboard cruisers and destroyers and like many of the other Japanese Second World War admirals, he travelled, in his case to Britain, attending the London Naval Conference with Isoroku Yamamoto in 1930. He was promoted to rear admiral on 1 December 1931, when he joined the naval staff. After several staff positions, Toyoda returned to sea as the commanding officer of the 4th Fleet, followed by a similar position with the 2nd Fleet, in both cases being responsible for providing support for the invasion of China. He subsequently claimed to be amongst those, such as Yamamoto, who opposed war with the United States, but he believed that it was not a naval officer's place to become involved in politics.

When Japan attacked Pearl Harbor, Toyoda was in command of the important Kure Naval Station and remained ashore from this time onwards. In November 1942, he joined the Supreme War Council, where he pressed the Army-dominated Imperial General Headquarters to allocate a higher percentage of Japan's industrial capacity to construct aircraft for the Navy. His pleadings were in vain, and, in frustration, he left the Supreme War Council in May 1943 to command the Yokosuka Naval Base.

Like his predecessor, and even Koga's predecessor, Yamamoto, he believed in the decisive naval battle, in which the US Pacific Fleet would be destroyed and the Imperial Japanese Navy would finally get the chance to use its large battleships. The plan was known as A-Go and involved drawing the Americans away from the Marianas to an area closer to Palau, which in itself recognized that his ships were so short of fuel that they could not give chase. The result was the disaster known as the Battle of the Philippine Sea. Unshaken by this, he then planned a further battle at Leyte Gulf, believing that Japanese air power and battleships combined would save the day, but with one of his commanders withdrawing early and Japanese air power no longer a match for the Americans, this was yet another disaster.

As the Americans landed on Okinawa, Toyoda launched Operation Ten-Go, with massed kamikaze attacks against the US warships and transports, with no less than 1,900 sorties between 6 April and 22 June, causing unprecedented Allied casualties. Nevertheless, in the Battle of the East China Sea that followed, the Japanese Mobile Fleet – in fact, the remnants of the Combined Fleet – was destroyed. The Battle of the East China Sea was in one sense the decisive naval battle for which so many Second World War admirals on both sides yearned. On the other hand, it was also the ultimate in kamikaze missions as Toyoda ordered the giant 64,000-ton battleship *Yamato*, with its 18-inch main armament, to sea with an escort of just one cruiser and eight destroyers as escort, without air cover and without enough fuel to return to port. This was desperate enough, but the sacrifice was in vain as the commander of the Thirty-Second Army ashore on Okinawa, Lieutenant General Mitsuri Ushijima, failed to follow the joint Army-Navy defence agreement of keeping the landing forces on the beachheads long enough to give the IJN time to amass both a kamikaze attack and heavy gunfire from the *Yamato*. Instead, he withdrew from the coastal area, so that the US troops encountered little resistance as they landed, while the Japanese forces were preparing defensive positions in the mountainous interior. On 7 April, 380 US aircraft from Task Force 58 attacked, quickly sinking the *Yamato*, the cruiser and four of the destroyers.

The kamikaze air offensive had started the day before, with 355 sorties on that day alone, and continued until 29 May, with no less than ten massed kamikaze attacks overall, mounted from Kyushu, one of the home islands, and a total of 1,465 sorties, of which 860 were JNAF and the remainder JAAF.

These kamikaze attacks proved to be the most concentrated of the war with no less than twenty-six Allied ships being sunk, albeit none of them larger than a destroyer, while another 164 ships were damaged. Those ships damaged included the aircraft carriers USS *Intrepid*, *Enterprise*, *Franklin* and *Bunker Hill*, as well as the British carriers HMS *Formidable*, *Indefatigable* and *Victorious*, and the battleships USS *Maryland*, *Tennessee* and *New Mexico*.

Enterprise was hit by a suicide aircraft on 11 April and was forced to suspend flying operations for forty-eight hours. *Franklin* was hit by six kamikaze aircraft, taking the lives of 700 members of her crew, with many more badly injured. The ship was also hit by two 550-lb bombs. It is generally accepted that this was the one Essex-class carrier that came close to being lost during the war. Although saved, she never returned to active service, spending some time after the war as an aircraft transport.

'When a kamikaze hits a US carrier, it's six months repair at Pearl,' commented an American liaison officer surveying the after effects of one such attack aboard a British carrier. 'In a Limey carrier, it's a case of "Sweepers, man your brooms!" '

This might have been an overgenerous appraisal of the situation, but it was certainly true that the Royal Navy's six fast armoured carriers proved the value of their armoured flight decks, hangar sides and decks during the kamikaze campaign.

Despite Japan being cut off from supplies of fuel, raw materials and food, Toyoda joined the anti-surrender faction, even after the atomic bombs had destroyed Hiroshima and Nagasaki, and when Prince Konoye lobbied for peace, Toyoda argued that they should defend the Japanese Home Islands until the last man. He retained his position as Commander-in-Chief until arrested for war crimes, and when tried by an Allied tribunal, he was acquitted on condition that he would never re-enter public service.

Toyoda died in Tokyo on 22 September 1957.

Chapter 32

Planning for War, Expecting Defeat

Fleet Admiral Isoroku Yamamoto (1884–1943)

Yamamoto had overall control of the attack on Pearl Harbor, including its planning. He firmly believed that Japan could not win an all-out war against the United States, not having the industrial power or manpower, or the natural resources. The paradox was that he was opposed to war with the United States, realizing that Japan could not match America's industrial might, her manpower or her natural resources. The best that could be expected was that Japan would win a major victory in the first year, but that by the second year the United States would have recovered and be able to move to the offensive. The Imperial Japanese Navy was stronger than the United States Navy in the Pacific, but it would be weaker than the United States Navy if it had to face the combined Atlantic and Pacific fleets.

Isoroku Yamamoto was the son of a schoolmaster and was born in Nagaoka in 1884 as Isoroku Takano. His forename, Isoroku, referred to his father's age when his son was born. In 1916, Isoroku was adopted into the Yamamoto family, taking the family name, following the custom for Japanese families lacking sons to adopt suitable young men in this fashion to carry on the family name. In 1918, Isoroku married a woman named Reiko with whom he had four children: two sons and two daughters.

On leaving school, he went to the Imperial Japanese Naval Academy at Etajima, from which he graduated in 1904. It was a good time to be joining the fleet as the Russo-Japanese War broke out in February 1904. Yamamoto served in the cruiser *Nisshin* during the war and was wounded at the Battle of Tsushima, losing two fingers on his left hand. Although all of the ships involved were pre-dreadnoughts, this was the first major naval battle of modern times and the only 'all-big-gun' battle that ever engaged the IJN. He returned to the Naval Staff College in 1914, emerging as a lieutenant commander in 1916.

After the First World War, Yamamoto was sent by the IJN to the United States so that he could learn English, a peculiarity of the IJN which expected its young officers to learn a foreign language. He lived in Boston and attended Harvard from 1919 to 1921, while he also spent some time at the US Naval War College, something that was possible because of Japan's role as a First World War ally. As well as learning the language, he learnt about the oil industry and became aware of the strength of US industry. On a lighter note, he also learnt to play poker, a game which appealed to his temperament. He seems to have enjoyed his period in the United States and returned home in 1921 well disposed to the country and its people.

In 1924, he was promoted to commander and appointed as executive officer of a naval air station, at a time when the former First World War ally was receiving the support and advice of a British naval mission. Despite his experience at Tsushima, he studied aviation and became one of the leading experts and proponents on the subject in Japan, with little confidence in battleships, even after the emergence of the dreadnought. Later, when his fellow senior officers claimed that only a battleship could sink a battleship, he responded with the old Japanese proverb: 'The fiercest serpent may be overcome by a swarm of ants.' His next appointment was as naval attaché in Washington in 1926. This brought him into close contact with the USN, of which he formed a low opinion, describing the peacetime navy as a club for bridge players and golfers. His regard for the strength of the USA, however, remained undiminished.

Clearly destined for senior rank, he was a rear admiral by 1930 and was sent as part of the Japanese delegation to the London Naval Conference. He resumed his connection with naval aviation on his return, being posted to Naval Air Corps headquarters in September 1930. In his new role, he concentrated on improving the quality and performance of naval aircraft, including the development of land-based naval aviation, particularly the G3M and G4M medium bombers. He specified long range and the ability to carry a torpedo, and insisted on the development of high-performance fighter aircraft, thereby starting a line of aircraft that culminated in the famous Mitsubishi A6M Zero, which possessed range and good manoeuvrability as well as speed. These qualities were incorporated at the expense of light construction and flammability that later contributed to the A6M's high casualty rates as the war progressed.

After returning to sea in 1933 in command of the First Carrier Division, with the rank of vice admiral, he also participated in the 1935 London Naval Conference, as the government felt that a naval specialist needed to accompany the diplomats to the arms limitations talks. In 1935, he became Deputy Minister of the Navy.

Meanwhile, he aroused the enmity of the pro-war faction as he had opposed the invasion of Manchuria in 1931, and the subsequent war with China which started in 1937, just as he later opposed the Tripartite Pact, negotiated in Tokyo but signed in Berlin on 27 September 1940, with Germany and Italy. In his role as Deputy Navy Minister, he apologized to the then United States Ambassador for the bombing of the gunboat USS *Panay* in Chinese waters in December 1937. When asked by the Prime Minister, Prince Konoe, about Japan's chances in a war with the United Kingdom and the USA, he responded that Japan's forces could 'run wild for six months or a year, but after that I have utterly no confidence.' He concluded that he hoped that the Prime Minister would try to avoid war with the USA. The year before, in 1939, a plot to assassinate him had been uncovered. His superiors decided that he would be safer at sea, and on 15 November 1940 he was promoted to admiral and given command of the Combined Fleet.

In his new role, Yamamoto oversaw the reorganization of Japanese carrier forces into the First Air Fleet, a consolidated strike force that gathered the six largest carriers into one unit. This provided unprecedented striking ability, but also concentrated the vulnerable carriers into a compact and attractive target. In addition, he formed a similarly large land-based organisation, the 11th Air Fleet, which would later use the G3M and G4M to cripple American air power in the Philippines and sink the Royal Navy's Force Z off Malaya. Earlier, he had opposed the construction of the two giant battleships as a waste of resources.

His continued progress was surprising given that many political observers thought that Yamamoto's career was essentially over when General Hideki Tojo was appointed Prime Minister on 18 October

1941. The two men had been opponents when Yamamoto had served as Japan's Deputy Navy Minister and Tojo was the leading advocate and planner of Japan's takeover of Manchuria. It was believed that Yamamoto would be appointed to command the Yokosuka Naval Base, described by one contemporary observer as 'a nice safe demotion with a big house and no power at all'. However, Yamamoto was left alone in his position as Commander-in-Chief of the Combined Fleet despite his open conflicts with General Tojo and other members of the Army's oligarchy who favoured war with the European powers and America. The main reasons for Yamamoto's survival were his immense popularity within the Navy where he commanded the respect of his men and officers, and his close relations with the royal family. Emperor Hirohito shared Yamamoto's deep respect for the West.

Given the superior strength of the United States, Yamamoto was faced with the problem of how to wage war given that the Government was determined on the opening of hostilities. He set his staff to examine the possibilities and the conclusion was that the only chance Japan would have would be to destroy the US Pacific Fleet and render its forward base inoperable at Pearl Harbor in a pre-emptive strike. Japan had in any case a history of not first declaring war, as in the Russo-Japanese War of 1904–1905. This proposal did not find immediate acceptance amongst the other admirals, who regarded the operation as being too risky, and threatened the loss of at least two or three aircraft carriers. Nevertheless, Yamamoto persisted, standing by the plan. It was probably the sheer audacity of the plan that made it workable. Eventually, unable to come forward with a better plan, the IJN adopted the idea of a pre-emptive strike on Pearl Harbor.

The battle that Yamamoto had to fight with his colleagues from January 1941 was that, since the end of the First World War, the Imperial Japanese Navy had been following the teachings of the USN's Captain Alfred T. Mahan. This meant that the naval general staff had planned for Japanese light surface forces, submarines and land-based air units to whittle down the American Fleet as it advanced across the Pacific until the Japanese Navy engaged it in a climactic 'Decisive Battle' in the northern Philippine Sea (between the Ryukyu Islands and the Marianas Islands), with battleships meeting in the traditional exchange between battle lines.

Yamamoto pointed out that this plan had never worked, even in Japanese war games. Painfully aware of American strategic advantages in military productive capacity, he proposed instead to seek a decision with the Americans by first reducing their forces with a preemptive strike, and then following with a 'Decisive Battle' fought offensively, rather than defensively. Yamamoto hoped, but probably did not believe, that if the Americans could be dealt such terrific blows early in the war, they might be willing to negotiate an end to the conflict. As it turned out, however, when the note officially breaking off diplomatic relations with the United States was delivered late, he realized that the Americans would be resolved upon revenge and unwilling to negotiate. The Naval General Staff proved reluctant to accept his appraisal and Yamamoto was eventually driven to capitalize on his popularity in the fleet by threatening to resign to get his way. Admiral Osami Nagano and the Naval General Staff eventually caved in to this pressure, but only insofar as approving the attack on Pearl Harbor. Surprise attacks have a long military tradition when starting a war, and Japan could clearly see that supporting such would give themselves six months to secure the resources of the Netherlands East Indies, free from any intervention by the USN.

Pearl Harbor and Beyond

Before the carrier fleet left – six ships in the First, Second and Fifth carrier Divisions, equating to British capital ship squadrons – Yamamoto visited them, worried that the young naval airmen might underestimate their opponents.

'Japan has faced many worthy opponents in her long history – Mongols, Chinese, Russians – but the United States is the most worthy of all,' he warned them. 'You must be prepared for great American resistance. Admiral Kimmel, Commander-in-Chief of the Pacific Fleet, is known to be farsighted and aggressive, so you cannot count upon surprise. You may have to fight your way to the target.'

What was widely perceived as the great victory at Pearl Harbor gave Yamamoto enormous prestige, but he realized that, by not sending a third and even a fourth wave later in the day, Nagumo had wasted an opportunity and that the attack had failed. It had brought the United States into the war, but with Pearl Harbor and the Pacific Fleet's aircraft carriers all intact. Nevertheless, the reputation of both men continued to grow with the rapid Japanese advance across the

Pacific and the Netherlands East Indies, as well as the fall of Malaya and the great fortress of Singapore, except, of course, that without a great fleet, the fortress itself was sadly inadequate. The one fly in the ointment was that the Doolittle raid on Japan had shown the country that even its home islands were vulnerable.

Yakamoto's next plan was to bring the US Pacific Fleet to a decisive naval engagement at Midway. When he first proposed this early in the war, once again the Naval General Staff rejected the idea, but the Doolittle raid changed their minds. A strong defensive ring was required and then the most direct maritime route between Australia and the United States had to be severed, so that Australia would be seriously, even fatally, weakened. Midway proved to be a step too far as Ultra intelligence forewarned the Americans of Japanese intentions, and the resulting naval engagement between aircraft-carrier forces was a massive victory for the USN with four Japanese carriers sunk in a single day. Along with Nagumo, Yakamoto's infallible reputation was badly dented at Midway.

For a while, at Guadalcanal and in the seas around it, it seemed that Yakamoto could once again save the day, flying his flag in one of the two giant battleships, *Yamato*, and, less often, *Musashi*, but despite a tactical victory in the Battle of the Santa Cruz Islands, Guadalcanal was lost by the Japanese. Not only had the USN regrouped and recovered from the setbacks at Pearl Harbor and the Battle of the Coral Sea, the IJN had lost the cream of its experienced aircrew and lacked the training organization to replace them quickly.

Moving ashore first to Truk, on 3 April 1943, he moved his headquarters to Rabaul. On 18 April, he left by air to inspect Japanese bases in the northern Solomons. Once again, Ultra intelligence alerted the USN to his plans, although strangely Nimitz decided first to ask Washington whether Yakamoto's aircraft should be shot down. Not surprisingly, the answer was in the affirmative, so, as his aircraft approached Bourgainville, it was shot down. He was being flown in a G4M medium bomber, lightly constructed and when fully fuelled, vulnerable to enemy fire, earning it the sardonic nickname 'the Flying Cigarette Lighter'.

There can be little doubt about Yakamoto's brilliance as a planner and a leader. Perhaps if he had entered politics instead of the IJN, Japan would have taken a different course and war might have been avoided, but we will never know. He seemed to have learned about Nagumo's mistake in not sending a third and even a fourth raid to

Pearl Harbor too late to correct the error, but it seems certain that had a third and fourth wave attack been mounted, Japanese losses would have been much heavier at Pearl Harbor than was in fact the case – which might have delayed the strike westwards.

In fact, what does become clear from this is that the inability to mount effective reconnaissance was a major failure for both sides early in the Pacific War. Good reconnaissance, supported by a picket line of ships or, even better, submarines, could have saved the heavy losses amongst American personnel at Pearl Harbor, and might even have given both navies a classic naval engagement. At Midway, effective reconnaissance could have saved the Japanese carriers, albeit only if they withdrew, but they failed to take the atoll anyway.

Chapter 33

Defining Leadership at Sea

What makes a great leader is something that is difficult to define. Our admirals varied in their characters as much as their political opinions. Only the British seemed to be completely apolitical, although the same could be said for Ozawa, and Toyoda claimed as much, despite belonging to the anti-surrender faction at the end of the Second World War.

Napoleon once said that when he was looking for a general, he always asked whether a candidate was lucky. Having good luck is probably more important in a leader than whether he is good humoured or bad tempered, patient or impatient, modest or arrogant. Halsey certainly had more than his fair share of good fortune, managing to be in the right place at the right time, and Cunningham would not have become First Sea Lord were it not for Fraser's modesty.

But there is more to it than that. Experience is also very important. Those with experience of action in the First World War tended to be greater and better leaders than those who had not. This was a weakness of the Japanese admirals. It was no help either that Dönitz never had the chance to command a fleet at sea in wartime, nor did he even have the opportunity to be close to a commander at sea during a major battle.

The problem with experience is that it can blind a commander to other possibilities. Many of those who had experience of the torpedo or the big gun thought that this was the way wars would be fought, not only in the present, but in future. At the beginning of the twentieth century, naval commanders were obsessed by the threat of the torpedo and were attracted by the power of the all big-gun battleship. These were weapons favoured by that great naval reformer, the British Admiral of the Fleet Lord Fisher, twice First Sea Lord at the British Admiralty, and father of the modern battleship, having dictated the design of HMS *Dreadnought*. On the other hand, few remembered Fisher's advice, which was that the future of warfare at sea would come from beneath the waves and from above them. Fisher was thinking of the airship at the time, but it was the aeroplane that reigned supreme.

The successful admirals were those who recognized the importance of the aeroplane and the submarine.

Closed minds have always been a weakness and there is no doubt that many of the Japanese admirals suffered from this. It is also apparent that Ernest King allowed his Anglophobia to cloud his judgement. During the First World War, American pressure finally helped to convince the Royal Navy that convoys were an essential element in the defence against the submarine, so it is even stranger that King was so reluctant to introduce convoys after the United States entered the Second World War. The fact that USN and USCG anti-submarine patrols operated to a timetable was also ridiculous, as was the failure to enforce a blackout in coastal towns, leaving ships backlit as they passed, giving the German U-boat commanders perfect targets.

What else is needed in a great wartime naval leader? Imagination and an open mind are important, so too is experience – but what else? Aggressive instincts are vital. When it came to the crunch, Nagumo lacked sufficient aggression to continue the attack on Pearl Harbor. The Italian admirals lacked the aggressive instinct that would have seen Malta bombarded and then invaded. On the other hand, Somerville can be forgiven for not being more aggressive with the French fleet at Mers-el-Kebir, although he certainly showed sufficient aggression against the *Bismarck* and later with his attack on Genoa.

Another factor that is important has to be good discipline. A senior commander expects discipline from his subordinates, but also needs to display it himself. Halsey showed a lack of discipline and a complete absence of regard for the rest of the US Navy in the Philippines when he chased after the retreating Japanese, leaving the fleet's flanks exposed. It was sheer good luck that disaster was avoided. There is a line to be drawn between seizing the opportunity or taking the initiative, and wilfulness. In the Royal Navy, it is said that the only excuse for disobeying orders is success. There is much that is true in that statement. Sometimes orders have to be changed and often only the commander at sea can see that the original plan was wrong. That is why those who interfere excessively with the commanders on the spot are wrong, and that is where Pound and Dönitz slipped up. Dönitz also exposed his submarine commanders to Allied attack by excessive communication.

The lack of communication was behind the inability of Jellicoe and the Grand Fleet to make the most of the opportunity presented by the Battle of Jutland. Senior officers at the Admiralty knew that the Germans were at sea but did not pass the information on. The excess of communication was behind the Allied ability to find and destroy German U-boats. Interference using modern communications enabled Pound to order Convoy PQ17 to scatter, so that ships were picked off by the Germans. Communication is there to provide information and up-dated intelligence more than commands, and only those commands that do not interfere with an operation should be sent.

A commander at sea needs to be able to absorb detailed information from a wide range of sources, and that includes the weather, something which the naval officer has to fight in peace and in war. Halsey's failure to heed meteorological information resulted in serious damage to several of his carriers and the loss of two destroyers.

Most senior commanders require good access to their political leaders and the opportunity to influence decision-making. While this was a problem for Raeder, Halsey was reckless with his ships, but there also has to be a willingness to take risks on the part of both politicians and naval commanders. The Germans and the Italians did not want to jeopardize the major warships in their fleets, so the ships were of little use in the end and simply a waste of resources. A deterrent that is not used and will not be used ceases to be a deterrent as its value is gone. Only the fact that the Allies did not dare make the assumption that the *Tirpitz*, for example, would not be used, enabled the ship to make some contribution to Germany's war effort by forcing the Royal Navy and the Royal Air Force to expend so much effort to ensure her destruction. This was a problem with the battleship, even during the First World War, when these large and expensive ships were seen as too valuable to risk, and the British and the Germans spent too much time agonizing over the balance of major fleet units.

Not committing ships to battle is different to pulling ships back when they can no longer make a useful contribution to a battle, and their survival is doubtful. Somerville did this in the Indian Ocean in 1942 and was right to do so. This is an important aspect both of courage and of judgement.

Most of all, a successful leader needs good health. Pound did not enjoy good health and brought himself into disrepute with his peers because, unable to sleep at night, he nodded off at meetings. No doubt some of his decision-making was also affected by his exhaustion, the pain from his hip and the developing brain tumour. Command in wartime does not work to a schedule – it is not a 9-to-5, Monday-to-Friday existence. The pressures are unrelenting and often unpredictable, and it is only a strong and healthy man who can cope with little or no sleep over several days.

That, of course, brings us to the USN and USAAF at Pearl Harbor. The Army and Navy commanders were taking the day off, not thinking about whether the Japanese might attack. It was sheer incompetence, even laziness, not to mount reconnaissance knowing that the Japanese Combined Fleet was at sea. Even if they did believe that it was heading in another direction, curiosity and the need for good intelligence at a time of crisis meant that they should have tried to find out. The weather north of Hawaii was bad, but cruisers could have been sent out on a scouting mission – which is why Admiral Kimmel is not included in this book.

Bibliography

Agawa, Hiroyuki (trans. Bester, John), *Reluctant Admiral: Yamamoto and the Imperial Navy*, Kodansho International, New York, 1979.

Angolia, John R. and Schlicht, Adolph, *Die Kriegsmarine*, 2 vols, San Jose, 1991.

Bekker, Cajus, *Das Grosse Bilduch der Deutschen Kriegsmarine 1939–1945*, Stalling, Hamburg, 1973.

——, *Hitler's Naval War*, London, 1974.

Bird, Keith W., *Erich Raeder, Admiral of the Third Reich*, Naval Institute Press, Annapolis, 2006.

Brodhurst, Robin, *Churchill's Anchor: The Biography of Admiral of the Fleet Sir Dudley Pound*, Pen & Sword Books, Barnsley, 2000.

Chalmers, W.S., *Max Horton and the Western Approaches*, London, 1954.

Cherpak, Evelyn M., *Register of the Raymond Ames Spruance papers*, Naval Historical Collection, Newport, Rhode Island, 1984.

Cunningham of Hyndhope, Admiral of the Fleet Viscount, RN, *A Sailor's Odyssey*, Hutchinson, London, 1951.

Dönitz, Karl, *Deutsche Strategie zur See im Zweiten Weltkrieg*, Bernard & Graefe, Frankfurt, 1972.

——, *Mein wechselvolles Leben*, Musterschmidt, Göttingen, 1968.

——, *Ten Years and Twenty Days*, Weidenfeld & Nicolson, London, 1959.

Elfrath, Ulrich, *Die Deutsche Kriegsmarine 1935–1945*, Podzun Pallas, Friedberg, 1985.

Gelb, Norman, *Desperate Venture*, Hodder & Stoughton, London, 1992.

Hickey, Des and Smith, Gus, *Operation Avalanche: Salerno Landings 1943*, Heinemann, London.

Hobbs, Commander David, *Aircraft Carriers of the Royal & Commonwealth Navies*, Greenhill Books, 1996.

Humble, Richard, *Fraser of North Cape: The Life of Admiral of the Fleet Lord Fraser*, Routledge & Kegan Paul, London 1983.

Ireland, Bernard, *Jane's Naval History of World War II*, HarperCollins, London, 1998.
Keegan, John, *The Price of Admiralty*, Hutchinson, London, 1988.
Kennedy, Ludovic, *Menace: The Life and Death of the Tirpitz*, Sidgwick & Jackson, London, 1979.
Lohmann, W., and Hildebrand, H.H., *Die Deutsche Kriegsmarine, 1939–1945*, several vols, Podzun, Dorheim, 1956–1964.
Macintyre, Donald, *Fighting Admiral: The Life of Admiral of the Fleet Sir James Somerville*, London, 1961.
Mallman Showell, Jak P., *The German Navy Handbook 1939–1945*, Sutton, Stroud, 1999.
Mitchel, Henri, *Francois Darlan: Amiral de la Flotte*, Hatchette, Paris, 1993.
Padfield, Peter, *Dönitz, The Last Führer: Portrait of a Nazi War Leader*, Victor Gollancz, London, 1984.
Potter, Elmer Belmont, *Nimitz*, Naval Institute Press, Annapolis, 1976.
Preston, Antony, *The History of the Royal Navy in the 20th Century*, Bison Books, London, 1987.
Raeder, Erich, *Struggle for the Sea*, William Kimber, London, 1959.
——, *My Life*, United States Naval Institute, 1960.
Roskill, Captain, S.W., *The Navy at War, 1939–1945*, O, London, 1960.
——, *The War at Sea, 1939–1945*, vols I-III, O, London, 1976.
Thompson, Julian, *Imperial War Museum Book of the War at Sea, 1939–1945: The Royal Navy in the Second World War*, IWM/Sigwick & Jackson, London, 1996.
Van der Vat, Dan, *Standard of Power – The Royal Navy in the Twentieth Century*, Hutchinson, London, 2000.
Vian, Admiral Sir Philip, *Action This Day*, Muller, London, 1960.
Winton, John, *The Forgotten Fleet*, Michael Joseph, London, 1960.
Woodman, Richard, *Arctic Convoys*, John Murray, London, 1974.
Woodward, David, *Ramsay at War: The Fighting Life of Admiral Sir Bertram Ramsay*, London 1957.
Wragg, David, *Plan Z – Germany's Bid for Maritime Domination*, Pen & Sword Books, Barnsley, 2008.
——, *Sink the French – At War with our Ally, 1940*, Pen & Sword Books, Barnsley, 2007.
——, *Royal Navy Handbook 1939–1945*, Sutton, Stroud, 2005
——, *Malta: The Last Great Siege 1940–1943*, Pen & Sword Books, Barnsley, 2003.

Index

Index